KINGDOM
ECONOMICS

REVIEWS:

Brett Johnson is a modern-day scribe highlighting the leaven that has penetrated the system but reminding the believer that Kingdom Economics should truly be Grace Economics.

Alan Louis, House of Louis

You may think this covers much ground, but it stretches the surface. Brett provides a lens to see through our present age into the rich history of God and His desire to fellowship with His people. I found Kingdom Economics encouraged me to search Scripture more and consider Christ in my work. In short, this fosters a deeper sense of who we all can be in Christ, starting with you and me."

Andrew Clark, Managing Director, Wherewithal

This was certainly an enjoyable and challenging read. Brett Johnson has the ability to condense a wide knowledge base and relevant Bible references into focus around the subject of Kingdom Economics. This book should be read by everyone that is thinking about heaven on earth. Every Christian believer in business will find their paradigm challenged, and if the penny drops, their world will be transformed. The writing is both thought-provoking and a practical guide to bringing a biblical worldview into daily business activity. But it is also so much more, as it challenges the economic systems of our day. Through Kingdom Economics the world of business becomes more than traditional capital and money. It discovers a whole new world of assets to be redeemed towards the restoration of a broken creation - all leading to a transformed society that makes heaven visible on earth.

Andre Holtshausen, CEO PayProp, London

I can only agree with what you provide in the book. It does speak to one's heart and I trust that there will be sufficient heart capital soon that will energize and activate people to depart Egypt and the Desert to enter the Promised Land.

Campher Serfontein, Senior Tax Advisor

All in all, a really good read that stretched my thinking on the subjects!

Chris McLellan, The Maclellan Foundation

The subject of the Kingdom of God and what that really means for an economically active committed Christian is in my view very poorly communicated in mainstream Christian communities, media and churches. Even more so, the concepts of Kingdom Economics is nearly unheard of and in the process, the perception of many Christians and the "world" is that the Bible does not have a view or a position on how to bring economic prosperity nor societal transformation through capital, finance, money and economics.

I found that Brett was able to connect and simplify many of these hard to explain concepts in Kingdom Economics in a systematic and very pragmatic manner to see the fundamentals of the Kingdom in the real economic reality of where we live...and where we want to and need to make difference.

Cobus Visagie, CEO, Africa Merchant Capital

I can think of no one person who has had a more formative impact on me and the way that I think about the confluence of faith, business and investing. I couldn't commend his teaching, and in particular, this book more.

Henry Kaestner, Managing Principal, Sovereign's Capital.
Founder, Faith Driven Investor

I absolutely love this book. It is very timely and relevant for the time we are living in. We are currently in a great transition with many moving parts. Presently with all the shaking going on, many are feeling insecure, fearful and uncertain of how to respond. Fear can lead to poverty and greed can lead to destruction and loss. Understanding kingdom economics and where God places value helps keep our priorities in the right place. Trusting God in times like this is premium and gives us the understanding we need.

I'm so glad you covered both the markets and crypto which are both manipulated systems but can be used for our benefit.

I believe we are on the edge of great wealth transfer, and we must be strategic in our investments and understanding of value.

I believe this is a must read for everyone.

Gene Strite, Author, Strategies for Financial Breakthrough, Not another richidea, Coins left over

As a Christ-following business leader I know that I am called to bring a kingdom perspective into business and into the marketplace. Yet developing the right perspective or lens through which to do this can often feel surprisingly elusive. Kingdom Economics is a great tool, rich with biblical insight and practical perspectives, to help us on this journey – to inform and shape our thinking, our decision-making and our leadership. It also empowers us as businesses leaders to see beyond our own businesses, to God's original design for business and its role in bringing about a just and flourishing society.

Pieter Faure, CEO, Mergon

We are in one of the most important times in our history. The accelerated pace of change has created an incredible opportunity for the Church to bring transformational shift that is deeply rooted in our faith and biblical principles to the world. Brett Johnson has written a well-timed handbook, Kingdom Economics, that is sacred and foundational for many, especially the kingdom builders for the modern era. Arise, Ekklesia! May the wisdom and revelation shared in this book empower you to take the next bold step. God will multiply your courageous obedience beyond our wildest imagination. May your hearts be ignited with God's love to bring heaven's economy on earth.

Susan Oh, Investment Director, PA Public School Employees' Retirement System

This is a must-read book if you want to integrate your financial life with your faith-based worldview.

Uli Kortsch, President, Global Partners Investments, Author,
The Next Money Crash and a Reconstruction Blueprint

We are in a season of divine wisdom, knowledge and understanding with a heightened focus on the Kingdom Economy. This book is an invaluable resource for marketplace leaders. It clearly articulates 50 Kingdom Economic Principles including the need to create communal funds for capital projects. The book highlights multi-generational thinking, intangible assets such as honor and reputation. The importance of inculcating the culture of honor including relationships and giving where we give as a matter of honor, not because of the needs of the recipient.

Dr. Zienzi Dillon, CEO, Carmel Global Capital, NY

God revealed himself through his work

Motivation for Work | Method of Work | Outcomes of Work | Collaboration with Mankind

Real work created wealth through Societal Value Chains

Bless — Store houses — Raw materials — Collect — Resources — Work — Products — Organize — Trade — Markets — Profits — Steward — Profits — Invest — Societal Assets

Three Economies Emerged

Babylon | Desert | Promised Land

The Promised Land Economy

Promises | Principles | Requirements | Safeguards | Outcomes

The Nations did not function on Kingdom Economics

Heart	Schemes	Mechanisms	Product Focus
• Greed deified • Mammon • Materialism • Independance from God	• Unrighteous scales, dishonest weights • Debt • Interest • No "Jubilee"	• Fractional Reserve Banking (FRB) • Fiat currencies • Returns skewed to Shareholder returns	• Financial Products • Derivatives • QE, National Debt

Wealth for the wealthy

The World System is failing, so they are looking to:

CSR | ESG | Climate Accords | MDGs > SDGs | IMF, World Bank, EU, etc | Emerging Econ Philosophies

The Opportunity: Believers with Kingdom Economics have answers at Fingertips

Holistic Capitalization | Repurposed Business: In God's Business | Households: Broad Stakeholders & Shareholders | 10-P Scorecard: Metrics for Today & Eternity | Giants toppled, Society Transformed | Nations Discipled

Dedication

To the growing community
who love the nations
and the planet
too much
to leave their money stuck
where it grows
but does not
change the world
for good.

Foreword

Brett Johnson's latest book - KINGDOM ECONOMICS - reflects the exceptional depth of understanding and revelation that God has gifted him on the subject. I first met Brett over fifteen years ago at a church in Johannesburg where he was a guest preacher. That night, I heard him speak about the confluence of faith, work and economics with such clarity as I had never heard before then. Till date, I still don't know anyone else with a deeper understanding of the subject of kingdom economics than Brett.

I have been privileged to hear firsthand from Brett several of the principles discussed in this book. Over the past fifteen years, Brett and I have worked collaboratively to propagate these principles, especially in my home country, Nigeria. One of such efforts resulted in the institutionalization of The Kingdom Summit (an annual kingdom economics and leadership summit) that currently holds in Nigeria, but which we plan to take to other nations.

In the KINGDOM ECONOMICS, Brett does not just discuss principles and great ideas, but is calling kingdom-minded persons to action. Capital is too important in God's agenda for this age to be left in the hands of people whose worldview does not accommodate God's own purpose. God is a businessman, and expects His people to be business-minded. Indeed, Jesus had a lot to say about the subject of money during His ministry here on earth. But Christ taught, and Brett amplifies those teachings in this book, that there is a higher calling to business than pecuniary profit. Kingdom minded people are charged by Brett to put faith and capital back together as God originally intended. Our mouth and our money must be aligned if we are going to make a success of the Great Commission which Christ gave us. The book concludes with a call to God's people on earth to wean themselves of all erroneous notions or concepts and become "kingdom capitalists".

I am persuaded that the next great move of God is not going to occur in the pews of our mega churches, but in the marketplace. I therefore strongly recommend this book to all believers in the marketplace, especially those who seek to be part of the coming move of God.

Ben Akabueze, Director General, Budget Office of the Federation, Nigeria

Table of Contents

This is the Story of the World

God revealed himself through his work

| Motivation for Work | Method of Work | Outcomes of Work | Collaboration with Mankind |

The first way we knew about God was seeing his work. It was good, like Him. We learned to work like God, with God. Value was created through good work. Raw materials became products, which shaped markets and then trade generated profits which created wealth. Societal assets grew for the good of all.

Societal Value Chain

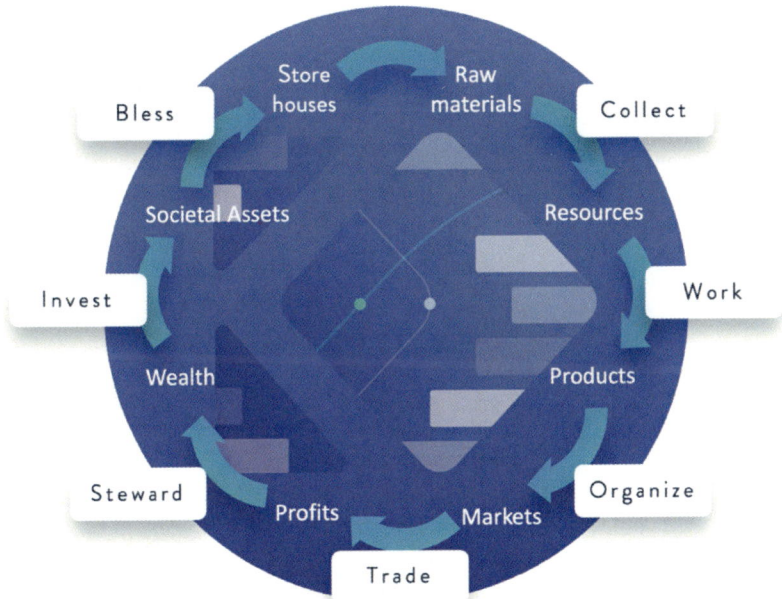

Store houses — Raw materials — Collect — Resources — Work — Products — Organize — Markets — Trade — Profits — Steward — Wealth — Invest — Societal Assets — Bless

Then we lost the plot. We made a god of greed, gave our allegiance to Mammon and connived clever ways for the rich to get richer...

God intervened to reset the Economy of the Promised Land which was polar opposite of the Babylon/Egypt system. Three systems are evident in history: Egypt, the Desert and the Promised Land. The promises and principles and potential of the Promised Land were simply amazing. Anyone in their right mind would leverage them to the hilt.

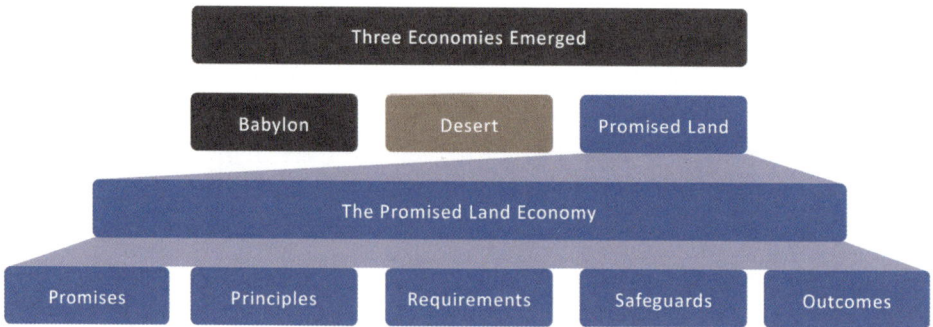

Human nature kicked in, however, and greed seemed more appealing. People became more cunning. Capital was amassed in the hands of relatively few at the expense of many. Central banks, international this, global that: systems were created based on dishonest scales and weights to enshrine the inequities God hated. Instead of focusing on investing in businesses doing real work we threw our offerings at the feet of stock market analysts who specialized in creating fictitious profits fueled by fiat currencies. Financial Capital that used to be a tool bounded by social, spiritual and human capital became king.

---

[1] Transforming Society, Brett Johnson

The Nations did not function on Kingdom Economics				
Heart	**Schemes**	**Mechanisms**	**Product Focus**	
• Greed deified • Mammon • Materialism • Independance from God	• Unrighteous scales, dishonest weights • Debt • Interest • No "Jubilee"	• Fractional Reserve Banking (FRB) • Flat currencies • Returns skewed to Shareholder returns	• Financial Products • Derivatives • QE, National Debt	Wealth for the wealthy

How did it get so bad?

We abdicated the world of Capital

Christians abandoned the world of capital in the 3rd Century, and today we see the results: materialism erodes our identity, the wrong financial foundation leaves us fearful of market fluctuations and "Causism" conscript capital for dubious ends. Greed and fear are rampant. We have lost sight of the purpose of capital; perhaps we have not grasped its essence. We are therefore ill-equipped for the massive changes taking place in worldwide economic systems that will impact you and me at a personal level.

People of faith are uninformed about the spiritual roots of capital; we therefore repeat the 1,000-year abdication of times past, or we embrace schizophrenia, having one set of rules for our finances, and another for our spirituality. God rules heaven but has no say on Wall Street or at the central bank. We can explain how to get to heaven, but we cannot explain how to handle capital (in its many forms) on earth.

At a societal level, we leave the funding of infrastructure projects to governments and international aid organizations because our micro-view of finance cannot stretch to the macro-needs of mankind. A personal view of salvation has stripped naked a communal view of capital. Warren Buffet and Bill Gates have a better grasp of "storehouse" than our local priest, rabbi or pastor. At best we outsource concern to charities; at worst we are paralyzed as global needs dwarf our personal resources.

The needs of man are an invitation for God. Sadly, we will not have the entry ticket to participate in the large events of humankind if we continue to play dumb on the subject of faith-based financing.

The World System is failing, and they know it

Shards of light are appearing. Anyone can see that the current systems are not sustainable. Debt will crush our children, systems will collapse under the weight of Trillions of Dollars of global debt, and the planet aches. People are grasping for solutions that will dampen the worst tendencies of mankind. CSR, ESG, MDG, SDG... none of this will be enough. Mammon is an insatiable master. If our money is made and invested in with Mammon it will not easily find its way into Kingdom Economics. "You cannot serve two masters."

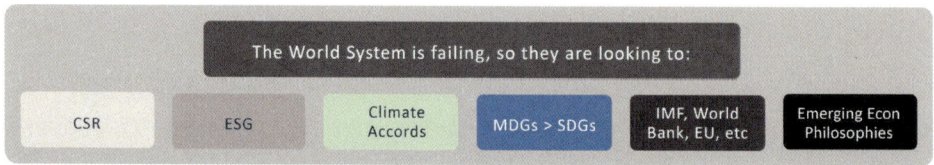

The World System is failing, so they are looking to:					
CSR	ESG	Climate Accords	MDGs > SDGs	IMF, World Bank, EU, etc	Emerging Econ Philosophies

We see the riotous effects of "new" philosophies hoping to replace what is with something different. There is hope. "In the last days..." says the prophet Isaiah. I will not delve into it much but, to quote what the late Benjamin Rogge said in 1965, "the typical American who calls himself a Christian and who makes pronouncements... on economic policies or institutions, does so out of an almost complete ignorance of the simplest and most widely accepted tools of economic analysis. If something arouses his Christian concern, he asks not whether it is water or gasoline he is tossing on the economic fire—he asks only whether it is well intended."[2] Are we not in an era where Christians applaud burning in the main streets of society in the name of being a social cause? We need to do better.

We may be closer to answers than we think

In the world of 2021+ the challenges are formidable, but if we look back for the fingerprints of God in recent decades we might see we are closer than we think to solutions. The people who said God's economy will become the main thing... perhaps they are righter than right. I believe we are closer to solutions than ever before, AND I believe it will take a concerted effort of a

---

[2] Benjamin Rogge, "Christian Economics: Myth or Reality?" The Freeman, December 1965

devoted few to press through until Kingdom Economics comes to life in our generation.

There's a day coming

    when the mountain of God's House

Will be The Mountain—

    solid, towering over all mountains.

All nations will river toward it,

    people from all over set out for it.

They'll say, "Come,

    let's climb God's Mountain,

    go to the House of the God of Jacob.

He'll show us the way he works

    so we can live the way we're made.3

The Opportunity: Believers with Kingdom Economics have answers at Fingertips

| Holistic Capitalization | Repurposed Business: In God's Business | Households: Broad Stakeholders & Shareholders | 10-P Scorecard: Metrics for Today & Eternity | Giants toppled, Society Transformed | Nations Discipled |

In short, today we are viewing capital more holistically. Movements in the marketplace are seeing thousands of businesses wanting to get into God's business. Shareholders are giving way to stakeholders, and the best metaphor, arguably, for stakeholder analysis is to recapture a biblical understanding of "households." Triple bottom line... it simply is not enough. We are going way beyond "people, planet, profits" to a richer set of metrics that are not only good for today, but good for eternity. Giants are being tweeted, hash-tagged and aimed at. Beyond the rants, images of

---

3 Isaiah 2:1-5 (The Message)

transformed societies are emerging from the mists of troubled global times. We have a shot at truly discipling nations in our generation.

It will not happen automatically. We don't get transformation by proclamation or wishful thinking. We have to return to biblically-rooted Kingdom Economics and seek out principles of sustainable transformation. Beyond the knowing of principles, we must learn the ways of God, recognize good and bad practices, and learn to write culture-changing policies that fuel the movement.

Read with three hats

I see three primary audiences for this book:

- Individuals curious about principles of finance and faith: whether they mix, and how teachings of ancient religions may inform life today.
- Societal reformers looking for better ways to build national assets with a view to addressing issues and uplifting people. These reformers know money in and of itself is not an answer unless it is accompanied by a worldview that undergirds sustainable economics; they also recognize that without capital economies will falter.
- Financing corporations, in all forms, seeking to do business in a manner both good for humankind and worth their while.

Capital is essential, but much of what we see in the many forms of capital today leads us to conclude that there is a definite and urgent need for Repurposing Capital. If you are starting kingdom-focused banks or seeking to shape financial policy at a central bank level, I recommend you read Repurposing Capital.

Act with one heart

The vast majority of people of followers of Jesus Christ are still trapped in the wrong financial system. Thankfully there are pioneers who are creating funds, platforms and metrics that help us shift into Kingdom Economics. Which system we live in is first a matter of the heart—where do we place our trust—and then a matter of priorities, obedience, praxis. Collectively we have many of the pieces, but we don't yet have all the answers. Will a new movement of kingdom capitalists fund adventures into the unknown, or will the scorecards of yesterday tether our capital to the sinking systems of this world?

Brett Johnson
2021

1

Work and the Value of Money

God works

Before we jump into the subject of economics, money, finance and capital we should restate some things that for you, an enlightened reader, may well be further glimpses into the blindingly obvious, so I will jot them down in bullet form:

- In the beginning, the only way humans surmised anything about God was through his work. There was no bible, no synagogues, certainly no churches and no religious media.
- They themselves were his handywork
- God gave man meaningful work, and they did it in collaboration with him

- Work was not a consequence of man's sin; it was not punishment for missing the mark. Work is a pre-Fall concept
- After he had done a brilliant job with creation, God put people on the earth to take care of it and bring it to its full potential
- The better we work on earth, the better our job will be in heaven.

It is true that work became more difficult after relationship with God was broken; many things got messed up in that debacle. We lost some of the meaning of work, the joy of unfettered collaboration with Mr. Creator, and meaning waned.

Types of work

Not all work is good. Like other things, we turned our attention away from value-creating enterprises to self-serving schemes, but I am getting ahead of myself. Let's be reminded that there were some finished goods in the Garden of Eden such as Farm to Table, Ready-to-Eat fruits and vegetables, all organic, mind you. But when Adam wanted to impress Eve for her birthday he couldn't pop down to the jewelry store and choose a ring. There was gold and there were precious stones and many other resources, but they were in raw material form. This is the Principle of Raw Materials. God gives us things in raw material form and our joy is to transform them, through work, into something else of greater value. Such work is value-adding, you might say redemptive.

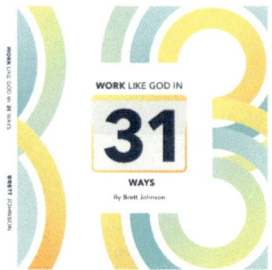

We were made to work. Work is not punishment for sin, but a privilege to do what we were designed to do and thereby reflect the essence of our creator. Just as nature reflects its creator, so our work reveals who we are and how we work with God, like God. I have covered this more in my book, Work like God in 31 Ways. Whatever our sphere of leadership our special privilege is to re-teach people to work the way they were designed to work. This is the essence of discipleship, restoring the image of God in humans and then redeploying them for noble purposes.

Societal Value Chains

The reason we need to understand Societal Value Chains is to remind ourselves of the purpose of money. We can then see how it has become corrupted over the centuries. The rest of this book will focus on how to get it back to its original design. So let's unpack the Societal Value Chain because later we will evaluate the work we do and the location of our investments around this chain.

_____

It might be useful to look at the work involved in getting Assets from a Raw Material stage—remember the accounting term—to Finished Goods, to market, to money to wealth etc. all the way through to a city or nation's storehouse.

- Raw materials are identified (or, in God's case, spoken into being). Sometimes this includes Inspired Innovations™, sometimes research, sometimes experimentation. The George Washington Carver question comes to mind: "Mr. Creator, why did you make the peanut?"

- Raw Materials are then collected into a critical mass: one ounce of gold does not constitute a refinery; one needs a critical mass to have Resources.

- Resources are transformed into Products through work. A bunch of grapes, to a wine maker, is not a Finished Good. Lots of work has to take place to transform a ton of grapes into bottles of wine.

- When wine makers get together and begin to market their wine to willing buyers, whether in their country or a faraway land, a market is developed. (Of course, it could be a buyer/agent or a customer that creates the market.) Nowadays, the markets for many goods and services are global and your customers can be anywhere.

- Markets give rise to Trade

- Trade leads to Profit, and raw material + sweat + intellectual capital has led to money in the bank.

- Money can get wasted, so in order for Wealth Creation to happen, there has to be Stewardship. Advanced leaders (those who have been successful and are asking, "What else do I do with my life to benefit others?") realize their job goes beyond making money, to stewarding what they have, to generate wealth that will be multi- generational.

- Stewarded wealth can then be invested for the good of humankind (that sounds grand, but insert your neighborhood, town, local hospital, or a collaborative of social entrepreneurs, and you get the idea), resulting in the creation of Societal Assets. This is where we spin out of the greedy cycle of thinking that what we can make is only for "I, myself and me."

- When a city or nation has created so much wealth that they are then able to bless other cities and nations, then they are finally getting to the promise of Genesis 12 where God shared his purposes with Abraham. "I will bless you, and you will be a blessing to all nations."[4]

---

[4] Transforming Society, by Brett Johnson – pages 114-115

The Role of Money

As economies advanced so did the sophistication of money. Those who claim that Israel was a collection of uninformed rabble who came from years of slavery fail to grasp the sophistication of the economics of history. Many of the elements of today's economy were present: debt, interest, letters of credit, economic slavery, taxes, ownership, lender and borrower nations, national treasuries, time value of money, collateral and more. It was therefore very important that instructions be given about what would and would not be permissible in the new economy.

Money was seen as a medium of exchange. Since work was good and money represented a person's work, it was not bad. It was there to facilitate real work, however, and not to become (as it is today) a vehicle to generate passive income. There were prohibitions on growing money from money, yet, when you look at the vast majority that takes digital flight around the world today a miniscule percentage is payment for goods and services. We have created sophisticated ways to make money from fake money. We have disconnected money from the early phases of the creation of value.

The Characteristics of Money

There are excellent books giving the history of money; I recommend Nial Ferguson's "The Ascent of Money: A Financial History of the World." Written in 2008, the last chapter is ominously called "The Descent of Money." Ferguson is not pessimistic, however, but believes that money and financial systems evolve to reflect what is happening in society.

I remain for than ever convinced that, until we fully understand the origin of the financial species, we shall never understand the fundamental truth about money: that far from being 'a monster that must be put back in its place,' as the German president recently complained, financial markets are like the mirror of mankind, revealing every hour of every working day the way we value ourselves and the resources of the world around us. It is not the fault of the mirror if it reflects our blemishes as clearly as our beauty.[5]

----

[5] The Ascent of Money, Nial Ferguson

If the world of finance reflects our blemishes and beauty, we do well to understand the nature of money. What makes money, or currency, valid and sustainable over time? Are some forms of money more moral than others? Has money been defiled? Can money be redeemed? During the course of this book you will find yourself answering these questions.

Sometimes a useful way to evaluate whether we are on track is to articulate the properties of money as it should be. In the book, Thank God for Bitcoin, the authors posit five properties money should have to be useful.

1. Divisible into small amounts so that scale is not a challenge.
2. Portable: easily transported.
3. Durable, "resistant to physical degradation over time"
4. Recognizable, "easy to verify its authenticity"
5. Scarce "so that the supply is resistant to manipulation over time. Money should hold its value and be able to pay for goods now but also into the future."

The introduction of coins in around 700 BC was a huge innovation that helped fulfill all these categories. Sadly, people found ways to debase the coins through clipping, sweating, shaving or mixing cheaper metals into the coins... which looked the same on the surface. The silver content in a denarius went from 4.5 grams to next-to-nothing over 450 years.

This enabled them to raise revenues without upsetting their populace by raising taxes, but there were unintended consequences. Prices inevitably rose following increases in money supply... Predictably, these Roman Emperors did not announce this debasement and it took time for the community to figure this out. In the meantime, the Roman government spent their coins for goods and services before the price increases, thereby redistributing wealth from citizens to state. ... This led to economic turmoil throughout the Roman Empire and eventually contributed towards its collapse. [6]

---

[6] Thank God for Bitcoin, Bitcoin and Bible Group

The authors contend that central control of a currency always leads to its debasement, and this is government theft. Nowadays, debasement of currency does not always involve changing the precious metal content of coins. We have more sophisticated mechanisms shakily built on the "foundation" of fiat currency. Money is printed by central banks at will, loaned to governments for nearly zero interest, and pumped into economies like cheap drugs. The side effects are horrendous: materialism, inflation and hyper inflation, devaluation of currencies, debt that stretches beyond the horizon, the devaluation of honest work, loss of entrepreneurship (since financial risk dwarfs business risk) and corruption, to name a handful of maladies.

We need a whack on the side of the head

We have fancy terminology about financial instruments, yields, returns, leverage, balanced portfolios and beating the index. We can talk terms and term sheets, exchange risk and exit strategies. We can beat the market, outperform the averages, mitigate risks and diversify our portfolios but... if we are doing it all in the wrong system, surely we are doing it wrong. We can become king of the mountain but if we are on the wrong mountain is it worth a hill of beans? If we run the race but are on the wrong path, are we not wasting our time?

The Lord said to his people:
"You are standing at the crossroads.
So consider your path.
Ask where the old, reliable paths are.
Ask where the path is that leads to blessing and follow it.
If you do, you will find rest for your souls."[7]

I left out the end of the verse because my hope is, for readers of this book, it will not apply to us. The Voice translation adds a little twist to Jeremiah's injunction:

---

[7] Jeremiah 6:16

Eternal One (to the people): Stand at the crossing, and consider the ancient path, for it is good and it leads to Me.

Walk on this path, and you will find rest for your souls.

But they have said, "We will not walk upon this road."[8]

Our pursuit in understanding Kingdom Economics is God himself: "...and it leads to me." The reason we work with anything, be it capital or clay, produce or people, is to get closer to God. Our work should take us back to the Garden daily, to get back onto the road.

To establish a new culture it helps to have a common glossary; in the next chapter we dig into some of the terms we will find useful as we explore God's economy.

---

[8] Jeremiah 6:16 (VOICE)

2

Introduction of Terms

Words can confuse and they can clarify. It stands to reason that we should discuss working definitions of some key concepts before we delve into the important subject of Kingdom Economics.

- Worldview
- The Kingdom of God
- The kingdom of this world
- Economics
- Capital
- Faith-Based Financing

Worldview

A good friend of mine has a master's degree in engineering and is building houses in India. He gives instructions to the foreman who explains things in Tamil to the workers. They then do whatever they want to do. They hear the words, but they do not have the cultural, business or technical framework in which to interpret the instructions. You could provide a set of plans to construct a building to contractors in different nations and the end product might look the same, but the building might fare radically differently in an earthquake or hurricane. Why would this be the case? There are several possibilities:

- The skill sets of the workers are not the same in each country
- The building codes vary
- The knowledge of local conditions causes an adaptation to what locals know will work—this could be good or bad
- The weights and measures may differ: 10 kilograms of cement is not the same as 10 pounds
- The assumptions about engineering could differ, and
- The foundations required—the underpinnings that are not visible to the naked eye—are different in each place. Where I live in earthquake-prone Northern California on a steep hillside, the pylons go 18 feet or more into the ground. That is what makes the house stable.

The same thing is true in the realm of finance, and even more so, because the products are less tangible. Unless the foundations are in place, the system will not work. In the case of the US I would argue that, despite complex regulations, we have departed from the Foundational Principles that should be underpinning the economy. There are some foreign nations seeking to buy banks in Europe and the US, for example. Does one simply ask whether they have the same banking regulations and ignore the context? One cannot assume that a term has the same meaning in China and Zurich. If we do this we will have the same banking products, but the customers will have a quite different experience, and when the pressure comes the bank will collapse. Why is this? One major difference is worldview—it is not the regulation book, but the lens through which one reads it.

What is worldview? It has gone by different definitions over the years.

- Weltanschauung—Immanuel Kant
- Mental model of the world—Toffler
- Sense of how the world works—Sowell
- Conceptual scheme—Nash
- Basic cognitive orientation—Mulder
- "A set of assumptions held consciously or unconsciously in faith about the basic make up of the world and how the world works"—Darrow L. Miller

Let me illustrate with a general business example. I sat with three businesspeople in India who were trying to explain to me that they did not need to do business planning. "Indians are so smart we do not need to plan." I pondered their proposal overnight and met with them the next day. "I suggest that the three of you are Christian in your religion, but Hindu in your worldview. You do not want to plan because your worldview is one of fatalism, not faith." One of the men, a formerly devout Hindu, thought through what I was saying and said, "You are correct. There is a Hindu saying, 'whatever will happen, will happen...' and many Christians have it on the walls of their offices."

A Chinese banker reading an American banking code book will interpret that code through a Communist, or Confucian grid, and the outcome will not be the same as someone who has a Judeo-Christian perspective. Likewise, a Christian who travels from Chicago with her Shari'ah banking handbook in hand to do financing in Pakistan will not interpret that handbook based on the same foundational understanding as her Muslim counterpart.

Cross-cultural Finance requires a Worldview Shift. If you are an investor in China—and China has a lot of money to invest nowadays—and you want to become a Venture Capitalist in Silicon Valley, first you will need to learn the worldview of Silicon Valley. It is partly about innovation, flat organizations, decentralized decision-making, empowered workers and casual clothes. But it is also about freedom of choice, including the freedom to choose one's religion, or no religion at all; it means that the youngest engineer has as much say as the oldest; it means transparency in relationships, trust in other colleagues, and collaboration. It assumes when one gives one's word, then one keeps it; when you call a meeting with one person, you go to the meeting on your own, without taking the five people who report to you. Competence trumps politics. Ideas trump ideology.

If you are a bank regulator in Switzerland and good people from Africa or India come over to start a bank, expect that they will bring their families with them. An African leader was asked what he thought about nepotism: "I believe in it," he said. Worldview is at work in each of us, and we have to realize, despite the many truths about globalism and international finance, we interpret and apply truth through our mental model of how the world works.

The Kingdom of God

Britannica describes it: "Kingdom of God, also called Kingdom Of Heaven, in Christianity, the spiritual realm over which God reigns as king, or the fulfillment on Earth of God's will. The phrase occurs frequently in the New Testament, primarily used by Jesus Christ in the first three Gospels." It is not heaven, it is not the Church, and it is not a physical place. Broadly speaking, it is the place where God rules as King, which includes the whole universe. There is present and "not yet" aspect to the kingdom of God which leaves many people grasping the "not yet" part and hoping for "pie in the sky when you die." Others focus on the "now" aspects of the kingdom of God. It is mysterious, it has to be recognized and received, and we enter the kingdom through faith in Jesus Christ. There is no other way in. Through re-birth one is transferred out of the kingdom of darkness and into the kingdom of light. Then one must learn the principles and practices of the kingdom of God. There are books written on this topic, so I will not expand on the emphasis Jesus placed on this new kingdom, nor its practices except to say kingdoms have economies.

As you might expect, the Kingdom of God has a unique economy. When Jesus came to usher in the kingdom of God and explain how its operations are plar opposite to business as usual, the same applies to monetary policy and financial principles. "It is better to give than receive" is a mind-blowing statement. We will contrast the two economic systems in the chapter covering 50 Principles of Faith-based Financing.

In his book, Secrets of the Kingdom Economy, Paul Cuny states, "The kingdom economy will soon be the dominant economic system on the earth." I had an opportunity to ask Paul about this in an interview for a podcast in the When Capital meets Eternity series. Paul indicated that he did not make this forecast based on his own analysis but on a "word" he sensed God speak to him.

"Paul, you wrote this in 2008: how close do you think we are to this becoming a reality?"

His reply was interesting. "We are already at the beginning of this taking place."

Of late I have been reviewing books by various authors who independently say that the world's systems will collapse. "Based on pure human logic and arithmetical possibilities, the financial world system is doomed to fail. That's it. The world is on the decline, on its way to destruction..." says Gottfried Hetzer. Norm Franz draws on scripture to say that Babylon's wealth will be "laid to waste." (Revelation 18:15-18)

The kingdom of this world

We would be forgiven for thinking that the kingdom of this world merely describes people who are "pre-believers" who do not yet know God. They are temporarily displaced citizens who may choose to follow God at some points, but they are not batting for the other team.

Scripture, however, refers to a kingdom that is the opposite of the Kingdom of God. It goes by names such as "kingdom of darkness" and "this age" and the "evil world" and is sometimes shortened to "the world." It has, like the kingdom of God, its own ways of operating, and it has an economic system.

———

"It is a system, built and maintained by unbelievers, and hosted, encouraged and promoted by Satan. The system is supposed to manage and cater perfectly for all aspects of our lives without help and interference from God."[9]

If we are to understand Kingdom Economics we must also understand the mechanics of the opposite system otherwise we will not recognize which systems is predominant in our lives. I will therefore devote some space to examining what is sometimes called Babylon or Egypt and the economic principles and practices at work there. For the moment you can assume that the Minister of Finance in the kingdom of darkness is Mammon, which

---

[9] Gottfried Hetzer, Finances-Who is in control? Page 101

means greed deified... making a god out of greed. Norm Franz describes three components of the World's Financial System.

> The world's financial system is made up of three interconnecting systems. On one side, there is the economic system, which is simply trade and commerce relating to the development, production, distribution and consumption of goods and services. Economics is simply the science of measuring and reporting trade in commerce. On the other side, there is the investment system, which consists of both real and paper assets. Real assets are natural resources such as precious metals, agricultural products, petroleum products, timber, real estate, etc. In contrast, paper assets consist of stocks, bonds, mutual funds, insurance products, futures, options, derivatives etc.
>
> In the middle of all this lies the monetary system, which is the engine that makes it all run. Without money, no one has the power to purchase either consumer goods or investments. However since all money is Federal Reserve Bank debt, it is actually the ever increasing bubble that keeps the economy and investment markets going.[10]

I recommend you listen to my podcast interview with Uli Kortsch on how this system works.[11] The bottom line is that it is based on debt, and interest is a mechanism for keeping people in bondage. Built into this system is the ability to destroy wealth through inflation, among other things.

Forms of capital

The focus of this book is financial capital. Like other forms of capital, financial capital does best when it intersects with other types of capital. A confluence of capital is essential in creating an impact. Without being exhaustive, the following strands of capital are important:

- Human capital
- Political capital

---

[10] Money & Wealth in the new millennium, Norm Franz
[11] https://www.youtube.com/watch?v=BdNM49L8_Aw&list=PLjLRWI_y1Hg1J4N3DcXa-s3Dk2nOaU7tX&index=2

- Intellectual capital
- Relational or social capital
- Environmental capital
- Financial capital
- Digital capital

There is a recently recognized form of capital that has existed through the ages which intersects greatly with financial capital—spiritual capital.

Spiritual capital is a concept that involves the quantification of the value to individuals, groups and society of spiritual, moral or psychological beliefs and practices. Proponents liken it to other forms of capital, including material capital (or financial capital), intellectual capital, and social capital. Some scholars such as Robert Barro see spiritual capital as simply another term for the power and influence generated by religion belief and practice, whilst others, such as Danah Zohar define it more broadly as the value of personal, social or cultural beliefs and meanings that stimulate creativity, encourage moral behavior and motivate individuals. It is often connected to the related concept of spiritual intelligence.

Faith-based Financing and Kingdom Economics deal, in part, with the intersection of many forms of capital, especially human, financial, and spiritual capital. Later, in our discussion of the broadening definition of economics and how we place a value on things, you will see why the confluence of the various notions of capital is essential.

Faith-based Finance

Faith-based Finance (FBF) is a set of values-based principles for economics, capital and finances rooted in the Heart of God and the Ways of God. These are universal laws, common good principles that apply to all people at all times. Jewish, Christian and Islamic Finance are all subsets of this greater reality of Faith-Based Financing. I have elaborated on this at length in Repurposing Capital and expand on this in the next chapter.

Faith-Based Financing Products

Features of FBF products

For sake of discussion, I have taken the universal principles and deduced what would appear to be key elements of faith-based financial products. Others may create a better set of criteria, but for the moment let's consider what might be the objective or structural elements of a FBF product, transaction, or arrangement.

From my perspective a FBF product should:

1. Have a noble purpose and create social value.
2. Have transparency of terms.
3. Clearly articulate the risk for all parties.
4. Foster long term positive relationships.
5. Grow the pie for all—generate wealth.
6. Empower all parties.

At the same time the transaction or product should not:

7. Invest in questionable industries.
8. Create a negative environmental impact.
9. Entrap the borrower.
10. Violate the requirements of appropriate index. (See next section.)

The Appropriate Interest Index

The rate of interest is a matter of subjective economic value. This does not mean it is a moral elective, but that it should be evaluated for appropriateness. In some cases the rate will be zero, and in other cases more. Interest is generally determined by three factors:

- Risk premium
- Inflation premium
- Time horizon

If I borrow $100 this morning and there is no inflation, and I am a wholly reliable person, and I leave you my $100 watch as security, and I repay it by noon, then the interest would be negligible, if anything. But if I borrow the $100 for 10 years, inflation is 10% per annum, and I give you my cell phone as security (which will be outdated next month) and I invest the $100 in chewing gum, then the rate will skyrocket. It is unfair to say the interest rate in both instances should be the same.

I believe there is a middle ground on the matter of interest. Some writings say it should be abolished completely; others say that the prohibition on interest is arcane. I would suggest that the right approach is to consider what is "appropriate interest" taking key factors into account.

1. The relative power of the lender and borrower.
2. The purpose of the loan or investment.
3. The extent of the equity position of the lender/investor.
4. The quality of the collateral.
5. The lender's intentions regarding the collateral.
6. The time horizon of the borrowing.
7. The win-win factor: whether there is gain for all parties. Whether the transaction results in unwarranted wealth transfer (versus mutual wealth creation.)
8. The social value of the related project or business or initiative.
9. The character and credibility of the borrower.
10. The borrower's accountability structure.

The matter of interest could become divisive to those seeking to practice FBF. The pragmatic solution may be first, the characterization of faith-based products, including the appropriate interest index, and second, the tiered approach to products mentioned elsewhere in this book. This would leave it to the conscience and purposes of the banks, rather than making it a matter of legislation.[12]

I have had a question about why they focus on interest versus other forms of returns. The reason is that the present banking system, which is supposedly in place to offer loans to businesses and individuals, is mainly based around lending at interest. Islamic Banking, private equity and direct investments (which I advocate) are less concerned about interest and more tuned into overall returns based on the success of the investee organization.

---

[12] Repurposing Capital, paragraphs 64 and 65

Kingdom Capital

Given the previous definitions it stands to reason that "kingdom capital" is capital generated according to God's principles and deployed solely for the purpose of extending His kingdom. It has the attributes of FBF products and operations and avoids the negatives of world systems.

Investor

When I was 12 years old I went through training to become a Sunday School teacher and my dad reminded us we all had three things we all invest: Time, Talents and Treasures. My understanding at the time probably focused on what went in the collection plate. In today's world there are technically two big buckets of investors: Accredited and Non-Accredited. By number, non-accredited investors make up the bulk of investors in the world. They are also spoken of as retail investors, and in the USA this means they hold less than $1 million in assets, apart from any value they have in their primary residence, and they earn under $200,000.

> A non-accredited investor is any investor who does not meet the income or net worth requirements set out by the Securities and Exchange Commission (SEC). The concept of a non-accredited investor comes from the various SEC acts and regulations that refer to accredited investors.
>
> An accredited investor can be a bank or a company but is mainly used to distinguish individuals who are considered financially knowledgeable enough to look after their own investing activities without SEC protection. The current standard for an individual accredited investor is a net worth of more than $1 million excluding the value of their primary residence or an income of more than $200,000 annually (or $300,000 combined income with a spouse).
>
> A non-accredited investor, therefore, is anyone making less than $200,000 annually (less than $300,000 including a spouse) that also has a total net worth of less than $1 million when their primary residence is excluded.[13]

---

[13] Investopedia

I have invested more time than money over the course of the last 65 years. In fact, I have invested 65 years. Have I invested well? In some ways, it is too soon to tell, and in other ways I can see positive and negative returns. My time and my talents are interrelated, and our journey in life is often one of building talents and discovering our calling in the early years. There have been many who have gone through to the end of their lives with little financial capital, even eschewing financial capital, and had a significant impact. We live in an era, however, where it is possible to add financial capital in ways not available to prior generations, so we have an imperative to consider what this means not so that we can amass capital, but so that we can propel "make the world a better place" from a slogan to a reality. A foundational premise of capital is contained in the promise to Abram in Genesis 12 summarized as "Blessed to be a blessing."

1 "Go out from your country, your relatives, and your father's household

to the land that I will show you.

2 Then I will make you into a great nation, and I will bless you,

and I will make your name great,

so that you will exemplify divine blessing.

3 I will bless those who bless you,

but the one who treats you lightly I must curse,

so that all the families of the earth may receive blessing through you." [14]

God's heart always includes the nations. This is part of the inheritance of Jesus, the return on investment for his sacrifice. In that heavenly interaction found in Psalm 2. "You are my son... I will assuredly give You the nations as Your inheritance." One of the key questions of this book is how we go on the journey to becoming those who participate in the fulfillment of this statement.

---

[14] Genesis 12:1-3 (NET)

My background as a management consultant for many decades, with perhaps a little finance and auditor thrown in, leaves me prone to charts and flow diagrams. The diagram below is from my book, Transforming Society and describes the journey to becoming a world changer. It is more a journey of royal identity than investing: we are people made in the image of God, placed in families, learning to work like God, with God, and hopefully being blessed to be a blessing through the stages of life.

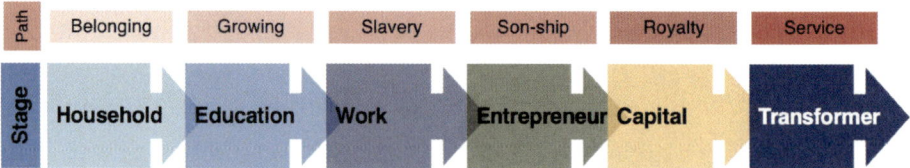

Path	Belonging	Growing	Slavery	Son-ship	Royalty	Service
Stage	Household	Education	Work	Entrepreneur	Capital	Transformer

There are, of course, quite a few people who accumulate capital but are still orphans. In fact, some build wealth to mask an unsettled identity. We will leave that aside for the moment, assuming we are whole people who have dealt with "the junk in the trunk" and are now on a path to figure out the often-neglected aspect of our faith journey: capital.

Hard money

A currency backed by a tangible commodity such as gold, silver, or platinum.

Soft money

A slang expression for creative financing techniques that involve no cash changing hands, such as seller financing.

Fiat currency

Money that is not backed by anything other than a government trust. Fiat money has no intrinsic value; it only has value at all because all participants in an economy agree to trust the government issuing the currency. All modern money is fiat money.

Fractional Reserve Banking (FRB)

"Fractional reserve banking is a system in which only a fraction of bank deposits are backed by actual cash on hand and available for withdrawal. This is done to theoretically expand the economy by freeing capital for lending" says Investopedia. If you deposit $1,000 in a bigger bank that may have to keep about 3% in reserve (the actual percentage varies), the rest can be leveraged to make loans to customers which, in turn, become assets in the bank's books. And so the cycle continues. If every customer demanded their money back at the same time, the bank would collapse (as happened during The Great Depression.) This is an oversimplification, of course, but we must note FRB in our conversation about Kingdom Economics.

Inflation

There are two aspects to inflation: Price inflation, which is generally reflected by the Consumer Price Index. The measures the increase in prices of a carefully selected basket of goods... and cleverly manipulated to appear as if it hovers around an "acceptable" 2% per annum.

Monetary expansion: as we alluded to in our short discussion of the debasement of coins, the increase in the money supply can happen electronically, or through the printing of money.

3

Expanding on Faith-based Financing

[Note to readers:

You may wish to skip this chapter if you are not concerned about the radicalization or spiritualization of capital. Since capital always carries an agenda, however, it might be wise to at least be familiar with these perspectives. I cover the similarities and differences between finance in the major monotheistic religions in depth in Repurposing Capital. It is there that I build the argument that principles of capital and faith draw from the heart of God and the ways of God and propose a set of Faith-Based Financing Principles.]

What on earth is "Faith-based Financing" (FBF)?[15] Can it be possible that finance and faith are mentioned in the same phrase? We should be acutely aware most financing transactions involve some degree of risk, and the conventional wisdom is that the potential for reward should equate to the degree of risk. Are faith and risk interconnected? And has there been a faith perspective on financing for centuries, millennia perhaps, that we have lost? What would our economy, with all of its complexity, look like if we employed ancient faith-related financial concepts? Are there different economic systems, or is "Western Capitalism" pretty much it? Islamic Banking (IB) is getting more press nowadays: are there other economic systems based on ancient writings, and if so, how prescriptive are they?

The emergence of Islamic Finance

There will always be numerous economic systems existing side by side. Increasing attention is being paid to banking products (and the related systems) that operate based on ancient writings and scriptures. With the large cash reserves built up due, in part, to rising oil prices there is a particular emergence of Islamic Finance (IF). Shari'ah-compliant Financing (SCF) is not the only emerging sector. In a recent book published by Oxford University Press the authors estimate that Protestant Christians in America have enough net worth to be considered a G7 nation.[16] The challenge has been that there is no separate group that gathers under banner of "Jewish financing" or "Hindu insurance" or "Christian capital" or "Buddhist banking." But that does not mean they do not exist. The first banks appear to have been temples. There has long been a correlation between religion and the amassing and deployment of capital.

---

15 This section is abstracted from the book Repurposing Capital by Brett Johnson, Indaba Publishing, 2010
16 Passing the Plate, Christian Smith, Michael Emerson, and Patricia Snell, Oxford University Press

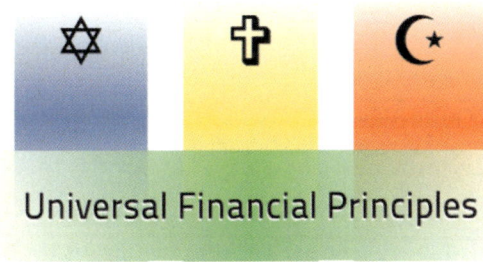

Figure 0.1 Major religions all draw from Universal Laws, Moral Laws, or Foundational Principles

Universal Financial Principles

In the 20th Century a new category has become more prominent, namely, Islamic Banking (IB). It is my contention that, while IB is getting good press, it is a very recent phenomenon. But this does not make it invalid at all. Thankfully IB has raised awareness of the possibility that financing can in fact be done in a manner useful to society. It is not, however, a uniquely Muslim or Islamic notion. Hundreds, if not thousands, of years before the Qur'an was written the Hebrew texts laid out many of the same principles. Christian practices followed these themes, and for over 1,400 years much of Christian banking was zero-interest. But times changed, trade became global, the time value of money became more of a factor, and modern banking emerged from the ghettos of Venice, among other places. Jewish bankers were the main players, but eventually Christians got back into the game. One thing led to another and we ended up with complex financial systems with Wall Street whizzes fabricating products even they could not keep up with, and engineering trails of paper money with questionable underlying value. The global economic crisis created a vacuum and the question began to be asked, "Is there a better way?"

On November 5, 2008 Worldnet Daily reported:

The US Treasury Department has announced that it will teach 'Islamic Finance' to US banking regulatory agencies, Congress and other parts of the executive branch today in D.C. – but critics say it is opening a door to funding of Islamic extremism. The UK is already well down the track of trying to become a hub for IB. The Financial Services Authority (FSA) has issued rulings in this regard. While Muslims tout the resilience of their stock markets in these troubled economic times, many Britons are concerned about the influence of IB on the values and way of life in the UK.

In the USA other agencies are considering this matter. For example, a former New York Federal Reserve Bank president, Bill Rutledge, stated in a speech at the Arab Bankers Association of North America (ABANA):

> At the outset, I would like to emphasize that we—and here I am referring broadly to US regulators—are open to Islamic financial products. Our mindset is to try to accommodate a variety of approaches to finance, focusing to the extent possible on the underlying substance—that is, focusing on what the implications for safety and soundness and consumer protection would be of a given product. Consistent with that approach, while we are committed to accommodating Islamic finance within the US structure, we will hold Islamic financial institutions to the same high licensing and supervision standards to which we hold conventional ones. Although we are certainly in no position to take a stance on issues of shari'a interpretation, it is important that we become more familiar with the principles and practices unique to Islamic finance in order to make our supervisory and regulatory judgments.[17]

The goal of the Federal Reserve seems to be to ensure that bank customers, whether depositors or borrowers, have adequate protection.

Since October 2008 we at The Institute have been exploring what the Bible says about economics and attempting to understand ancient financial truths. In 2001 we published an article called Networking Charitable Capitalists, and later authored another paper called Kingdom Capitalists. The line of inquiry in all of these endeavors has been to find the ancient truths as taught in scripture about finance, banking, borrowing, lending, interest, debt and more, and to explore which of them are still relevant today. Many others have been asking the same questions.

---

17   http://www.sukuk.net/news/print.php?newid=9379

Nations in general, and the central banks or similar authorities, in particular, need insight on how to accommodate Islamic Banking under its many names. As other countries, such as China and India, emerge as major powers it is inevitable that their banking systems will rise with them. Such systems may or may not be grounded in principles familiar to us.

Beyond Islamic Banking

I suggest we broaden our thinking on this matter to cover major religions that deal with ancient banking concepts and do not just limit the thinking to Islamic finance for several reasons:

- The very term "Islamic Banking" is emotive and elicits negative responses from many quarters. The heated discussions around whether to have a mosque near Ground Zero, site of the September 11 attacks, illustrates this clearly.
- Many of the principles contained in IB are also found, to one degree or another, in other religious teachings.
- While devoted Muslims have revived their ancient trading ideas in recent times, they are not alone in their development of alternative products. In fact, IB is a fairly recent development in the latter part of the 20th Century, and yet Christian and Jewish-led banks have existed for centuries.
- There are significant areas of common ground between Muslims, Christians and Jews when it comes to finances in particular. There are also areas of difference. Note: I am not saying that the faiths themselves are substantially similar, because there are real differences between various religions or faiths. What I am contending is that, when it comes to economic principles, the teachings of IB are not unique or new.
- If the US or other nations provide a wholesale endorsement of IB they become, by definition, subject to the opinions of religious leaders and governing bodies that participate in deciding whether new IB products are "Shari'ah-compliant" (although some in IB do not like this term). Leading Muslim officials have admitted as much to me: there simply are not enough knowledgeable Muslim scholars to go around when it comes to matters of IB.

If, however, nations understand ancient truths as they pertain to banking and finance, then a set of Foundational Principles and products can be articulated, and a new category of financing can emerge: Faith-based Financing.

There is a lack of consensus among Muslims about some basic items such as whether interest is totally forbidden. Central banking authorities, in my view, cannot get embroiled in these arguments, and have to set their own standards.

Rutledge in his address to ABANA reinforces the fact that IB is a new phenomenon:

> At present, the approach of United States regulators to Islamic Banking has been fairly ad hoc—with individual regulators dealing with specific issues as they are presented. This has been the case because the industry is still relatively new in this country. Despite the industry's impressive growth in recent years, there are only a small number of providers and a relatively limited array of services available.

The purpose of this book is to open a dialogue among those looking at ancient banking constructs with the suggestion that we do two things:

- First, broaden the topic beyond Islamic Banking to Faith-based Financing (FBF)
- Second, that we discuss the idea of defining the "box" within which Islamic, Jewish and Christian banks can operate within the US and other nations as FBF institutions.

We also have to debunk the simplistic notion that financial capital is bad, and that any self-respecting religion would have harsh things to say about capital and capitalists. In fact, we have to see that capital, properly deployed and stewarded, is essential to the wellbeing of families, cities and nations. In order to fully consider the topic of FBF we have to go back to the nature of capital, and its role in society—we must be engaged in the business of Repurposing Capital.

If your mind has already flitted to the redistribution of wealth and the forced redistribution of capital you are, in my view, going in the wrong direction. We will discuss more about the purpose of capital later, but it suffices to say, capital has always played a major role in the three main religions that I will cover in this book.

For sake of simplicity this book discusses three major monotheistic religions or faiths—choose your own vocabulary—as they offer the clearest teaching on the topic of debt, capital, wealth creation, charity, interest and lending, to name just some topics. I am not saying that these three religions are the same. Each is entitled to their specific views. I am, however, saying that if the principles of any of them are correct, then they will stand up to scrutiny. Beyond that, I believe we can articulate a set of Foundational Principles that are both spiritual and pragmatic—workable in the real world because they are truth, because they make sense, and not because Moses, Jesus and Mohammed said so. The corollary is also true: where we have come to assume that certain principles of finance, economics and banking are sound, but the fruit of these principles is rotten, then we should reexamine what we have taken to be generally accepted principles.

You may be saying, "This will never work. How are we ever going to get the major religions to agree? We cannot even get Protestants to agree with Protestants (their very name stems from the word protest) let alone Catholics and Protestants to agree. Various groups within Islam are not agreed on primary matters such as riba (interest). Orthodox and modern Jews have differing views. What will get Jews, Muslims and Christians aligned?"

Before I venture towards a framework in which we can work out pragmatic solutions, let us first acknowledge the fears these three groups have, and then the concerns groups such as the Federal Reserve, the FSA and central banks have regarding these matters.

Each group has concerns, suspicions

There has been a rapid growth of liquidity and hence funds seeking investments in the Muslim world thanks mainly to oil revenues. Certain Muslims are concerned that there is a downside to the emergence of IB.

- Muslims are concerned that materialism is on the increase.
- The increased liquidity is seeking diversified investment options and could be going into investments that are not to their liking.

- Islamic Banking (IB) products are relatively new and are evolving quickly. The initial products often mimic regular banking products.
- There are concerns among conservative Muslims that the IB products are departing from the spirit of the Qur'an.
- There are also some Muslims that hold the view that their participation in modern financial markets will result in the dilution of Muslim culture.
- Others believe that there is a strong Jewish influence in the Western markets, and this concerns them.
- They believe that opening Shari'ah banks or banking windows in Western banks is the West's way of toppling Islam.

An article by Imran Nazar Hosein gives a perspective on the historical ills of riba (interest) and how they have impacted Muslim society and the associate fears of today's systems.[18]

The prophecy of the Prophet (sallalahu 'alaihi wa sallam) concerning the universal prevalence of Riba has today been fulfilled. Indeed it has been fulfilled in our own miserable lifetime! Specifically it has been fulfilled during the time that has elapsed since the Ottoman Caliphate was abolished in 1924. Up to 1924 the Riba-based capitalist European economy could not succeed in penetrating the economy and the market of the Muslim world. But Europe did succeed in enticing the governments that presided over the affairs of Muslims to enter into Riba. The Ottoman Caliph, for example, had borrowed considerable sums of money on interest from Europe. His financial and economic difficulties grew to such an extent that he was forced, as a desperate means of preventing the collapse of the Empire, to seek membership in the new European secular State system. He achieved this in the Paris Peace Agreement of 1856. But the price he had to pay was to succumb to a financial blackmail that extracted from him the abolition of Jizyah and Ahl al-Dhimmah in all the territories of the Ottoman Empire. This was also a quid pro quo for

---

18   Imran Nazar Hosein - www.imranhosein.org

debt and interest payment relief. In doing so the Caliph betrayed Allah Most High Who had Himself established the jizyah tax in the Qur'an (al-Tauba, 9:29).

The success of Euro-Jewish bankers in targeting the Ottoman Caliph was a classic example of the financial imperialism, which is made possible through Riba. Henry Kissinger was the author of the same strategy that eventually led to the collapse of a super-power in modern times, the Union of Soviet Socialist Republics (USSR).

That event should have opened the eyes of the 'Ulama of Islam. It did not! As a consequence, the same strategy continues to be pursued by the International Monetary Fund and the World Bank, and by so many others.

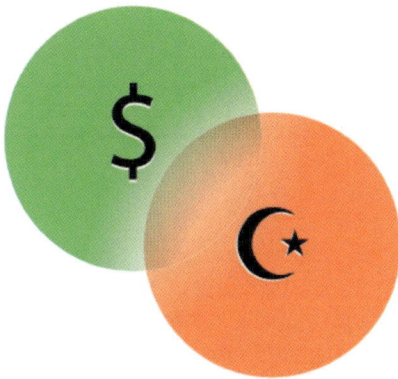

Figure 0.2: Muslims fear a tainting of Islam by Western Materialism.

Perhaps the clearest statement of a purist application of the principles of riba (interest) is found in the momentous ruling of the Supreme Court of Pakistan.

It was a momentous event, as big as the creation of the country itself. On 14 Ramadan 1420, the Shari'ah Appellate Bench of the Supreme Court of Pakistan gave its landmark decision banning interest in all its forms and by whatever name it may be called. Thus fifty-five years after its creation in the name of Islam (27 Ramadan 1365), Pakistan became the first Muslim country to officially declare modern (and rampant) bank interest as ar-riba, declared haram by Qur'an.

The court also specified a step-by-step approach to rid the country of the evil of interest. As a consequence of this judgement, certain laws will cease to take effect from 31 March 2000, some other laws from 31 July 2000, and all other laws permitting or condoning interest from 30 June 2001.

The Federal Shari'ah Court of Pakistan had declared the laws allowing interest repugnant to Islam in 1991. The Federal Government of Pakistan and certain banks and financial institutions filed 67 appeals against this judgment in the Shari'ah Appellate Bench of the Supreme Court. This decision is a disposition of that appeal. It is the final verdict of Pakistan's highest court.

The report went on to conclude:

In the light of the detailed discussion above, there is no difference between different types of loan, so far as the prohibition of riba is concerned. It also does not make any difference whether the additional amount stipulated over the principal loan or debt is small or large. It is, therefore, held that all the prevailing forms of interest, either in the banking transactions or in private transactions do fall within the definition of "riba."

Pakistan is one of only three countries to adopt this stringent position. (The others are Iran and Saudi Arabia.) Not all Muslims agree with their position, of course. In an article titled Partnership, Equity-Financing and Islamic Finance: Whither Profit-Loss Sharing? Mohammad Omar Farooq writes:

Proponents of Islamic financial institutions (IFIs) regard their conventional counterparts as Islamically unacceptable, because the latter are interest-based, not based on fair profit-loss sharing (PLS) and risk sharing. Idealization of the PLS mode is questionable as it is not explicitly mandated in Islam's primary texts. The preference for PLS is based on juristic interpretation that evolved in response to the prohibition of riba, commonly equated with interest. Contrary to theory, IFIs in practice have marginalized PLS modes and instead adopted mark-up type, interest substituting, risk-avoiding modes of finance. In this paper it is argued that despite the theoretical idealization, IFIs as businesses are rational in avoiding PLS modes.

Partnership is the least common form of business organization for practical reasons. In this context these reasons also cover equity-financing. IFIs are organized as banks, but rather than being financial intermediaries, they are primarily merchant banks. Accordingly, this paper contends that legally restricting or religiously idealizing PLS modes is untenable. The conclusion is that, while paying lip service to PLS modes to define themselves as interest-free, a.k.a., Islamic entities, IFIs continue to marginalize PLS, packaging conventional banking products under Islamic labels.

It therefore seems clear to me one cannot rely on the label placed on Islamic Banking products to determine whether they comply with the spirit of scripture. One has to examine the nature of the transaction to see whether it complies with the Foundational Principles that are inherent in Faith-based Financing. The same would be true for products that purported to be "Christian." There have, after all, been failures of several banks in the US claiming to be Christian.

Certain Christian groups also have fears

There are some Christian groups who are concerned about the entry of IB into the United Kingdom, specifically, and the West generally.

- They see IB as a precursor to Islamic inculturation of their countries.
- They suspect that the goal of IB is proselytizing.
- They are seeing restrictions placed on Christians while simultaneously more freedom is being given to Muslims as the UK, EU and US open up to Islamic Banking.

An article by Helena Christofi in February 2007, she stated the following:

London is the leading Islamic banking center in the West. Islamist clerics with terrorist connections and a mission to Islamize Europe are infiltrating the United Kingdom through its banking system, and British officials are encouraging them. HSBC, Lloyds TSB, and Citigroup have opened Islamic banking units and branches throughout England. In 2005 the first stand-alone British Islamic bank, Islamic Bank of Britain, opened its doors. Middle Eastern Islamic banks have also set up shop in the UK.

Islamic banks are managed according to shari'a law, the defining principle being the prohibition of interest in all monetary transactions as commanded in the Qur'an. The other defining feature of Islamic banks is their operation of shari'a advisory boards comprised of Islamic scholars and clerics whose job it is to ensure that the banks' activities comply with shari'a law. Proponents of the Islamic economic model (of which Islamic banking is a central pillar) argue that the Islamic system is superior to capitalism because it is structured around a strict code of ethics prohibiting exploitative practices, such as the charging of interest, with the aim of constructing a moral society. Capitalism's single-minded focus on money, they argue, produces the social ills we see in the West whose manifestation would become impossible under the Islamic model.

Sheik Yousef Al-Qaradawi, a leading Sunni cleric, spiritual leader of the Muslim Brotherhood, and instigator and financier of terrorism in Europe and the Middle East, heads the fundamentalist European Council for Fatwa and Research, several of whose most prominent members sit on every major British Islamic bank's shari'a board. Both Al-Qaradawi and the Council have expressed their hope that "Islam will return to Europe as a conqueror" by way of "preaching and ideology" or "by the sword."

In a paper entitled Financial Jihad: What Americans Need to Know, the author, Christopher Holton, expresses concerns about those providing governance in issues of Shari'ah banking.

Mufti Taqi Usmani. Usmani is one of the most famous—or infamous—Shari'ah scholars. Until recently—after his Jihadist tendencies were revealed in National Review, Human Events, Investor's Business Daily and other publications, Usmani was on the board of the Dow Jones Islamic Index (IMANX). He is still on the Shari'ah advisory boards of several other Western financial institutions, including Swiss RE, Arcapita, UBS-Warburg, and HSBC. It has been revealed that Usmani is an officer of a Deobandi madrassa (a type of Muslim academy) in Karachi, Pakistan which is essentially a jihadist factory, educating young Islamic extremists. Usmani has advocated jihad by Muslims in the West ("The purpose of Jihad aims at breaking the grandeur of unbelievers and establish that of Muslims.") Earlier this year, he publicly endorsed suicide bombing and the Taliban.

There is a second element to the fears of Christians and Muslims alike, namely, the broad influence of Secular Humanism.

- They see faith-based organizations being marginalized
- There appears to be increasing government intervention and control both in the markets and in life in general
- There is, in their view, a departure from scriptural frameworks
- Many Christians in the US are concerned that the efforts to counter the excesses of the "free markets" will stifle entrepreneurship, free enterprise, private ownership, and a good return for labor.

Cultural and Religious Takeover on the back of Islamic Banking

Figure 0.3: There is a fear that Islamic Banking is a front for radical Islamization.

Jewish elements also have fears

The field of mistrust is not limited to Muslim vs. Muslim, or Christian vs. Muslim. The Jewish people are suspicious of:

- Christians who go to Israel as missionaries trying to make converts of Jews.
- The adversarial Muslim agenda coupled with growing influence through amassed petro-dollars.
- They, along with Christians, are concerned that Islamic Banks are using their zakat giving to fund anti-Israel activities.

Islamic banking took off in the 1970s but was first concocted by Muslim Brotherhood founder Hassan al-Banna in the 1920s. The stated goal was to penetrate the Western finance system, corrupting it from within in hopes of creating a parallel system to re-establish a global Islamic empire governed by Islamic law (Shari'ah). Islamic rules of commerce (fiqh al-muamalat) forbid interest (riba) and investing in a prohibited (hara'am) enterprise. They also mandate tithes on wealth (zakat). However, the Koran fails to precisely define these concepts. Imams and ayatollahs differ, for example, on whether riba prohibits all interest or only usurious interest.

While the overhaul of American and Western banking regulations is urgent, Islamic banking cannot be the answer because Muslim clerics—not US laws and regulators—make the rules. In 1969, the Saudis created the Organization of the Islamic Conference (OIC), which is now leading the charge for global expansion of Islamic banking and has established new regulatory, accounting and auditing organizations to govern such banks. Notably, the OIC's charter is to "liberate Jerusalem and Al-Aqsa [mosque] from Zionist occupation.[19]

One cannot dismiss the capital concerns of Israel since they represent a large venture capital market and are active in international capital markets. So their views on finance have to be taken into account in the consideration of faith-based programs, should they have specific requirements.

Figure 0.4: Jews fear being squeezed by the growing Islamic finance push.

---

[19]   Islamic banking: Is Treasury complicit? Rachel Ehrenfeld and Samuel A. Abady (Thursday, December 11, 2008)

Conventional bankers have concerns

Western and conventional bankers have concerns about IB, many of which revolve around the practical matters of risk management. "While Islamic finance has grown substantively in the last few years, appreciation of its risk architecture and profile is still evolving."[20]

Muslims differ in their definitions of what constitutes IB. For example, Tarek El Diwany, keeper of the website Islamic-banking.com, writes an article titled Islamic Banking isn't Islamic.[21]

"The contractum trinius was a legal trick used by European merchants in the Middle Ages to allow borrowing at usury, something that the Church fiercely opposed. It was a combination of three separate contracts, each of which was deemed permissible by the Church, but which together yielded a fixed rate of return from the outset." He goes on to say, "The above set of legal devices is nothing other than a trick to circumvent riba, a modern day Islamic contractum trinius. The fact that the text of these contracts is so difficult to come by is one shameful fact of Islamic banking."

- They differ on what constitutes riba.

- Many of the guidelines for IB products are set by religious councils whose laws are set outside the jurisdiction of the US or other non-Muslim nations.

- These matters are open to religious interpretation and Western bankers are ill-qualified to argue the more subjective aspects of IB.

The Kuwait Finance House (KFH) Global Islamic Finance Directory for 2008 points out that availability of human capital is a challenge.

20   Risk Analysis for Islamic Banks, Hennie van Greuning and Zamir Iqbal, 2008, The International Bank for Reconstruction and Development, World Bank
21   http://www.islamic-finance.com/item100_f.htm

The IB sector worldwide is growing at a much faster rate than it is acquiring and developing new talent. The significant growth in the industry in the last few years, combined with the establishment of new players in non-traditional markets is taking a toll on the sector's already limited pool of human resources.[22]

Risk management practices are another concern due to the unique risks of Islamic finance. The guiding principles established by existing standards bodies are, according to KFH, "rarely embraced wholeheartedly."

As William Rutledge of the New York Fed stated, "we are certainly in no position to take a stance on issues of Shari'ah interpretation." He went on to point out specific challenges for US regulators.

There are several other features of US banking law that could potentially hold back Islamic finance. One example is the set of restrictions placed on the range of permissible investments that commercial banks may hold. To ensure that banks do not assume unnecessary risk, their investments are generally limited to fixed-income, interest-bearing securities, which are prohibited by the shari'a. In addition, commercial banks must meet numerous disclosure requirements in order to comply with regulatory policy such as the Truth in Lending Act. These requirements typically mandate advance disclosure of APR and other terms that do not fit the principles on which Islamic finance is structured. On top of these issues, an Islamic financial institution that intends to finance the purchase of a home or a car according to murabaha or ijara structures may need to consider whether state law requires the institution to qualify as a licensed leasing company or auto lender.

The difficulty for Muslim consumers in obtaining shari'a-compliant insurance presents another hurdle to the accessibility of Islamic finance in Western markets. As I mentioned earlier, both Fannie Mae and Freddie Mac have purchased Islamically structured mortgages. However, both entities require

---

22   KFH Research Ltd. Global Islamic Finance Directory for 2008 – page 108

property insurance and private mortgage insurance to be held on the securitized mortgages they purchase. This requirement forces customers of Islamic financial institutions to purchase traditional insurance for these mortgages that I understand is not compliant with the shari'a. Beyond the legal issues regarding the activities a bank is permitted to conduct, bank supervisors have issues to confront in how to assess the safety and soundness of individual Islamic banks. A flexible approach to these issues corresponds with a larger trend toward a more adaptable, risk-oriented strategy in which supervisors are evaluating the specific risks and risk management practices of individual institutions. This manner of supervision can allow for an accommodative approach to Islamic banking that is based on its unique structure and related risks.[23]

So Islamic banking is clearly not a foregone conclusion. But it is a growing market and will therefore receive attention.

━━━━━━

But challenges remain. If Islamic finance is to move deeper into mainstream global finance, the industry needs to improve transparency and foster credibility by harmonizing standards and practices. Not least, shari'a interpretation varies between regions and even institutions. Regulatory oversight need to be sharpened as well. These measures – and others – could be critical in broadening the appeal of Islamic finance and bridging the gap between Islamic and conventional financial systems.

The Islamic finance industry needs to work on innovation, too. Shari'a-compliant products can be more complex than conventional ones because every transaction is backed a non-financial trade. Many instruments are still lacking, including corporate treasury and derivatives products. As UIB's Pace points out: "We [in the industry] need to change our perception of R&D and view it as a core ingredient of success." But at the same time, innovation is hampered by the limited number of Islamic scholars able to vet financial products for Shari'a compliance.[24]

---

[23]   KFH Research Ltd. Global Islamic Finance Directory for 2008
[24]   Is Islamic finance at tipping point? By Christopher Watts, The Economist

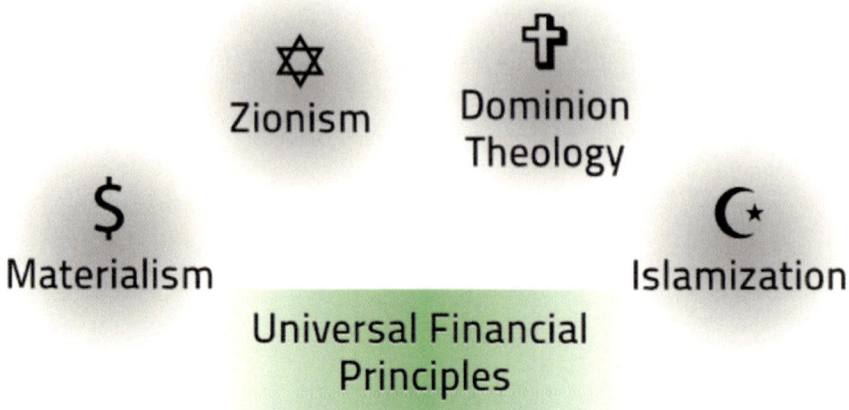

Figure 0.5: Finance does not do well in a climate of fear.

There is also a serious concern that IB lacks the compliance skills and depth of resources to govern or monitor IB efficiency. Compared to the US and other developed nations, the IB compliance functions are very short-handed.

Economies do not thrive under fear

Someone remarked to me recently that he had been through three economic downturns in his career, but this one felt different. "This time the fear is palpable." Certainly there is cause for many to have concern about the world economies in general. If fear and suspicion of "other" groups is added to the mix, a wave of fear can paralyze meaningful economic progress.

The radical actions of central banks often do not help the situation. People are leery of heavy-handed intervention in financial markets, in part because the initiative gets taken from the hand of those working in the markets, or at least from what Adam Smith called "the invisible hand of the market." Uncertain times can breed isolationist thinking.

The fears, or concerns, mentioned in the sections above can be seen as the possible cascading of consequences of opening one's system to alternate banking products:

- Infiltration: the "others" will use their way of finance to infiltrate "our" way of life
- Inculturation: the requirement that we adopt their worldview and way of life
- Dilution: once we adopt their financing mechanism it will not be long before our own culture is diluted
- Domination: this will lead to "them" dominating "us"
- Marginalization: eventually we may become a marginalized minority in our own country

What can banking authorities do to mitigate the specific (sectarian) fears? In my view, the Central Banks of nations entertaining IB and other FBF (including the Federal Reserve Bank in the USA) must start with the area they know well—banking. They must then lay out a framework allowing the major interests of faith-based groups to flourish while ensuring the governing laws of their particular country remain intact. The prudential responsibility of the central banks and other governing entities could be to define which facets of FBF they are willing to accommodate, and which ones fall "outside the box."

A FBF approach could encourage faith-based organizations to plough new ground in launching institutions and products that serve their constituents. But they would need to do so consistent with laws of the land in which they operate without imposing external laws on the sovereign nation within which they bank.

Faith is the antidote to fear

Some of the fears I have described are the inevitable result of globalization as nations get greater exposure to diverse people groups. Unfortunately there is enough evidence on all sides to support the fact that radical groups do have less-than-transparent agendas. Despite these fears there is nonetheless an opportunity to draw wisdom from these ancient truths and bring into one's own environment those principles and practices that could serve one's people and economy well.

How does one address the potential fears of all parties? Faith is the antidote to fear. The discussion of the potential fears of those considering the possibility of FBF is not to say one should not have FBF. On the contrary. Faith-based is the antithesis of fear-based.

A second antidote is love. There is a saying, "Perfect love casts out fear." FBF should be open, transparent, clear in its practical and humanitarian objectives, and respectful of the views of those from differing faiths. Moderates in each of the faiths espouse principles of tolerance and love. The Guardian carried an article covering the teaching of a Muslim cleric, Ghanaian-born Sheokh Ahmed Tijani Ben Omar.[25]

> According to Sheikh Omar who identified himself as a student and servant of Imam Cisse of blessed memory, it is a case of spiritual bankruptcy for a Moslem to ever cast a scornful look at a Christian, and worse still, to say in his heart: 'these are kafir,' infidels just as it is simple-mindedness for a Christian to see a Moslem as unsaved.

The report went on to say, "although Mecca and Medina would retain their status as the center of spiritual significance of Islam, the United States is the place where the brilliant illumination of Islam will rise and shine... any Moslem who attacks or plans to attack America is not a true Moslem." Omar went on the say:

> It is easier to practice Islam in America because it is the land of freedom. It is only in America you could practice whatever religion you so choose without any form of hindrance. And they made it clear that there should be no compulsion in religion.

This may not be the love that American Christians or Jews want to hear, but it points out there are Muslims who are not anti-American. And truth remains truth: we are to love our neighbors as we love ourselves, and neighbors include those from other religious groups. In a moment I will

---

25   A Messenger of Peace, The Guardian, Saturday May 23, 2009, by Ajibola Amzat

explore the difference between faith and ideology: any group can shift from relationship with God to ideology.

In overseeing the banks offering such products, the guidelines should hold FBF practitioners to the standards they espouse: being hopeful, loving, expecting the best, and simultaneously mitigating the potential risks of FBF.

What is "faith-based"?

Faith-based means seeing things with a different set of eyes. It has nothing to do with "just believing without seeing" or suspending rational thinking or logical inquiry. We talk about a "leap of faith" as doing something that involves taking a risk without knowing all the facts. Anyone in business and finance will know that one never has all of the facts. To be in business involves some level of risk, and the joy of business and finance is getting a reasonable return for the risk involved. FBF entails seeing the world of finance through lenses informed by a scriptural worldview. This impacts time horizons (eternal rather than temporal), the manner of structuring transactions (transparent rather than opaque), integrity (required because of higher accountability), and much more. I unpack the Foundational Principles of financing and capital in Part 9 of this book. At the outset, however, I simply want to point out that "faith-based" is a matter of seeing differently, and not a case of not seeing and hoping for the best.

The former President of Harvard University, Charles W. Eliot, said:

———

All business proceeds on beliefs, or judgments of probabilities, and not on certainties.

Worldview, Faith and Ideology

Financial markets are, by and large, global. The financial crisis of 2009-2010 had ripple effects into most nations on the globe and revealed some of the positive and negative effects of globalization. Is globalization good or bad? People will line up behind both sides of this argument. Is finance a weapon wielded by some at the expense of others? This has always been the case throughout history. You may be concerned that those who masquerade as people of faith will use FBF as a vehicle to accomplish their agendas at the expense of others. I believe this is a valid concern, and the question is how we can discern the difference between those with noble intentions, and those who would use finance to advance questionable aims.

Some of the answer can be found in differentiating between faith and ideology. At the core, however, will be whether we try to understand the common ground without simplistic polarizing. Having said this, the tendency of Western diplomats to assume the best of every radical group is alarming. The recent embrace of the Muslim Brotherhood in Egypt is an example, despite its motto: "Allah is our objective; the Prophet is our leader; the Qur'an is our law; Jihad is our way; dying in the way of Allah is our highest hope."

This book is written at a time when there is turmoil in many Arab or Muslim nations, yet countries are considering IB for one reason or another. The initial assumption, driven by tolerance and pluralism, is the god of the Jews, Christians and Muslims is the same, so there can be no harm in allowing IB products or banks into one's country. Banking authorities need to step outside their comfort zones and consider the question (Is the god of Islam the God of the Bible?) if they are to make an accurate determination about the wisdom of allowing IB. If banking regulators are familiar with the Judeo-Christian God, then they can rightly demand that the motives and behaviors of those proposing IB would be consistent with what they know of God. If banking authorities are in Islamic nations and Christians or Jews are proposing opening faith-based financial institutions, then the host banking authorities should likewise examine the question.

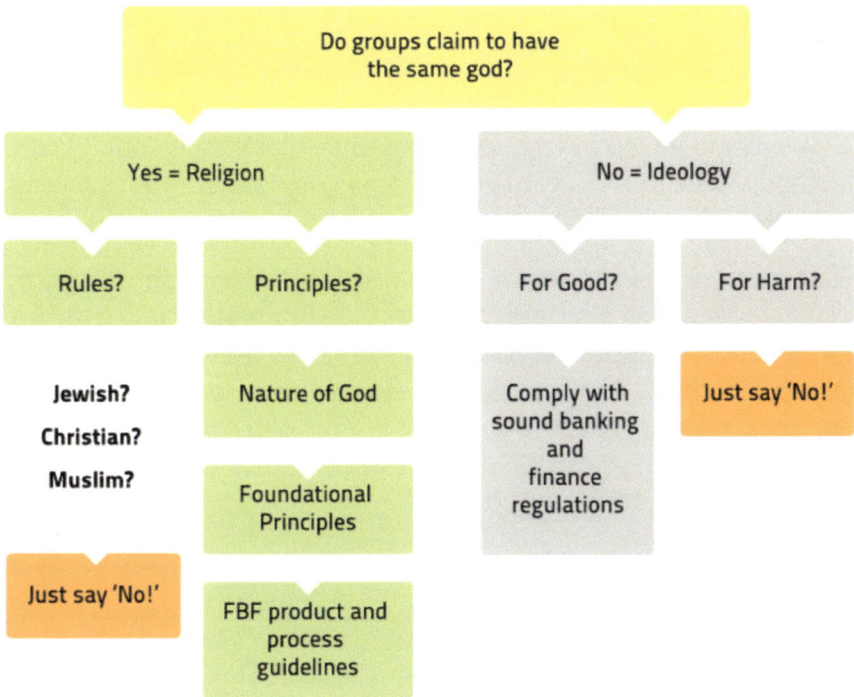

Figure 0.6: How similar is the faith of Jews, Christians and Muslims? Moderates claim similarity: what are the implications?

You might say, "We are in a nation where anyone can practice whatever religion they like and do so freely. What difference does it make?" Common sense dictates, however, that if I am using my religion to spread an agenda that does not build up the host nation and the ideals of that nation, then the host nation is quite within its rights to established banking, disclosure and reporting regulations that moderate my banking or financing practices that are an expression of my religion such that they do not harm the host nation. I can believe whatever I want to about God, salvation, charity and ritual, but when it spills over to the way I do finance, then my financial practices have to comply with banking regulations.

The tree diagram (Figure 0.6) asks a series of questions:

- Is the God of the Jews, Christians and Muslims the same?
- Should one follow rules or principles?
- What principles emanate from the nature of God?
- How do they inform financing products, practices and purposes?

If the god of the Muslims, or other religions, is not the same as that of Jews and Christians (setting aside the question of the identity of Jesus Christ), one must ask, "Is Islam a peaceful religion, or an ideology?" The tree diagram (Figure 0.7) explores the alternatives. By the way, we have seen our fair share of Jewish and Christian radicals who claim to be mainstream but who have moved themselves into the category of ideologues rather than followers of the Law, or of Jesus.

If you are a central banker, how do you sift through the religion vs. ideology question? This is particularly important because few groups are going to say, "We have bad intentions and we are aiming to ruin or overtake your country." It is more likely that any religious organization will say, "Yes, we are a religious group, but we exist for the good of mankind and you should allow us to express our religion freely. By the way, our religion dictates that we should have our own financial systems."

Mark Siljander is a former US Congressman who claims that there is much common ground between Christians and Muslims. His book, The Deadly Misunderstanding: A Congressman's Quest to Bridge the Muslim-Christian Divide, contends that there are political differences, but many overlaps at the spiritual level that could form the basis for meaningful dialog. He has traveled extensively in Muslim nations and believes that there are misunderstandings that empower radical Muslims, whom he says are a small percentage of the population.[26] He is a controversial figure, but still has the support of many Christians.[27]

We often hear politicians say, "We all worship the same god." President Bush, in an interview with Al Arabiya television in October 2007, said, "I believe in an almighty God, and I believe that all the world, whether they be Muslim, Christian, or any other religion, prays to the same God." In the same interview he said, "I believe there is a universal God. I believe the God that the Muslim prays to is the same God that I pray to. After all, we all came from Abraham. I believe in that universality." Not everyone agrees. Nowadays the conflicts between the ideological aspects of Muslims and Westerners is at

---

26   A Deadly Misunderstanding: A Congressman's Quest to Bridge the Muslim-Christian Divide, Siljander, Mark D. (October 2008). New York: HarperOne. ISBN 9780061438288

27   According to Wikipedia, Mark Deli Siljander (born June 11, 1951) is a former Republican US Representative and deputy United Nations ambassador from the state of Michigan who was convicted of obstruction of justice and acting as an unregistered foreign agent related to his work for an Islamic charity with ties to international terrorism. Siljander pleaded guilty to the charges in Federal court on July 7, 2010.

the fore. The view expressed by President Bush is seen as Universalist, not Christian.

Other Christians and Jews contend that the Hebrew God, YHWH is not the same as the Muslim God, Allah.

We are well aware that the name Allah is used by Arab speaking Christians for the God of the Bible. In fact, the root from which the name is derived, ilah, stems from the ancient Semitic languages, corresponding to the Mesopotamian IL, as well as the Hebrew-Aramaic EL, as in Ishma-el, Immanu-el, Isra-el. These terms were often used to refer to any deity worshiped as a high god, especially the chief deity amongst a pantheon of lesser gods. As such, the Holy Bible uses the term as just one of the many titles for Yahweh, the only true God. Yet the problem arises from the fact that Muslims insist that Allah is not a title, but the personal name of the God of Islam. This becomes problematic since according to the Holy Bible the name of the God of Abraham is Yahweh/Jehovah, not Allah. God spoke further to Moses and said to him, "I am Yahweh (YHWH) and I appeared to Abraham, Isaac, and Jacob, as God Almighty; BUT BY MY NAME, YAHWEH, I did not make myself known to them." Exodus 6:2-3 Therefore, Christians can use Allah as a title but not as the personal name for the God of the Bible.[28]

Yet others put the burden of proof on Muslims since the Hebrew and Jewish scriptures pre-date the Qur'an.

The Qur'an alleges that the God of Islam, Allah, is indeed the God of Abraham and hence the God of Scripture, Yahweh Elohim. But is this the case? Are we to assume that just because the Qur'an states that Allah is Yahweh of the Bible that both Jews and Christians are obligated to believe this to be true? Or do we examine the nature and attributes of Allah in order to compare them with the biblical portrait of Yahweh to find if this is the case? This process of examination is essential since our objective is to discover the true nature of

---

[28]   Is Allah the God of the Bible? http://www.answering-islam.org/Shamoun/god.htm

God, a process whose outcome entails eternal consequences in regards to man's future destiny in the afterlife. After all, if Allah is the God of Abraham then Jews and Christians are wrong for not embracing Islam.

But if Allah is not Yahweh, then Muslims are not worshiping the same God only with a different name. We will examine certain qualities of Allah as stated in the Qur'an and briefly compare them to Yahweh and see where the evidence leads us. The reason why we are comparing Allah to Yahweh as opposed to contrasting Yahweh to the Koranic portrait of Allah, using the Qur'an as the standard, is due to the fact that it is Islam that claims to worship the same God of the Holy Bible. Thus, the burden of proof rests upon the Muslims to defend this contention since they believe Allah is the same as Yahweh.[29]

Governments have a responsibility to determine what is best for their countries. China, for example, has conducted extensive studies and determined that Christianity could make a positive difference in their nation, at least economically. It is reasonable to examine a religious system (setting aside the fact that people say, "I have a faith, not a religion") and determine whether it produces good outcomes.

Recently, the Arab League reported that "nearly one-third of Arabs are illiterate, including half of Arab women." The report also points out that "it's not just the older generation: Three quarters of the 100 million illiterate people in 21 Arab countries are between the ages of 15 and 45." By contrast, 99 percent of Americans 15 years and older are literate, according to the latest government figures. Western nations have for centuries had the most literate populations and literacy rates in the US have been among the highest in the world going back as far as the 1600s when it was estimated that "the literacy rate for men in Massachusetts and Connecticut was somewhere between 89 and 95 percent..." And for "women in those colonies it is estimated to have run as high as 62 percent in the years 1681 – 1697." (Postman, Amusing Ourselves to Death, 1985)

29   http://www.answering-islam.org/Shamoun/god.htm

Where Christianity spreads, literacy inevitably follows. A Ugandan university study published in 2007 reveals that while "Arab Muslims were the first to introduce written information (texts) in Uganda, they did not make any effort to teach reading and writing... Literacy in the Roman alphabet was introduced into Uganda by Christian missionaries in the late 19th century." The report goes on to add that within contemporary Ugandan culture, "Christianity provides the impetus for local literacy practices..." Another study by the Organization of the Islamic Conference on the status of scientific research in its 57 member states reveals a similar shortcoming in the area of scientific accomplishment.

Of the more than 11.5 million scientific papers published worldwide each year; Muslim countries contribute just 2.5 percent. There are more than 1.5 billion Muslims living across the Islamic world — about a quarter of the world's population — and yet they have generated barely more than one percent of the world's scientific literature and produced only two scientific Nobel Prize winners.[30]

By 2006 there were 165 Jewish Nobel Prize winners compared with 6 Muslims.[31] Craven's point is not about racial superiority, but about systems that produce innovation and wealth. If we are espousing FBF, from whatever vantage point, we should back up the demands with proof of benefits to society.

This view is confirmed by Dr. Farrukh Saleem, Pakistani Executive Director of the Center for Research and Security Studies, who wrote in a 2009 blog:

Interestingly, the combined annual GDP of 57 OIC-countries is under $2 trillion. America, just by herself, produces goods and services worth $12 trillion; China $8 trillion, Japan $3.8 trillion and Germany $2.4 trillion (purchasing power parity basis). Oil rich Saudi Arabia, UAE, Kuwait and Qatar collectively produce goods and services (mostly oil) worth $500 billion; Spain alone produces goods and services worth over $1 trillion, Catholic Poland $489 billion and Buddhist

30   Christianity & Islam: Two Worldviews and Why They Matter, S. Michael Craven, January 28, 2008
31   http://www.jewishmag.com/99mag/nobel/nobel.htm

Thailand $545 billion. (Muslim GDP as a percentage of world GDP is fast declining).[32]

If IB, Materialism, Zionism and Dominionism are adopted willy-nilly without serious consideration of the fruit of the philosophy the consequences could be disastrous for an economy over the long term.

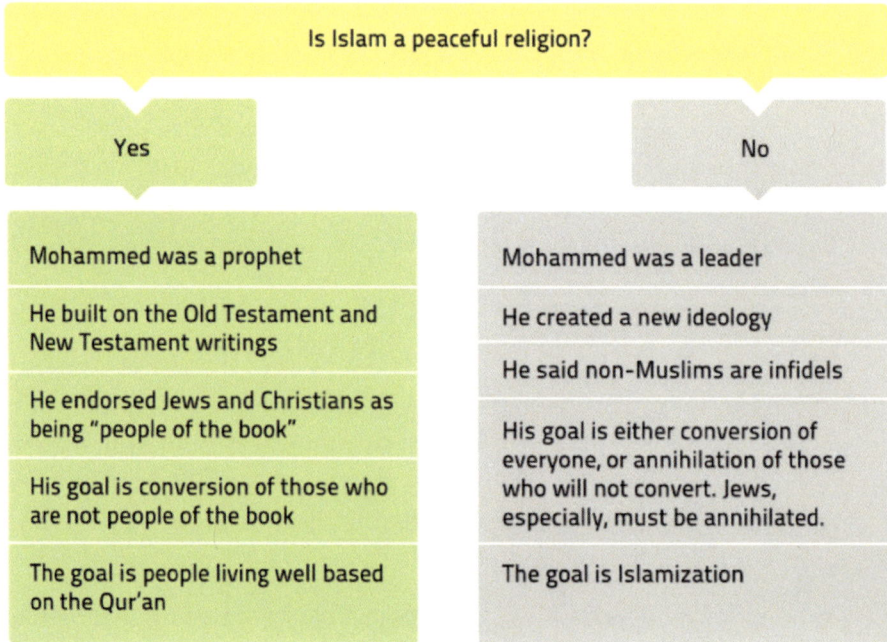

Is Islam a peaceful religion?	
Yes	**No**
Mohammed was a prophet	Mohammed was a leader
He built on the Old Testament and New Testament writings	He created a new ideology
	He said non-Muslims are infidels
He endorsed Jews and Christians as being "people of the book"	His goal is either conversion of everyone, or annihilation of those who will not convert. Jews, especially, must be annihilated.
His goal is conversion of those who are not people of the book	
The goal is people living well based on the Qur'an	The goal is Islamization

Figure 0.7: Is Islam a peaceful religion? Central Banks should address this question before opening their systems to Islamic Banking.

If we take the fork on the decision tree that says we worship the same God, then we are still left with the decision as to whether we will pursue a rules-based approach to finance, or a principles or values-based approach. The rules-based approach is not practical if we are talking about religious rules. We will examine why this is the case.

---

32   http://ibnmahadi.wordpress.com/2009/01/12

If faith is indeed a factor in finance, we are then left with the best alternative being the pursuit of principle-based FBF. These principles should inform the purpose, products and operational processes of all manner of finance.

If you are a Muslim and hold the view that the God of Jews and Christians and Allah of the Qur'an are different, this poses another set of challenges when it comes to asking Western nations to be accepting of IB. If you are a radical Christian or Jew, you face the same issues. I believe the burden of proof rests with those seeking to enter countries that have a different financial system than their own. If I want to open a bank in an Islamic nation or in Israel, I have to prove that I will operate for the good of their nation and consistent with established banking regulations. I cannot say, "Because I am a Christian you must make special arrangements for me." Yet this is precisely the stance of many who seek to set up IB in non-Islamic nations. There needs to be a high standard for all who wish to engage in FBF.

Those of us in the Western world may find it hard to actually state that the ideology of an organization, of whatever religious creed, is harmful. Political correctness, tolerance and freedom of religion are powerful concepts, and we are reluctant to violate them. Looking at the outcomes of a group's faith and trying to discern whether the fruit is good can seem judgmental. There is a desperate need for clear thinking in the issues of finance, however, so we must ask the tough questions.

If you are a person working in the world of finance and your religion is producing positive results for society, there is still a need for self-reflection at the personal level. The majority of Christians would not call themselves secular, yet they are infected with what is commonly referred to as the secular-sacred dichotomy. This is the notion that some things are spiritual (or sacred) and other things are not: they are secular, or pragmatic. For many Christians, best practices trump biblical principles. Rationalism triumphs over religion when it comes to everyday work. To their credit, this is less the case for Muslims and for practicing Jews. If faith is not something isolated to the religious closet in our lives, we should be asking, "Should my faith impact my work in finance?" If there is not a clear connection between your faith and your work in finance then you are most likely, for practical purposes, a secularist, regardless of your religious affiliation. If you are a Christian in terms of salvation, your worldview is probably Christian-humanist when it comes to finance.

Is the fruit (outcome) of the FB group good?

Yes = Religion

No = Ideology

Rules?

Principles?

Yes

No

For Good?

For Harm?

Jewish?

Christian?

Muslim?

- Based on character of a good God

- Abstracted to Foundational Principles

- Translated to FBF guidelines

- Focused on outcomes, not just mechanics

- For the public good

- Subject to governance and scrutiny

Just say 'No!'

Comply with sound banking and finance regulations

Just say 'No!'

The outcomes are positive?

Yes

No

Consider positive principles, application

Reconsider why you should cater to it

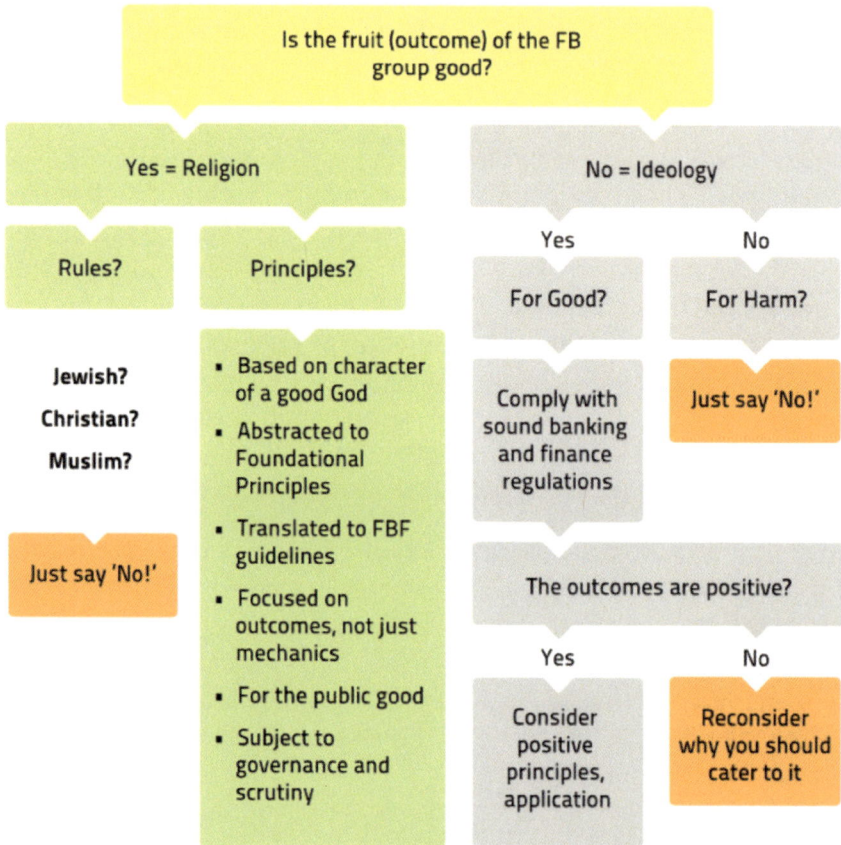

Figure 0.8: Is my religious group producing a good outcome? If an outsider looked at the outputs rather than the inputs, would they conclude that the fruit was good?

In The Everlasting Man the prolific English author, GK Chesterton cautions against this dualistic thinking:

In reality the rivers of mythology and philosophy run parallel and do not mingle till they meet in the sea of Christendom. Simple secularists still talk as if the Church had introduced a sort of schism between reason and religion. The truth is that the Church was actually the first thing that ever tried to combine reason and religion.

Many Jews claim to be secular Jews. Yossi Beilin has served in many roles in Israel's government. He says "secular Jews are not a marginal group in Jewish life. We are the mainstream."[33] I have met many Muslims in Indonesia, for example, who are secular Muslims. Work and faith are routinely separated by those who are religious. This posture will not bring the benefits of faith-based perspectives on today's pressing financial challenges. We need to reconnect the dots between our faith and finances. It is my belief that Finance is a gift from God for the good of the world. Like any gift, it can be misused. What started as a set of faith-based practices has given way to greed and self-enrichment. Is there a way to recapture the essence of FBF and make a positive contribution to the world?

We will explore this question throughout this book. We will also lay a framework for considering:

- Are historical writings practical today?
- Can we agree on a set of Foundational Principles common to many religions?
- What about interest and usury?
- Is capitalism the same as Christianity?
- What makes a product faith-based?
- What makes a financial institution, be it a retail bank or private equity firm, faith-based?
- What outcomes would you expect in a corporation, or a nation, that embraces FBF?
- How can one comply with the laws of the land and operate consistent with Foundational Principles?
- Are there any examples of where this has worked in history?

As we explore these questions, and many others, the authorities in the nations where we work should be entitled to judge whether our faith-informed financial products and practices serve the good of society at large or are simply a different way for us to promote personal or religious agendas. Having a faith should not be a free-pass to avoid intellectual scrutiny.

---

[33] His Brother's Keeper: Israel and Diaspora Jews in the Twenty-first Century, Yossi Beilin, Schocken Books, 2009

Capital comes in many forms, and it serves many purposes. It has potential for good and for harm; in order to be constructive in society it needs a context.

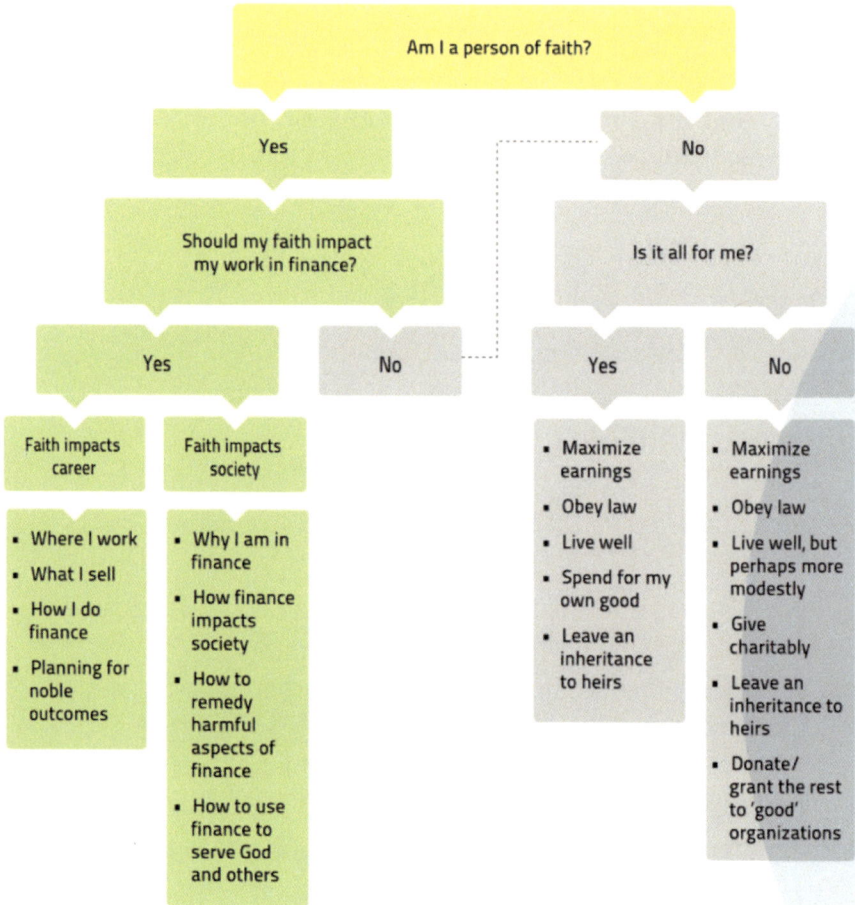

Figure 0.9: Does my faith make any difference to my role in the world of finance?

4

Should economics and religion co-exist?

How the world outside the USA views religion

In the Western world there has been a distinct effort to rid the marketplace of religion. The fact of the matter is there has been an upsurge of spirituality in the marketplace, regardless of what is happening in traditional churches. The secular press has reported on the phenomenon of believers who are seeking to merge faith and work.

SUB-SAHARAN AFRICA

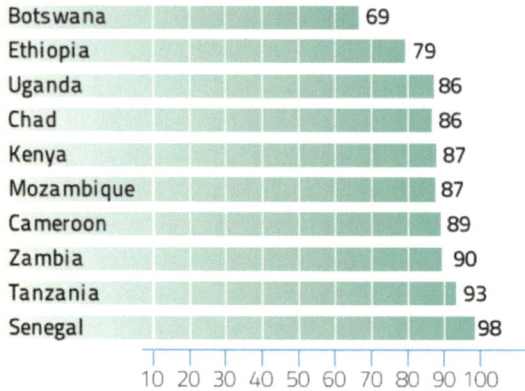

Botswana	69
Ethiopia	79
Uganda	86
Chad	86
Kenya	87
Mozambique	87
Cameroon	89
Zambia	90
Tanzania	93
Senegal	98

10 20 30 40 50 60 70 80 90 100

Figure 9.1: "How important is religion in your life?". Source the Pew Forum on Religion and Public Life.

The divide of work and worship is not as pronounced in other parts of the world. A study by the Pew Forum on Religion and Public Life offers interesting insights. The vast majority of people in many sub-Saharan African nations are deeply committed to the practices and major tenets of one or the other of the world's two largest religions, Christianity and Islam. Large majorities say they belong to one of these faiths, and, in sharp contrast with Europe and the United States, very few people are religiously unaffiliated.

In this part of the world, Christianity and Islam also coexist with each other. Many Christians and Muslims in sub-Saharan Africa describe members of the other faith as tolerant and honest. In most countries, relatively few see evidence of widespread anti-Muslim or anti-Christian hostility, and on the whole they give their governments high marks for treating both religious groups fairly. But they acknowledge that they know relatively little about each other's faith, and substantial numbers of African Christians (roughly 40% or more in a dozen nations) say they consider Muslims to be violent. Muslims are significantly more positive in their assessment of Christians than Christians are in their assessment of Muslims. There are few significant differences, however, in the degree of support among Christians and Muslims for democracy.[34]

---

[34] www.pewforum.org

Sweden	8
France	13
Britain	19
Spain	23
Italy	24
Germany	25

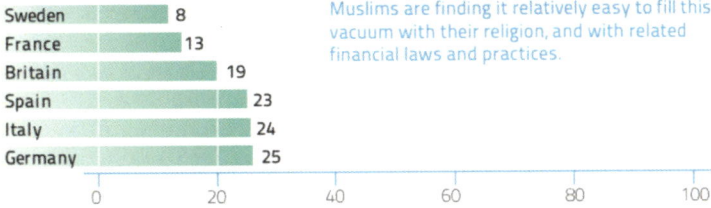

Chart: Looking at the statistics for Western Europe, a vacuum of belief is developing and Muslims are finding it relatively easy to fill this vacuum with their religion, and with related financial laws and practices.

0   20   40   60   80   100

NORTH AMERICA

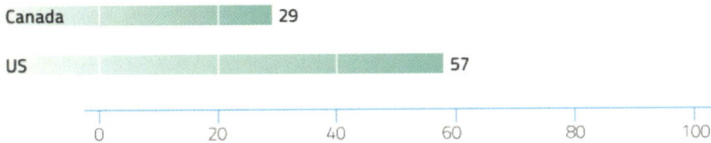

Canada	29
US	57

0   20   40   60   80   100

So much for the religious side of things: what did the report say about how a country, and by implication the finances of a nation, should be governed? Should faith be separate from public life? After 25,000 in-person interviews the Pew report found that 60% of Africans surveyed believe scripture should be the basis of their nation's laws. I have selected a sampling of countries where there were respondents from both Christians and Muslims. This chart indicates the percentages wanting their nations to be governed by the Bible or Islamic Law.

At the same time, the survey finds substantial support among Muslims and Christians alike for basing civil law on the Bible or sharia law. Although this may simply reflect the importance of religion in the region, it is nonetheless striking that in 13 of 16 countries with a sufficient number of Christians to analyze, half or more Christians favor making the Bible the official law of the land. And in 12 of 15 countries where analysis of the Muslim population is possible, half or more of Muslims favor establishing sharia, or Islamic law, in their countries. Support for religiously based civil law is highest, at roughly eight-in-ten, among Muslims in Djibouti (82%) and among Christians in Zambia (77%).

Significant minorities of Christians in 15 countries and at least half of Muslims in every country also support allowing leaders and judges to use their religious beliefs when deciding family and property disputes.[35]

ASIA PACIFIC

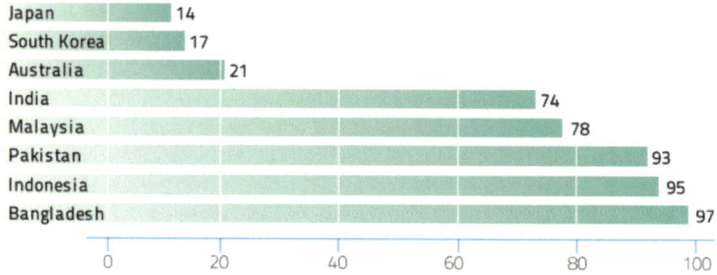

MIDDLE EAST

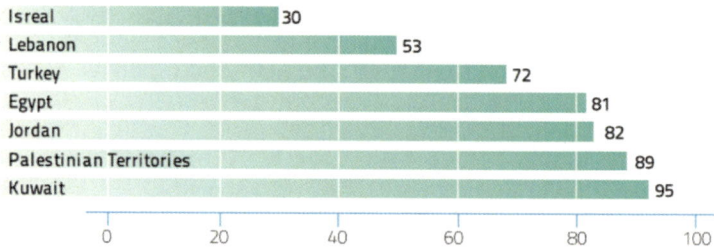

Chart: What seems notable about these charts is the nations least given to religion, with the exception of the US, are the ones with the most developed financial services sectors. The humanists would argue, on the surface of things, this proves that faith and economics do not mix. The truth is many European nations are still benefiting from the fruit of centuries of faith-based influence on their societies.

[35]   Page 57 of the detailed Pew report

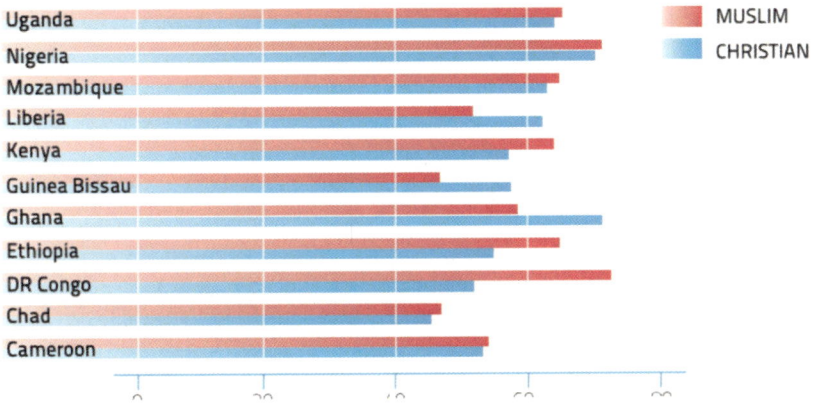

Table: Percentage of people who believe scripture should be the basis of national law.

Eras of Capital: understanding the times

I have outlined different eras of capital in the book, Repurposing Capital, because it gives us a sense of the historical context of capital and addresses the co-existence question. We are in an era of the Spiritualization of Capital and therefore have no choice but to consider the integration of faith and capital. If we do not do so others will fill the philosophical void and coopt capital for their own purposes: in fact, they already do. The question is how we, as followers of Jesus, get back into capital with a biblical worldview of money, finances, wealth and more.

Eras of Capital

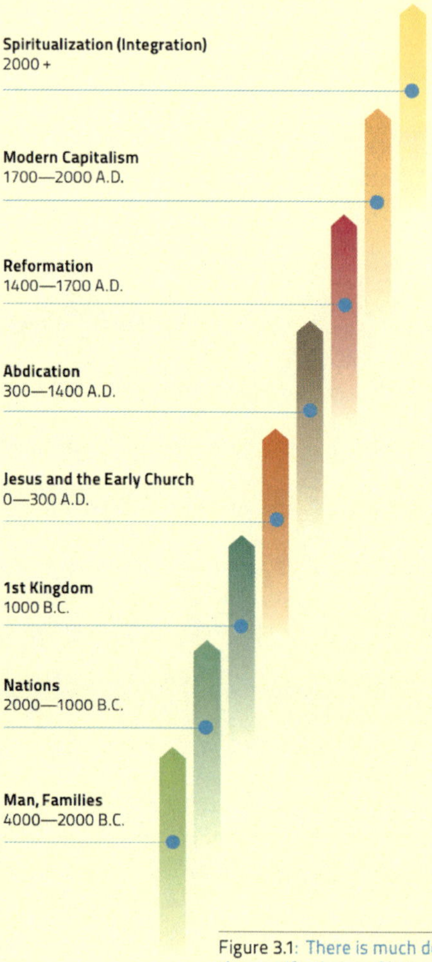

Spiritualization (Integration)
2000 +

Modern Capitalism
1700—2000 A.D.

Reformation
1400—1700 A.D.

Abdication
300—1400 A.D.

Jesus and the Early Church
0—300 A.D.

1st Kingdom
1000 B.C.

Nations
2000—1000 B.C.

Man, Families
4000—2000 B.C.

Figure 3.1: There is much debate about the specific timing of historical events; Eras of Finance are depicted in broad increments to give an approximate sense of the timelines.

Capitalism
- Wealth created
- Freedom to buy and sell
- Value set by willing buyer
- Risk and reward
- Return on capital
- Values-based
- Self-interest, not greed
- REALISM

Interventionism
- Government involvement
- Undue favor
- Wealth protection at expense of free market workings
- Forced redistribution of assets
- IDEALISM

Socialism
- Government thinks and acts better than individuals
- Wealth is static: pie is divided, not grown
- Forced exchange
- Risk, reward irrelevant
- Power, politics > economics
- COMMUNISM

We have passed the era of Modern Capitalism. Even though it seems some would like to drag society back to Socialism their agenda is more spiritual than economic, and we are in the tumultuous season of the Spiritualization of Capital. We therefore cannot avoid the questions of faith and economics. In fact, our present era gives us the opportunity to recapture, implement and propagate God's view of finance more than ever before.

Materialism	Islam	Causism
▪ Wealth as status	▪ Islamic Finance	▪ Causes abound
▪ Worshipping work	▪ Amassing of assets	▪ They conscript Capital for their ends
▪ Treadmill	▪ Mandatory charity (2.5%)	
▪ Restlessness	▪ Integration of work, faith, worldview	▪ Necessary evil; inherent good (Creative Capitalism)
▪ Expanding wish-list	▪ Clear goals	
▪ Lack of contentment	▪ Deliberate investing and spending	▪ Rise of NGOs
▪ Mammon: greed deified	▪ ISLAMIZATION	▪ Squishy funding
▪ DEIFICATION		▪ RADICALIZATION

You may be wondering whether there is another era beyond capitalism. I believe that there is, and that we are already partly in it. I have called it The Era of Spiritualization, but it could also be called The Era of Integration. The lines between work and leisure are being blurred, as are the boundaries between office and home. (I cover these trends in more detail in my book, Convergence.) People are recognizing that work has spiritual value, and they are working at their spirituality. There is a yearning for a greater integration of all facets of life. This greater openness to spiritual things, coupled with the rediscovery that work is a calling, has had some interesting consequences. The post-capitalism era (and here I speak of capitalism in its tainted form) has given way to three facets of The Era of Spiritualization:

▪ Materialism
▪ Islam
▪ Causism

In Materialism, we have made money a god. This is not a new thought. When Jesus Christ walked on earth he warned his followers that they had a binary choice: "You cannot serve both God and Mammon." Modern versions of the Bible will say "God and Money" but Jesus referred to Mammon as a spirit-being, a god, not just a concept. Mammon means "greed deified"—making a god out of money.

In more recent decades Islamic Finance has underscored that money can have a spiritual purpose. The West's dependence on oil has streamed dollars to Arab nations. Islamic law requires 2.5% of income be given as charity. Some of this has gone to noble causes, and some less noble. Either way, the Muslims have been more integrated than many Christians in their view of finance, integrating it into the whole of life rather than carving it off as something separate from their faith. Investing has been consistent with the goals of their faith. Christians often view finance as something which is theirs to give or keep, and rarely something to be deployed in the advancement of a specific cause. Many Muslims do not suffer from this dualism. The spiritualization of capital can, however, lead to Islamization as the goal, that is, advancing an aggressive Islamic agenda. Ideology is the enemy of theology, so while the idealization of money (whether by Jews, Christians or Muslims) may look harmless, it is not.

The final sector in the Era of Spiritualization is what I have called "Causism." There has been a new wave of venture philanthropy in recent decades. Social Entrepreneurship is the buzz on many college campuses, and a Fourth Sector is emerging. People are taking on causes. Examples include Bill Gates and team throwing billions at clean water or malaria projects, but there are many others that include ordinary people starting do-good enterprises, many of them for-profit, that are aiming at addressing needs in society. Once again, the outcome can be good or bad depending on what cause is being promoted. The Causism itself is not bad, of course, and underscores the intrinsic knowledge of humankind that we were indeed made for a purpose. In the Era of Spiritualization, if we do not have a clear purpose, we invent one, and fund it ourselves. Or we pour money into someone else who articulates a cause.

The era of Integration is a wonderful opportunity for those seeking to seamlessly blend faith and finance. There is great openness to good capital; people, corporations and nations are sick and tired of the twisted versions of capitalism. For people of faith to repurpose capital, we need to first take a deeper look at Capitalism, Socialism and Interventionism. How well does FBF sit with what we know as capitalism today? Are they one and the same... or were they at some point in history?[36]

---

[36] Repurposing Capital, pages 109-110

Capital always has an agenda

Our naïve notions of church-state separation have left us prone to dichotomy and silent on matters of work-faith integration and the use of capital to further the cause of the gospel. Capital always has an agenda. This is not a positive or a negative but simply a reality. When you look at the major NGOs and they work in developing nations their contributions of capital always have terms and conditions. They have an agenda. When the Chinese invest in Africa it is not for altruism; they have an agenda. when Muslims extended interest free loans to entrepreneurs, they have an agenda. And when Christian missionaries invest in hospitals and schools and water projects... They also have an agenda. The notion of neutral capital is nonsense. While avoiding the evils of colonization and its present form of asset colonization we can still use capital productively to positively shape societies. Scripture is under no illusion that wide scale societal change can be achieved without an economic component whether as a driver or as a consequence. Capital can be inserted at the front end of societal change, or it can be the fruit of genuine revival that overflows into economic prosperity. Either way, capital is integral to societal transformation. If we have a capital parked passively in mainstream investments without considering the spiritual implications of how those investments are used, we are on the wrong bus.

5

50 Biblical Economic Principles

There are numerous foundational principles of FBF spread throughout this book. They are summarized in this chapter to help readers see them as a whole. The scriptures of the Hebrews and Christians were written over a period spanning about 1,600 years by 40 authors. The process of recording and preserving these ancient texts is meticulously detailed in other writings. In my discussions with some people of the Muslim religion they have told me that the Jewish and Christian writings were lost for hundreds of years and then re-written from memory. They argue, because of this perceived lapse, the rewritten scriptures are filled with errors and contradictions. Any serious student of the scriptures will recognize that this is a myth, and there is no evidence to support this theory. On the contrary, there were very strict laws regarding the preservation of the authenticity of ancient Jewish texts, and the New Testament writings went through a rigorous process of selection. Archeological findings of ancient texts, such as The Dead Sea Scrolls, verify the fact that there are no major discrepancies between the scriptures we have today and the copies from thousands of years ago. The scriptures were recorded by a diverse group of people over a protracted period of time in many different locations. It was the collaborative effort of prophets, poets, physicians, historians, rich, poor, the disadvantaged and the privileged. The consistency of themes, teaching and focus argue for Divine inspiration. It is a body of work complete in and of itself and has been translated into over 2,000 languages (contrast Shakespeare at 50 languages) and The Holy Bible, as it is generally called, is still the bestselling book in the world.[37]

The gist of this section is extracting the principles, not hard and fast rules, from the ancient texts. This chapter lays out a sampling of financial principles and gives some referential support; for sake of brevity, the chapter is not exhaustive.

1. Principles, not laws

There are some who would rather live by a set of rules than understand the desires of someone else and make choices to please them. Throughout scripture we see God as desiring the relationship route more than the rule-based alternative. Scripture speaks of God writing his laws on the hearts of man, rather than in rule books. Prophets even point out the compounding of "rule upon rule" is an outcome of less relationship with God, not more relationship with him.

---

[37] At the time of writing it had sold 2.5 billion copies, three times more than the next book on the list. Source: http://en.wikipedia.org/wiki/List_of_best-selling_books.Other sources put the number at 6 billion: http://home.comcast.net/~antaylor1/bestsellingbooks.html

That said, scripture is under no illusion about the nature of man. In the Hebrew and Christian writings God understands that, left to his own devices, man does not have the capacity to stay within the bounds of the desires of God's heart. So scripture offers principles and precepts that enlighten the eyes, guide the conduct and renew the thinking if taken to heart.

We live in an age of choice and an age of risk. God is a risk taker at many levels. Even though he is sovereign and all powerful, he has opted to leave men and women with the freedom to exercise choices about how they live their lives, and whether they will relate to him. There is no coercion for those who choose to ignore him. Generally speaking, the good and the bad (however you define this) get the sunshine and the rain, and God does not intervene every instant when we contravene his express or implied will.

This leaves us firmly in the camp of considering principles relating to FBF, and not dictating a set of laws having absolute application regardless of circumstances.

2. Three different systems

Earlier in the book I referred to the differing economic systems of Egypt and the Promised Land. By way of recap, there were three different geographic locations, each with a different economic model:

- First, there was Egypt: it had a particular way of doing business that was influenced by the culture, the spiritual roots, and the geography.

- Second was the Desert: the nomadic lifestyle of Israel for 40 years was coupled with miraculous provision of water, manna and quail.
- Third was the Promised Land: it too had a different economic model.

Deuteronomy 11 picks up the story, and I quote it extensively because it contains truths regarding three economic systems. If you are a person of faith reading this book—and most people have some type of faith—think carefully about what system is native to the way you do business or handle finance. Many Christians I know, for example, have one philosophy for "salvation" and yet still live in the Egypt or Desert model.

> Observe therefore all the commands I am giving you today, so that you may have the strength to go in and take over the land that you are crossing the Jordan to possess, and so that you may live long in the land that the Lord swore to your forefathers to give to them and their descendants, a land flowing with milk and honey. The land you are entering to take over is not like the land of Egypt, from which you have come, where you planted your seed and irrigated it by foot as in a vegetable garden. But the land you are crossing the Jordan to take possession of is a land of mountains and valleys that drinks rain from heaven. It is a land the Lord your God cares for; the eyes of the Lord your God are continually on it from the beginning of the year to its end. So if you faithfully obey the commands I am giving you today—to love the Lord your God and to serve him with all your heart and with all your soul—then I will send rain on your land in its season, both autumn and spring rains, so that you may gather in your grain, new wine and oil. I will provide grass in the fields for your cattle, and you will eat and be satisfied.[38]

In the years immediately prior to leaving Egypt the nation of Israel, which had been incubated within Egypt, lived in a pleasant part of the country, had plots of arable land, and a predictable income stream: "where you planted

---

38 Deuteronomy 11:8-15

your seed and irrigated it by foot as in a vegetable garden." Although they were a semi-religious people in that their ancestor Abraham was a man of faith, in practice they could live without economic dependence upon God. The River Nile flowed continuously; they took their bucket, retrieved the water, irrigated their vegetable patch, and grew their provisions. People who manage their finances to avoid dependence on God are usually reflecting the Egypt Model.

Once the nation of Israel had miraculously exited Egypt, taking a trove of jewelry and spoils with them, they found themselves in a nomadic cycle where their certain supply was gone. In fact, they had to depend on God for miraculous provision of daily necessities, such as water. They lived in tents, had no fixed address, and could not build dams or granaries. They lived from hand to mouth. Many people of faith think this is the ultimate economic model—one of total dependence on God. They embrace the idea of only having enough for today in order to stay dependent on God. There is no doubt that for specific seasons of life—and for some people, their entire lives—this Desert Model is a chosen path. The sad reality is that many people live with the mind-set of Desert Economics simply because they do not understand the third alternative: The Promised Land Model.

The Promised Land had elements of Egypt and the Desert, but it was different from both. People were allocated land and had a capital base for wealth creation. This was similar to Egypt in "the good old days" when they were still treated with favor. The catch, however, was that there was no River Nile.

> But the land you are crossing the Jordan to take possession of is a land of mountains and valleys that drinks rain from heaven. It is a land the Lord your God cares for; the eyes of the Lord your God are continually on it from the beginning of the year to its end.[39]

---

[39] Deuteronomy 11:11

The good news: you have land. The bad news: unless God sends the rain, you have a drought. In the Promised Land everyone had a capital allotment, or a capital base from which income could be produced. That said, there was no guaranteed water supply outside of obedience to God. Scripture then lays out the conditions upon which God would water the land.

So if you faithfully obey the commands I am giving you today—to love the Lord your God and to serve him with all your heart and with all your soul—then I will send rain on your land in its season, both autumn and spring rains, so that you may gather in your grain, new wine and oil. I will provide grass in the fields for your cattle, and you will eat and be satisfied.[40]

You will note that the Promised Land was a blend of capital and faith (in contrast to Egypt, which was capital and no faith, and the Desert, which was no capital and faith).

Understanding these three different systems is essential to FBF. I mentioned earlier that faith is seeing things differently. When we understand Promised Land economics, we have a better basis for interpreting the many laws, precepts, commandments, instructions and tenets of scripture. The intent of faith-based economics is a working collaboration between God and man that meets the needs of man abundantly while furthering God's purposes. The Deuteronomy explanation of the three economic systems was then reinforced with a promise and a warning:

If you carefully observe all these commands I am giving you to follow—to love the Lord your God, to walk in all his ways and to hold fast to him—then the Lord will drive out all these nations before you, and you will dispossess nations larger and stronger than you. Every place where you set your foot will be yours: Your territory will extend from the desert to Lebanon, and from the Euphrates River to the western sea. No man will be able to stand against you. The Lord

---

40   Deuteronomy 11:13-15

your God, as he promised you, will put the terror and fear of you on the whole land, wherever you go.

See, I am setting before you today a blessing and a curse—the blessing if you obey the commands of the Lord your God that I am giving you today; the curse if you disobey the commands of the Lord your God and turn from the way that I command you today by following other gods, which you have not known.[41]

The challenge for people of faith is how to live with capital, growing an asset base, and still remaining faithful to God and dependent on him. There is a world of difference between these three economic systems, and simply having a rule book without grasping the nature of faith will not be enough.

Financial Inclusion & The Promised Land

You might be wondering how this applies to us today. One of the buzzwords in the banking world is "financial inclusion." According to Investopedia, "Financial inclusion refers to efforts to make financial products and services accessible and affordable to all individuals and businesses, regardless of their personal net worth or company size. Financial inclusion strives to remove the barriers that exclude people from participating in the financial sector and using these services to improve their lives. It is also called inclusive finance." The sad truth is that roughly 2 billion adults are outside formal financial systems. A recent World Bank report claims:

Globally, 1.7 billion adults remain unbanked, yet two-thirds of them own a mobile phone that could help them access financial services. Digital technology could take advantage of existing cash transactions to bring people into the financial system, the report finds.[42]

Biblical economics prevents financial exclusion. We might look at laws about debt forgiveness every seven years and the return of land to its original

41   Deuteronomy 11:26-28
42   https://www.worldbank.org/en/news/press-release/2018/04/19/financial-inclusion-on-the-rise-but-gaps-remain-global-findex-database-shows

owners as being relics of the past, but the Jubilee principles (including the 50 Year Reset) ensure financial inclusion. No one in Israel could remain asset-less for long... perhaps just long enough to reflect on how they messed up so that, in the next 7-year cycle, they could better steward their assets.

There are various reasons for the Financial Inclusion problem: technology, culture and gender are all important factors. We cannot ignore, however, the stringent "Western" rules that are imposed on people in developing nations that would prevent them from passing through the fine screen of KYC (know your customer) and other bankability filters. In a later conversation with Mark Moss we will discuss how cryptocurrency might just be the thing needed, in addition to mobile money, to foster financial inclusion.

Today, 69 percent of adults around the world have an account
Adults with an account (%), 2017

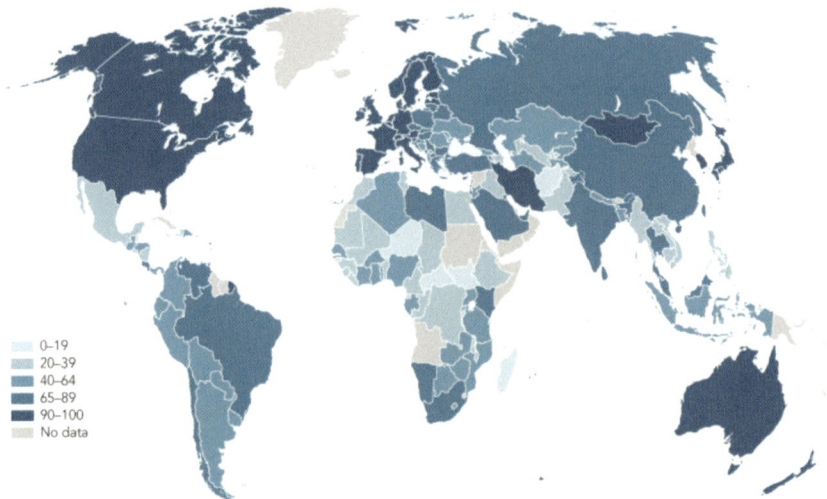

- 0–19
- 20–39
- 40–64
- 65–89
- 90–100
- No data

Source: Global Findex database.

3. Foundational Principles

The founding documents of the United States contain the phrase, "We hold these truths to be self-evident..." Not every nation, in fact, relatively few nations on the planet, hold the same set of truths to be "self evident."

When in the Course of human events it becomes necessary for one people to dissolve the political bands which have connected them with another and to assume among the powers of the earth, the separate and equal station to which the Laws of Nature and of Nature's God entitle them, a decent respect to the opinions of mankind requires that they should declare the causes which impel them to the separation.

We hold these truths to be self-evident, that all men are created equal, that they are endowed by their Creator with certain unalienable Rights, that among these are Life, Liberty and the pursuit of Happiness. — That to secure these rights, Governments are instituted among Men, deriving their just powers from the consent of the governed, — That whenever any Form of Government becomes destructive of these ends, it is the Right of the People to alter or to abolish it, and to institute new Government, laying its foundation on such principles and organizing its powers in such form, as to them shall seem most likely to effect their Safety and Happiness.[43]

These self-evident truths were articulated in the context of "their Creator" who had endowed people with "inalienable rights." Just as truths about liberty and the pursuit of happiness are logical because the Founding Fathers determined that God was the source of truth, not a foreign government or sovereign, so the Faith-based Financing Foundational Principles are the "self evident" principles that can be deduced in the context of faith in a God who has articulated principles of finance.

The US Constitution allows for and encourages freedom of religious choice and expression, but this is because of the faith of the Founding Fathers, not because they did not have a faith. A friend was involved in drafting a new constitution for a young nation and told his colleagues, "You can separate church and state, but you cannot separate God and government." Likewise, you can (and should, in my view) ensure that the church does not run the economy, but you cannot separate finance and faith. The principles of honesty, wealth creation, free exchange of goods and services, property

---

43   The Declaration of Independence. http://www.ushistory.org/declaration/document/

rights, hard work, financial liberty, giving to others, flow-through and enjoyment of the results of one's labor are biblical constructs. And they work for any economy in any nation in the world, so we can rightly call them "Foundational Principles" that will create a basis for building individuals, communities and nations. Foundational Principles are objective truths that are universal in nature, but local in application. Just as the Federal Government can draft legislation that has to be interpreted and applied at a State level, so the financial Foundational Principles are neither American, nor Western Capitalism, but are broader than both, and have a local application that may not be the same as one might find in the US or other Western nations. Put another way, if truth is indeed truth, then it should be applicable in every culture or economy.

I have arranged the Foundational Principles in the following manner:

- Sources
- Uses & Nature of finance
- Stewardship & Spending
- Generosity & Giving
- Investing
- Remedial action

SOURCES

Where does wealth come from? Faith holds many paradoxes, and this is clearly seen in the matter of the sources of wealth. On the one hand, everything is a gift from God. On the other hand, he expects us to work for a living. We, on one side, are finite, but God is infinite. Our finances, like our lives, are temporal and yet we live with an eternal life expectancy. Our approach to finances is generally driven by what we choose to have as our dominant reality. This is particularly true regarding our perception of the Source of Capital and provision.

4. God is the source

To understand FBF one must start with the premise that God is not just the rightful owner of everything, which he then entrusts to man to steward, but he is also the source of everything.

Don't be deceived, my dear brothers. Every good and perfect gift is from above, coming down from the Father of the heavenly lights, who does not change like shifting shadows.[44]

To the rationalist this may sound like a platitude, but to be free from a fear of not having money—and therefore be able to handle finances with faith—one has to make a huge shift in one's perception regarding the source of wealth. The differences in perception of source are highlighted in the table, "Where wealth comes from."

WHERE WEALTH COMES FROM	
Self-reliance	Dependence on God
Calculation	Revelation
Finite	Infinite
Debt	Real assets
Temporal	Eternal
Natural	Supernatural

---

44   James 1:16-17

Running out	Running over
Lack	Abundance
Scorns source	Remembers source
Man, nature, self as source	God as source

One thing from this table requires some clarification: on the last point, since mankind is made in the image of God, designed to work with God, and intended to work for his glory, then this is a legitimate source of income. And, since we are under-performing as humankind, if we learned to work like God[45], humankind working in the image of God is perhaps the greatest potential source of new income.

5. God is not limited to any one source of funds

There is a tendency to favor overly "spiritual" sources of money: the widow whose oil was supernaturally multiplied by the prophet Elijah, or the coin found in the mouth of a fish (at the instruction of Jesus). To some, both seem more "spiritual" than money earned from a hard day's work. The historical record shows sources of funds used for initiatives in which God was involved were extremely varied, without one being more "spiritual" than another. A small selection of God's diverse funding strategies include:

- Jewelry taken from Egypt by Israelites
- Generosity: Boaz and Ruth, gleanings
- Miraculous provision: Gold coin in mouth of fish, widow's jars of oil, multiplication of loaves and fish, manna and quail in the desert for 40 years
- Foreign kings or rulers
- Spoils of war
- Public offerings for special occasions, such as the building of the temple

---

[45] I cover this in my book, Work like God in 31 Ways, Indaba Publishing, 2021

- Routine giving, such as tithing
- Selling of property and pooling of funds (as in the Book of Acts)
- Government funding, plus local sweat equity (today we would call this Public Private Partnerships, as in the case of Nehemiah and the project to rebuild Jerusalem)
- Gifts from the Magi at the birth of Jesus
- Work
- Donations, offerings received
- Women who helped fund Jesus' work on earth.

6. Faith leads to action

There is a misconception that faith and economics do not mix. Business, finance and economics is all about dealing with uncertainty and risk, and these are so closely allied to what one might call "the life of faith." Many of the best decisions are made by instinct, gut feelings or intuition and not necessarily logic. Some might call it faith; let us examine faith in a bit more detail before we reach this conclusion.

In the context of FBF, faith is not just a vague notion that good happens, but a belief that God has spoken, and a conviction this is definite enough to spur one to action, regardless of whether it seems logical. Scripture puts it this way, "Faith comes by hearing the [spoken] word of God."[46] A principle on its own may not be enough to cause a businessperson or financier to spring into action. A precept or commandment may not, in and of itself, convince a venture capitalist to make an investment. Having done all of one's research, having weighed the probability of success, the person of faith will still ask, "God, is this what you want me to do?" If the answer is "Yes" this produces a measure of faith, and fuels further activity.

You will notice from this definition that this is not faith in faith itself, faith in a principle, or faith in business school models. This is faith in a God who, in the context of a relationship, speaks a specific instruction.

The instruction given to a person of faith may or may not be logical. This is beside the point. The main point is "did God say...?" and in the process of

---

answering this question there is plenty of room to be analytical, logical, inquiring, skeptical and tentative. At the end of the day, however, if a transaction, product or corporation is to be faith-based then it must fuel faith through continuous consulting with the God who speaks. In the economy of God, hearing his voice is a core competence.

The other element of FBF is that God often requires that one respond to negative actions with a counter-intuitive positive action or attitude.

> If someone drags you into court and sues for the shirt off your back, giftwrap your best coat and make a present of it. And if someone takes unfair advantage of you, use the occasion to practice the servant life. No more tit-for-tat stuff. Live generously.[47]

It takes faith to respond in an opposite spirit when one has been taken advantage of, but it tests whether we really believe that God is one's source, and not this or that transaction. This "turning the other cheek" is not done in order to be nice, but to change the spiritual climate in which business or financing (or life, for that matter) is practiced. The pragmatist reading this will say, "Well, won't you just get ripped off, and won't the whole economy collapse?" You may well get taken advantage of in the short term, but the economy will not collapse because true capitalism is based on trust, and faith-based financing is based on faith in God, not man. It recognizes that man will do things to take advantage of other people, but the answer is not more rules and grabbing what you can but being constrained by the character of God.

Why would you do this? Those involved in FBF have an eternal perspective. The time horizons for returns are not at the end of today, tomorrow or the quarter. They are eternal, and this colors all of their dealings.

The final aspect to FBF is that it is not fear based. In the recent global economic crisis it appeared people were being paralyzed by fear. There has been a palpable angst perhaps because of the enormity of the mess. In the

---

47   Matthew 5:40-42, The Message

2008-2010 financial crisis the initial advice was "spend more." It is patently obvious you do not solve a crisis of overspending, by under-saving and living beyond one's means (personally and nationally) with more spending. There is some truth to the "spend more" statement if it is an indicator of true faith, and not just an assumption of perpetual growth. When the prophet Jeremiah was in prison and his city was under siege God told him to buy a piece of land as a statement of faith that things would be better in the future. FBF is realistic about the state of things, but does not trade in fear by preying on the anxieties of others.

Spending in faith must be balanced by responsible consuming; Westerners, in particular, should curb their appetites and spend less on non-essentials. The famous John Wesley saying is apt: "Make all you can, save all you can, give all you can."

7. Resources are not necessarily scarce

Many economists assume resources are scarce. A definition that captures much of modern economics is that of Lionel Robbins in a 1932 essay:

> ... the science which studies human behaviour as a relationship between ends and scarce means which have alternative uses.[48]

Unfortunately, many people of faith accept this view as gospel. A truer definition, from a faith-based perspective, does not include the scarcity mind-set espoused by Robbins. The term economics comes from the Ancient Greek, oikonomia, "management of a household, administration" which has several parts: oikos, "house" + nomos, "custom" or "law", hence "rules of the house(hold)." Since God is the Father of the household—"yet for us there is but one God, the Father, from whom all things came and for whom we live"[49]—the concept of household management, or economics,

---

[48]   An Essay on the Nature and Significance of Economic Science. London: Macmillan and Co., Limited., p. 16, Robbins, Lionel (1945).

[49]   1 Corinthians 8:6

stems from him, and he has no scarcity. So, in FBF, the basic definition of economics has to counter the "scarce means" view of Robbins.

Regeneration of resources is a second aspect of this principle. Many facets of life, from the human body to economics, involve a regeneration. There are species that are extinct because of the exploitation, mismanagement or ignorance of mankind. But in FBF, as in the assumptions behind a healthy stock market, resources are not always simply depleting. Mankind will continue to discover new ways of doing things, since we are made in the image of God.

The third aspect of this principle is that resources on the planet are not necessarily in their final form, and man has a creative contribution to make. Diamonds in a shaft several kilometers below the surface of the earth are not in their final form. Value can be added by man. When man begins to manufacture diamonds, this adds another twist to the availability of resources.

A misapplication of this principle can be seen in the "creation" of financial service products, such as derivatives, that have little inherent value if the trust inherent in the underlying contract or security is broken. For example, when a financial services firm sells clients products and then bets against the products' success, trust is broken. The same is true for the printing of money, a practice devaluing what already exists.

A final thought: it is essential in FBF to slough a poverty mindset. God is not poor and does not purpose for us to be paupers. The corollary is this: God is not a cosmic vending machine jostled into dispensing by our so-called proclamations of faith. Prosperity is God's desire, but it is not the automatic right of principle-less people.

8. God rewards initiative

Humankind can take initiative, make choices, and act with purpose to improve a situation. God expects us to proactively initiate and do so in faith. Work itself should be an expression of faith as it contains the belief that initiative carries rewards.[50] God often requires man to take a first step before he will intervene. Whether you recall the story of Jonathan and his armor bearer taking initiative to fight in the face of overwhelming odds, or the

---

[50]   1 Thessalonians 1:3

nation of Israel stepping into Jordan, or Moses raising staff to part Red Sea, all required initiative, or at least a response in faith, on the part of man.

9. Business risk can be an expression of faith

Technically you might argue, since he is sovereign and powerful, God has never had to risk anything. There is no question that he knows everything. For mankind, however, we are left with many unknowns, and yet God requires action on our part. This action includes trusting him and moving forward based on the knowledge of his character and his will. In the parable of the talents Jesus commended the servant who risked his capital and said he was "faithful." An unwillingness to risk, which in this case was evidenced in hoarding, was condemned. Risk motivated by love is an especially powerful combination.

10. Hard work creates value

Work is valuable, not a punishment for sin. Work is a "pre-Fall" reality, not just a consequence of man being out of relationship with God. In fact, work should be done in relationship or collaboration with God. In contrast, laziness is condemned in scripture. "Go to the ant, you sluggard; consider its ways and be wise."[51] Again the proverbs say, "Lazy hands make a man poor, but diligent hands bring wealth."[52] The writer of Hebrews says, "We do not want you to become lazy, but to imitate those who through faith and patience inherit what has been promised."[53] The apostle Paul states, "For even when we were with you, we gave you this rule: 'If a man will not work, he shall not eat.'"[54]

11. You reap what you sow

Anyone who has attended a Christian church service might have heard the phrase "sowing and reaping" and come to equate it with an admonishment to give because the phrase is often used just before the collection plate is passed. This is tremendously unfortunate because it short-changes our

---

[51] Proverbs 6:6
[52] Proverbs 10:4
[53] Hebrews 6:12
[54] 2 Thessalonians 3:10

understanding of an important principle related to life in general. Seed is crucial to God. Even a cursory look at scripture will reveal that God places a high value on the seed of trees, of man, and of finances. The concept of sowing and reaping is inherent in biblical economics, and this also applies to the area of investing. A sampling of verses dealing with the topic includes:

The wicked man earns deceptive wages, but he who sows righteousness reaps a sure reward.[55]

He who sows wickedness reaps trouble, and the rod of his fury will be destroyed.[56]

Do not be deceived: God cannot be mocked. A man reaps what he sows.[57]

Well known texts dealing with sowing and reaping cover other topics too, including generosity, the difference between capital and working capital, the ability of God to multiply resources, and God being the source.

Remember this: Whoever sows sparingly will also reap sparingly, and whoever sows generously will also reap generously. Each man should give what he has decided in his heart to give, not reluctantly or under compulsion, for God loves a cheerful giver. And God is able to make all grace abound to you, so that in all things at all times, having all that you need, you will abound in every good work. As it is written:

"He has scattered abroad his gifts to the poor; his righteousness endures forever." Now he who supplies seed to the sower [Capital] and bread for food [Working Capital] will also supply and increase your store of seed and will

---

55   Proverbs 11:18
56   Proverbs 22:8
57   Galatians 6:7

enlarge the harvest of your righteousness. You will be made rich in every way so that you can be generous on every occasion, and through us your generosity will result in thanksgiving to God.[58]

The principle is clear: sowing what you have increases your supply of seed. Actively utilizing finances to generate wealth and give to the needy is God's way.

USES & NATURE OF FINANCE

12. Money is a tool, not a goal

The popular view of money is that it is neutral, being neither positive nor negative in nature. Others argue money is like a chameleon taking on the nature of the person possessing it. A third perspective is that the source of the money determines its nature, much as "blood diamonds" would make an otherwise beautiful stone a horrible commodity.

The nature of money should be considered in the context of both the purpose of money and the nature of work. If work is good—and we have already established that work done for the right reasons and in the right way is good—then the money given as a representation of that productive work must surely also be good. If a man builds a good wall and gets paid for his labor, is the money bad? When an artist paints a beautiful picture is his or her work good? How then can the money for that artwork be neutral?

When we pursue money for its own sake hoping it will bring prestige, favor or security then the pursuit is bad, but it does not make the money bad. The problem is us, not the money. "The love of money is the root of all kinds of evil."[59] The pursuit of anything as a "first love" before the love of God is evil,

---

58   2 Corinthians 9:6-11

59   1 Timothy 6:10

whether it be career, family, fame, ministry or anything else. The first commandment is clear: love God first.

The word money sometimes goes by the name Mammon in scripture, and this is an entirely different kettle of fish. Mammon is talked about as being a force, a spirit, or a demonic being that is served. "You cannot serve both God and Mammon."[60] As a reminder, Mammon means "greed deified" and carries the connotation that when we make greed our god we give ourselves over to the dark side of finance, namely, making a god of money and becoming subject to the spiritual forces that fuel the deification of money. If we believe this perspective, and some do, then money is very important because it is either a force for good, or when it is worshipped, it becomes an alternative to God, and hence a force for evil. Money, in the FBF world, is a tool, not a goal.

> God's purposes on earth require change in the human heart sufficient to cause mankind to prioritize love of God over love of money.

13. Money must serve the right purposes

The evolution of money over time has diversified work possibilities and broadened the horizons of trade. The growth of trade between geographically disbursed markets necessitated letters of credit. Banks holding money on deposit learned that they could not just lend what was given to them for safekeeping, but leverage what they had since it was highly unlikely that all depositors would want their money back at once. So they loaned money, pocketing the spread between what they collected and paid in interest. Money went from being static to dynamic.

None of this explanation of the utility of money, simplistic as the explanation may be, lends much insight into the real purpose of money from a FBF perspective. A fairly common view of money sees it simply as a medium of exchange. To tap the depths of the purpose of money, however, we must consider the purpose of man. In the FBF context, the purpose of man is to know, enjoy and give honor to God.[61] As people made in the image

---

60   Matthew 6:24

61   This assumes that God is personal and has revealed that he wants to be known. How we get to know him—the basis of faith—varies by religion.

of God and drawn into relationship with him, our view of money and the uses to which we put it should be aligned with our purpose. We should be making, investing, giving and spending money in order to work with God in accomplishing his purposes. Practically, as a person of faith I do not head into an investment simply because it produces a good return; this is not enough. I do not just buy something because I feel like it; this is also not enough. I do not take the higher paying job if it does not honor God. Money, like other assets on the planet, should be serving the desires and purposes of God. I have often heard it said, and have repeated the statement myself, "God does not need your money." Is this true? Jesus Christ said, "Where your treasure is, there will your heart be also."[62] So perhaps God does need our money since it is an indicator of whether he has our hearts. For our own sake, we need God to mean more to us than our money.

Another purpose of money is to help us fulfill our destiny. We are called with a specific and unique calling (beyond the general call to glorify God) and it is a good use of money to invest in our own calling, and in the callings of others.

A third purpose of money is to give God the reward to which he is entitled. You are probably reading about FBF because you have some concept of investment, risk and return. God invested heavily in us and is entitled to a return. Your view of God's investment will determine the level of return to which he is entitled. Since we are stewards, it is not a question of just giving God a return on what we already have, but also a matter of seeing things God wants, and working with him to bring those under his control. If God, for example, wanted a building to be used for an orphanage, then he may want you to buy it. If he wants a factory in order to create meaningful employment, he may want you to invest in it on his behalf. This requires risk and faith, most likely, but will bring something back into God's portfolio that was abdicated, sold or otherwise forfeited. Money can fulfill a redemptive purpose. Some corporations may need to be acquired before they are repurposed.

Another purpose of money is to meet our own basic needs. God simply cares about our daily necessities and knows that money is essential for living. There is nothing wrong with this practical view, and spending money to meet daily needs is no less spiritual than buying an orphanage.

---

62   Matthew 6:21 (NKJV)

The purpose of money is also to meet the needs of others, and, better yet, help them get into a position where they can meet their own needs. Capital invested in a business providing income for households is capital well invested.

A final purpose of money is building relationships. Giving opens doors because it opens hearts. (Misused, you could call it bribery; used rightly, a better word is generosity.) God wants us to be generous because we will then reflect his nature. Jesus told a story of a shrewd manager who was about to get fired and had debtors settle their accounts for pennies on the pound so that, once he was out on the street, the debtors would remember him kindly. The manager understood one of the purposes of money, namely, building relationship.

───

If money does not build the kingdom [of God], then it perverts, spoils and destroys its owners.[63]

14. Financial capital is not king

In an earlier chapter we examined many forms of capital. Some countries prize intellectual capital over financial capital. Others value relational capital. Many people in capitalist societies have bought into a definition of success that puts financial capital at the top of the pile. This is not true for those seeking to be involved in FBF. "A good name is to be desired more than riches."[64] There are two equal and opposite errors: exalting those who have financial capital as having "arrived," and disdaining those who have financial capital as having "got it at all costs." These polarized views are simply nonsense. Having capital is a reflection of God's nature, and our being made in his image. As Creator he made tangible and intangible things. In his wisdom he did not put everything on the earth in its final form and invited mankind into a relationship of creative development to bring fruit, gold, horses and human beings to their full potential. Capital is simply part of his resource base. It is not everything, but it is not nothing either.

---

63   Money won't make you rich, Sunday Adelaja, Charisma House
64   Proverbs 22:1

15. Capital and working capital are different

A key principle of FBF is the differentiation of capital and working capital. "Now he who gives you seed for sowing, and seed for bread, will increase your harvest..."[65] The context for this verse is the encouragement of inter-city generosity. People in Jerusalem were in need, so Paul wrote to the church in Corinth and urged them to be generous givers. He reminds them that God is the source of both capital—"seed for sowing"—and working capital—"seed for bread." When we eat what we should be sowing we do not have a harvest the following season. Our consumer society urges us to eat what should be investing. We have a negative savings rate, and we are completely fine with buying consumer items on credit. This would have been an anathema to prior generations, and it is coming back to haunt us. The biblical principle is simple: invest what you can, and purchase discretionary items from what you earn on your investments.

The parable Jesus told about the ten minas or talents is a further illustration of the truth that God expects capital to be risked (or deployed) to produce a good return. The risking or investment of capital was deemed to be "faithful" behavior. As indicated earlier, the Christian Church has lost sight of investing at the corporate level: seed for sowing has been terribly misconstrued as simply the Sunday offering.

16. Wealth creation is normal

A quick glance at major stock markets over the last fifty years will reinforce that the world economy is growing steadily. Conspiracy theorists will say it is only a few who are getting wealthy, but the statistics do not support these presuppositions. The fact is that God intends us to create wealth. "It is he who gives you the ability to create wealth."[66] The whole passage in Deuteronomy 8 is informative both regarding wealth creation, and the source of wealth.

---

65   2 Corinthians 9:10

66   Deuteronomy 8:18

When you have eaten and are satisfied, praise the Lord your God for the good land he has given you. Be careful that you do not forget the Lord your God, failing to observe his commands, his laws and his decrees that I am giving you this day. Otherwise, when you eat and are satisfied, when you build fine houses and settle down, and when your herds and flocks grow large and your silver and gold increase and all you have is multiplied, then your heart will become proud and you will forget the Lord your God, who brought you out of Egypt, out of the land of slavery. He led you through the vast and dreadful desert, that thirsty and waterless land, with its venomous snakes and scorpions. He brought you water out of hard rock. He gave you manna to eat in the desert, something your fathers had never known, to humble and to test you so that in the end it might go well with you. You may say to yourself, "My power and the strength of my hands have produced this wealth for me." But remember the Lord your God, for it is he who gives you the ability to produce wealth, and so confirms his covenant, which he swore to your forefathers, as it is today.[67]

Wealth creation is a covenantal matter: the Jews have not forgotten this, and Christians and Muslims are lagging.

17. Finances grow people

It is a huge temptation for those with money to entrap those who have little. This is true at the personal, the business and the national level. There are 27 million slaves today, by most estimates, and many are in slavery due to debt. Sometimes a very small debt can enslave generations of people in a family. The contrasting truth is we are to use finances to build relationships, empower people and move them to a higher level. Sadly, much money invested or given by people of faith has strings, not wings.

18. Be careful when using collateral

Collateral, or pledges, are to be used sparingly, and with concern for the disadvantaged. Loan sharks take collateral assuming the borrower will

---

67   Deuteronomy 8:10-18

default, and with the hope that the lender can seize the borrower's assets. Scripture has a different view.

> If you take your neighbor's cloak as a pledge, return it to him by sunset, because his cloak is the only covering he has for his body. What else will he sleep in? When he cries out to me, I will hear, for I am compassionate.[68]

> When you make a loan of any kind to your neighbor, do not go into his house to get what he is offering as a pledge. Stay outside and let the man to whom you are making the loan bring the pledge out to you. If the man is poor, do not go to sleep with his pledge in your possession.[69]

19. "The bottom line" is not the bottom line

Scripture encourages the building of wealth but discourages misplaced confidence in wealth. One could go further and say The Bible redefines success. On the financial front, success is not measured by what you amass, but by what you allow to flow through your hands to others.

> Command those who are rich in this present world not to be arrogant nor to put their hope in wealth, which is so uncertain, but to put their hope in God, who richly provides us with everything for our enjoyment.[70]

Scripture also reminds us that wealth is temporary.

> But the one who is rich should take pride in his low position, because he will pass away like a wild flower. For the sun rises with scorching heat and withers

68   Leviticus 22:26-27
69   Deuteronomy 24:10-12
70   1 Timothy 6:17

the plant; its blossom falls and its beauty is destroyed. In the same way, the rich man will fade away even while he goes about his business.[71]

God's Message: "Don't let the wise brag of their wisdom. Don't let heroes brag of their exploits. Don't let the rich brag of their riches. If you brag, brag of this and this only: That you understand and know me. I'm God, and I act in and delight in those who do the same things. These are my trademarks."[72]

20. Be content

Without contentment, one never has enough. "But godliness with contentment is great gain."[73]

"Note well: Money deceives. The arrogant rich don't last. They are more hungry for wealth than the grave is for cadavers. Like death, they always want more, but the 'more' they get is dead bodies. They are cemeteries filled with dead nations, graveyards filled with corpses. Don't give people like this a second thought. Soon the whole world will be taunting them:

"Who do you think you are—getting rich by stealing and extortion? How long do you think you can get away with this? Indeed, how long before your victims wake up, stand up and make you the victim? You've plundered nation after nation. Now you'll get a taste of your own medicine. All the survivors are out to plunder you, a payback for all your murders and massacres."[74]

21. Have Integrity: honest weights and measures

Scripture points out that God himself is the source of honesty and expects us to act in a like manner.

---

71   James 1:10-11
72   Jeremiah 9:23 (The Message)
73   1 Timothy 6:6
74   Habakkuk 2:5-8 (The Message)

Use honest scales and honest weights,
an honest ephah and an honest hin. I am the Lord your God, who brought you out of Egypt.[75]

You must have accurate and honest weights and measures, so that you may live long in the land the Lord your God is giving you.[76]

Honest scales and balances are from the Lord; all the weights in the bag are of his making.[77]

The businessmen engage in wholesale fraud. They love to rip people off! Ephraim boasted, "Look, I'm rich! I've made it big! And look how well I've covered my tracks: not a hint of fraud, not a sign of sin!" "But not so fast! I'm God, your God!"[78]

Disclosure of terms, clear contracts, and unconditional honesty are hallmarks of FBF. I remind readers of Norm Franz's contention that fractional reserve banking (FRB) is a modern expression of dishonest scales. Sir Josiah Stamp, former President of the Bank of England in the 1920's, spoke at the Commencement Address at the University of Texas in 1927.

Banking was conceived in iniquity and was born in sin. The Bankers own the earth. Take it away from them, but leave them the power to create deposits, and with the flick of the pen they will create enough deposits to buy it back again. However, take it away from them, and all the great fortunes like mine will disappear and they ought to disappear, for this would be a happier and better world to live in. But, if you wish to remain the slaves of Bankers and pay the cost of your own slavery, let them continue to create deposits.[79]

---

75   Leviticus 19:36
76   Deuteronomy 25:15
77   Proverbs 16:11
78   Hosea 12:7-9 (The Message)
79   http://libertytree.ca/quotes/Josiah.Stamp.Quote.69BB (I reference it here because there is some good debate on the site)

22. Gainful employment: get it, create it

It is fair to say God hates unemployment. The parable of the workers in the vineyard highlights this truth. Using finances to create jobs and draw people into meaningful work is entirely biblical. If you can alleviate unemployment, consider it carefully. At the time of writing, Africa has 90 million SMEs (small and medium-sized enterprises). If each one could add one or two employees it would go a long way to tackling a giant.

23. Ignorance can lead to poverty

King Solomon is the classic example of someone who sought wisdom and knowledge and gained great riches. Isaiah 5:13 puts the counter truth this way: "Therefore My people go into exile for their lack of knowledge."[80] Many people are in financial exile because of a lack of knowledge concerning the foundational principles of finance from a biblical perspective. Not all poverty, by any stretch, is related to ignorance or a lack of knowledge of financial principles, of course. The principle: wealth and wisdom are close cousins.

STEWARDSHIP & SPENDING

The very rich tradition of capitalism in the United States has at its foundation a set of presuppositions that have, unfortunately, been all but ignored in the various run-ups to market crashes. Greed has overtaken self-interest, and financial products with little real value have been part of bubbles that inevitably burst. Many of these issues could have been overcome, as I would argue later, if we had held to a proper notion of stewardship.

The Characteristics of Faith-Based People table (below) highlights contrasting perspectives of people governed by faith-based principles, and others who do not hold the same constructs at a practical level. This does

---

80   Isaiah 5: 13 NASB

not contrast Americans and Arabs, for example, but people who profess to follow God, but who are governed by temporal, self-centered thinking, and those who live out different principles. I think you will admit advertising is aimed at making us insatiable. We favor short term gains over long-term benefits, and we live as if we are not accountable to our fellow man, or our God. We will continue to do so, in my view, until we who are wealthy—and that will be most people reading this book— acknowledge having a responsibility beyond our immediate circle.

CHARACTERISTICS OF ORDINARY AND FAITH-BASED PEOPLE	
Restless	Calm
Postured to speak	Positioned to listen
Demanding	Grateful
Protecting	Freeing
Hurrying, hustling	Resting
Boosting myself	Blessing others
Elevating myself	Consecrating
Working	Favor
Personal legacy	God's glory

24. Stewardship supersedes ownership

We have already examined the constructs of ownership and stewardship elsewhere in detail. Stewardship frames the moral context for capitalism. Without it we inevitably resort to greed.

25. Save to invest

It is a radical misconception that "faith" equates to living hand to mouth. Cutting down on expenses and setting aside money for investment is crucial to building wealth. There are exceptions but as a general principle scripture encourages self-discipline and delayed gratification. We save in order to invest; what we choose to invest in will vary. Investments become future assets.

26. Exercise personal freedom with societal responsibility

There is a world of difference between self-interest and selfishness. Self-interest is encouraged in scripture. Jesus told people to love others in the same way that they loved themselves. This is an "and" not an "or" concept: love yourself and love your neighbor.

You can look after your own self-interest and care about the betterment of society, particularly if you remember all biblical principles taken as a whole: God is the source, everything is his, he rewards generosity, sowing and reaping is a principle, risk taking is better than hoarding, etc.

27. Distinguish between self-interest and selfishness

Proverbs 18:1 says, "An unfriendly man pursues selfish ends; he defies all sound judgment." In other words, it is counter to the logic of scripture to be selfish. In scripture, selfishness is often coupled with the word "ambition." One passage lists it among a litany of wrong behaviors:

> The acts of the sinful nature are obvious: sexual immorality, impurity and debauchery; idolatry and witchcraft; hatred, discord, jealousy, fits of rage, selfish ambition, dissensions, factions and envy; drunkenness, orgies, and the like. I warn you, as I did before, that those who live like this will not inherit the kingdom of God.[81]

Capitalism expects self-care, and God condemns selfish ambition.[82] As indicated earlier, if we do not have a healthy fear of God and are not placing the kingdom of God as a priority over our own wishes, then our self-interest will quickly descend the slippery slope to selfishness. Deuteronomy 8

---

81   Galatians 5:19-21 (emphasis added)
82   Philippians 2:3, James 3:14-16

cautions us regarding this downward spiral, and gives three antidotes: thankfulness, humility, and a remembering our source:

When you have eaten and are satisfied, praise the Lord your God for the good land he has given you. You may say to yourself, "My power and the strength of my hands have produced this wealth for me." But remember the Lord your God, for it is he who gives you the ability to produce wealth, and so confirms his covenant, which he swore to your ancestors, as it is today. If you ever forget the Lord your God and follow other gods and worship and bow down to them, I testify against you today that you will surely be destroyed.[83]

28. Respect property rights

Abraham purchased property as a burial site. Israel purchased property in Egypt, and laws were given regarding protection of property.

If a man gives his neighbor silver or goods for safekeeping and they are stolen from the neighbor's house, the thief, if he is caught, must pay back double. But if the thief is not found, the owner of the house must appear before the judges to determine whether he has laid his hands on the other man's property. In all cases of illegal possession of an ox, a donkey, a sheep, a garment, or any other lost property about which somebody says, 'This is mine,' both parties are to bring their cases before the judges. The one whom the judges declare guilty must pay back double to his neighbor.[84]

83   Deuteronomy 8:10, 18-19
84   Exodus 22:7-9

Do not move your neighbor's boundary stone set up by your predecessors in the inheritance you receive in the land the Lord your God is giving you to possess.[85]

Scripture is also clear there should not be a forced sale and redistribution of land. Generosity is a choice, not a mandate from spiritual leaders, nor government. (This is a line between taxing people to provide services and redistributing their wealth.) A telling example is given of a husband and wife, Ananias and Sapphira, who sold property and pretended to give all of the proceeds away. When the apostle Peter confronted them he clearly spelled things out: the property and the proceeds were always theirs.

Then Peter said, "Ananias, how is it that Satan has so filled your heart that you have lied to the Holy Spirit and have kept for yourself some of the money you received for the land? Didn't it belong to you before it was sold? And after it was sold, wasn't the money at your disposal? What made you think of doing such a thing? You have not lied to men but to God."[86]

29. Foster freedom of exchange

The basic concept of "freedom of choice" goes back to the Garden of Eden and extends to our current day where God gives people the freedom to choose whether to serve him. There is no coercion or forced religion in God's book. Similarly, scripture allows for buying and selling, done fairly.

If you sell land to one of your countrymen or buy any from him, do not take advantage of each other. ...Do not take advantage of each other, but fear your God. I am the Lord your God.[87]

Scripture encourages the mutual agreement of seller and buyer, the preservation of relationship, and the meeting of genuine needs (or the

---

85   Deuteronomy 19:4; 27:17, Proverbs 22:28; 23:10
86   Acts 5:3-4
87   Leviticus 25:14-17

avoidance of deception). A Muslim man explained to me that unbelievers can be coerced to convert to Islam through seizure of property and even physical violence. If he is correct in his understanding, not only is this contrary to human rights, but it is also counter-FBF.

30. Avoid certain types of debt

We have already discussed how debt is to be avoided, especially consumer or consumption debt. "The rich rule over the poor, and the borrower is servant to the lender."[88] It is, however, realistic to take on certain debt when dealing with capital assets that will produce a greater return than the amount borrowed (including interest). It appears, from Leviticus 25, even in the cases of capital-asset debt, the targeted repayment period should be short, as in six or seven years.

You can argue for matching the life of the debt to the life of the asset. But doesn't it make sense to have the debt-life shorter than the shelf-life? When leading a community of faith in South Africa I developed payment plans encouraging people to pay off home mortgages in seven years. This involved delayed gratification on current spending, but the payback was enormous.

31. Be cautious with interest

We have already seen that interest was outlawed in certain instances, but not prohibited outright. The objective truth is debt and interest can ensnare people, corporations and nations. All of the associated negatives of interest are to be avoided. Having said this, a combination of truths leads me to conclude that "appropriate interest" is a concept supported by and consistent with scripture. The combination of thinking includes: the broad view of economics covered earlier in this book and the related idea of subjective value, the combination of the Old Testament writings leaving an opening for interest, the Early Church participation in banking in the first three centuries, the changing nature of money and commerce over time and the fact the Jesus did not outlaw interest (although I do not believe that he specifically condoned it, as some conclude from the parable of the talents).

---

88   Proverbs 22:7

GENEROSITY & GIVING

32. Give to God first

The first of everything belongs to God. How one determines the percentages or portions varies, but the principle is that the first part of a return belongs to God. In a FBF transaction strong consideration should be given to setting aside an agreed portion for God. Do it in writing, as part of the contracts where possible.

You must present as the Lord's portion the best and holiest part of everything given to you.[89]

33. Giving is a given

A cursory reading of scripture could cause one to focus on laws or rules about giving, percentages, frequency of giving and the intended recipients. This misses the heart of the matter because scripture actually intends there to be a culture of generosity and a mind-set of abundance. In fact, there are many forms of generosity encouraged throughout scripture, and many types of gifts. These include first fruits, tithes, offerings, gleanings, and more. Jesus summarized it this way:

Give, and it will be given to you: good measure, pressed down, shaken together, and running over will be put into your bosom. For with the same measure that you use, it will be measured back to you.[90]

---

89   Numbers 18:29
90   Luke 6:38 (New King James version)

First-fruits were given at the beginning of the season as an expression of faith that God would bless the harvest, even before the harvest was determined. (You could liken it to a form of crop insurance, with God backing their acknowledgement of him.) Tithes were given at the end of the season. Money was given to individuals, to the disadvantaged, and for national capital projects. Inherent in giving was an acknowledgment that everything was God's, and a faith that he would provide, and would reward generosity because it was a reflection of his nature.

Scripture by no means proposes that we should do all our giving through a local synagogue or church: much of it should be done through our own household or business, including giving to the poor. Consider this statement made by a pastor of a large church in the Ukraine:

———

> When Christians teach that the only way to be prosperous is by giving to the church or ministry, the only person who becomes wealthy is certainly not the giver but rather the person or group at the helm of the ministry.[91]

34. Sowing and reaping: Giving and gaining

Scripture is replete with examples of sowing and reaping. Sowing is an act of faith done believing that the result will outweigh the input; the payback will exceed the cost. The following table outlines some examples of sowing and reaping. The term generally refers to generosity but has a broader application.

---

91   Money won't make you rich, Sunday Adelaja, Charisma House

	SOWING	REAPING
Creation	God sowed a word	And reaped a creation
Adam	Sowed a rib	And got a woman
Abraham	Sowed self-help	And got Ishmael
Joseph	Sowed a dream that died	And reaped a harvest of a dream fulfilled
Hannah	Sowed a child	Reaped a prophet
David	Lust, murder	Judgment and a dead son
God	His Son	Many sons

35. Care for the poor

Not everyone in scripture was eligible for "handouts" and those who could work were encouraged to do so. Families were responsible for their own family members, and they did not palm off responsibilities on the state or the church. Scripture did not encourage showing partiality to the rich or the poor. "Do not pervert justice; do not show partiality to the poor or favoritism to the great, but judge your neighbor fairly."[92]

Scripture realistically recognizes people have different capacities and can make bad choices; poverty could be the result. Instruction was given to treat the poor kindly. For example:

---

92   Leviticus 19:15

When you reap the harvest of your land, do not reap to the very edges of your field or gather the gleanings of your harvest. Leave them for the poor and the alien. I am the Lord your God.[93]

If one of your countrymen becomes poor and sells some of his property, his nearest relative is to come and redeem what his countryman has sold.[94]

If one of your countrymen becomes poor and is unable to support himself among you, help him as you would an alien or a temporary resident, so he can continue to live among you.[95]

If one of your countrymen becomes poor among you and sells himself to you, do not make him work as a slave.[96]

He who is kind to the poor lends to the Lord, and he will reward him for what he has done.[97]

Do not exploit the poor because they are poor and do not crush the needy in court.[98]

The righteous care about justice for the poor, but the wicked have no such concern[99]

---

93   Leviticus 23:22
94   Leviticus 25:25
95   Leviticus 25:35
96   Leviticus 25:39
97   Proverbs 19:17
98   Proverbs 22:2
99   Proverbs 29:7

Sell your possessions and give to the poor. Provide purses for yourselves that will not wear out, a treasure in heaven that will not be exhausted, where no thief comes near and no moth destroys.[100]

But when you give a banquet, invite the poor, the crippled, the lame, the blind...[101]

INVESTING

In the matter of investing, it is a good reminder that the faith-based view of investing is aligned with the tenets of capitalism, but it goes well beyond the logic and reasoning of man. Biblical investing is based on obedience, not logic. When God instructed the prophet Jeremiah, who was in prison in a city under siege, it was illogical for him to buy real estate, but he did it because he was obedient. Ultimately, FBF is done for God's glory not man's legacy. Nonetheless, scripture is clear that God wants us to invest.

36. Expand with God

Any of these principles can be misused. Nonetheless, it is important to point out how it follows from "wealth creation" that wealth is not static, and we are not in a zero-sum game. Many posit that if one gains, the other loses. Capitalism is based on a win-win scenario. FBF is also based on a win-win proposition: everyone wins from growing financial and other assets. The notion of expansion is directly tied to God's intention to re-establish his influence on the earth through the very people who yielded it to God's enemy in the first place. The expansion of assets makes sense where it is tied to

---

100   Luke 12:33
101   Luke 14:13

the increase of God's influence through men and women who steward those assets.

BUSINESS-AS-USUAL VS. THE KINGDOM OF GOD	
Logic	Obedience
Fear	Trust
Greed	Generosity
Debt	Cash
Credit	Hard Assets
Owning	Stewarding
Personal Legacy	God's glory

37. Avoid financial schemes

A modern translation of the Bible says it best:

> Work your garden—you'll end up with plenty of food; play and party—you'll end up with an empty plate. Committed and persistent work pays off; get-rich-quick schemes are rip-offs.[102]

Unfortunately, religious people are (a) prone to schemes because the element of "faith" can make them hopeful, and (b) willing to prey on other people of faith. The World Christian Encyclopedia has had a team of statisticians tracking what they call Religious Financial Fraud for over twenty years. While many will not agree with their analysis, it highlights a growing global problem. Any development of FBF must include safeguards

---

102   Proverbs 28:19-20 (The Message)

against such trickery. The prophet Amos carries a clear caution that sounds eerily like a warning against televangelist tactics:

I can't stand your religious meetings.

I'm fed up with your conferences and conventions. I want nothing to do with your religion projects, your pretentious slogans and goals. I'm sick of your fund-raising schemes, your public relations and image making.

I've had all I can take of your noisy ego-music. When was the last time you sang to me? Do you know what I want?

I want justice—oceans of it.

I want fairness—rivers of it.

That's what I want. That's all I want.[103]

38. Create communal funds for capital projects

People of the Christian faith have all but lost the notion of a central storehouse funding initiatives consistent with their faith. Muslims and Jews are much better informed and coordinated in this regard. Part of this is the flabby, if not misleading, teaching that equates the local church to the storehouse, overly spiritualizing what was intended to be a practical topic. Another issue could be lack of planning. A further obstacle to implementing the storehouse principal could be rugged individualism. Whatever the reason, FBF should include the establishment of storehouse-equivalent investment funds.

The building of the tabernacle and the temple are examples, but we ignore them because they are "religious" in nature. The rebuilding of Jerusalem goes beyond a "religious" project and is an example of a Public Private Partnership that used funds from multiple sources, including a foreign government, and promptly reinstated the storehouse in Jerusalem.

---

103   Amos 5:21-24 (The Message)

I am not suggesting for a moment that local pastors manage the money in the storehouse. They may or may not have the skills to do so. Spiritual leaders could be part of the management team, bringing a needed perspective, but they will most likely not be effective money managers on their own. Even the early Church apostles delegated financial management to suitably qualified deacons.[104]

39. Practice Self-governance

The biblical progression involves moving from infancy to maturity, from central control to being guided by the Spirit of God in daily matters. The complement to the central treasury or storehouse is the idea of avoiding centralized control, whether by church or state. We tend to substitute rules for relationship. Religious organizations may be even more prone to use money to manipulate because they have less political power than government, in most nations. Bear in mind, however, having a king was not God's first choice for the nation of Israel. Samuel, the prophet, warned how the installment of a king would lead to taxes and many other issues. Government is necessary; how much government is the question.

> One of the more effective ways of mitigating the effects of human sin in society is dispersing and decentralizing power. The combination of a free-market economy and limited constitutional government is the most effective means yet devised to impede the concentration of economic and political power in the hands of a small number of people.[105]

40. Treat relationships as covenants

While we tend to be fairly casual and temporary about business and other relationships, scripture treats relationships as covenants. Financial relationships binding people to each other for periods of time should be regarded as mutually beneficial covenants where each party looks out for

---

104   Acts 6:1-7
105   A Biblical Economics Manifesto, Gills and Nash

the interests of the others. They should be characterized by trust, commitment, and mutual discipling. Investing is a relationship of trust, requiring either a belief in an individual, a company, a market or a system. Kingdom investing believes that, sooner or later, God is the rewarder.

41. Engage in multi-generational thinking

Throughout scripture God presents himself as a multi-generational God with purposes spanning beyond individuals and their immediate generation. While this sounds obvious, it has implications for the way we view the stewardship of assets—including intangible assets such as honor, reputation and calling—across generations. In the FBF arena it extends to an appropriate view of finances across generations.

▬▬▬

God also said to Moses, "Say to the Israelites, 'The Lord, the God of your fathers—the God of Abraham, the God of Isaac and the God of Jacob—has sent me to you.' This is my name forever, the name by which I am to be remembered from generation to generation."[106]

42. Plan to leave an Inheritance

There is an interesting case in scripture where daughters of a deceased man brought their case to Moses. It illustrates the rights of giving and receiving an inheritance, and the role of the state in protecting this right.

▬▬▬

The daughters of Zelophehad ... approached the entrance to the Tent of Meeting and stood before Moses, Eleazar the priest, the leaders and the whole assembly, and said, "Our father died in the desert. He was not among Korah's followers, who banded together against the Lord, but he died for his own sin and left no sons. Why should our father's name disappear from his clan because he had no son? Give us property among our father's relatives."

So Moses brought their case before the Lord and the Lord said to him, "What Zelophehad's daughters are saying is right. You must certainly give them

---

106   Exodus 3:15

property as an inheritance among their father's relatives and turn their father's inheritance over to them. "Say to the Israelites, If a man dies and leaves no son, turn his inheritance over to his daughter. If he has no daughter, give his inheritance to his brothers. If he has no brothers, give his inheritance to his father's brothers. If his father had no brothers, give his inheritance to the nearest relative in his clan, that he may possess it. This is to be a legal requirement for the Israelites, as the Lord commanded Moses."[107]

Note the healthy respect God himself had for women's rights. Others, like the woman who anointed Jesus with perfume, had fewer physical assets yet built spiritual capital and secured a place among God's history-makers.

I know wealthy Christians who say, "I want my last check to bounce!" Their goal is to give their wealth away in their lifetimes. Decide what type of inheritance you want to leave your children. I will expand on this later.

A good man leaves an inheritance for his children's children, but a sinner's wealth is stored up for the righteous.[108]

REMEDIAL ACTION

People get into debt; nations pile up national debt and print money at the cost of every citizen. The global economic crisis has made nearly everyone debt-literate, at least in terms of understanding that bad debt is, well, bad. We agree less on the remedies for debt. Those who do not hold a particular faith persuasion, like the IMF, tend to be more pragmatic: fix your underlying economic policies and practices, and we will lend you more money. People of faith tend to say, "Have good intentions—or a crisis of some form—and we

107   Numbers 27:1-11
108   Proverbs 13:22

will forgive your debt." Are there a set of FBF principles providing better guidance for remediating financial catastrophes?

43. Restitution, where economic harm was done

Scripture requires restitution be made if someone else's property is defamed or devalued, and there is usually a penalty clause. Exodus 22 deals with this extensively. This is in stark contrast to the immunity from consequences given to banks today after their role in the crisis, let alone the bonuses paid to executives of banks who benefited from a crisis for which they are responsible, at least in part.

44. Jubilee: Avoid financial captivity

One cannot leave the topic of biblical principles for finance without addressing the matter of the Jubilee year and the principles surrounding it. The fiftieth year was the year of Jubilee, and in that year certain lands and properties were to be returned to their original owners. The properties in question were generally agricultural land. Houses in cities were usually exempt from the 50-year Jubilee program. There were several premises behind this Jubilee stipulation, the first being that the Israelites did not own the land: God owned the land. "The land must not be sold permanently, because the land is mine and you are but aliens and my tenants. Throughout the country that you hold as a possession, you must provide for the redemption of the land."[109] The same premise underpinned the instruction to not permanently enslave people: "Even if he is not redeemed in any of these ways, he and his children are to be released in the Year of Jubilee, for the Israelites belong to me as servants. They are my servants, whom I brought out of Egypt. I am the Lord your God."[110] The takeaway is clear: Israelites were to regard themselves as stewards of that which God owned. They were to grow, increase wealth, make improvements, but at the end of the day, God owned the land...and no-one owned people.

Another principle, which is perhaps greater than ownership and stewardship, is redemption. What was contained in the Old Testament was not a prohibition against property ownership but an illustration of

---

109   Leviticus 25:23-24
110   Leviticus 25:54-55

redemption. Christians believe that this foreshadowed the fact that people themselves would be redeemed, set free from slavery by the sacrifice of Jesus Christ. This re-established his rightful ownership of man and was the ultimate Jubilee.

The facts today are along these lines:

- According to the United Nations Working Group on Contemporary Forms of Slavery, an estimated 20 million people were held in bonded slavery as of 1999. In 2010 the number was estimated at 27 million.
- In 2004, there were more slaves in the world than were seized from Africa during four centuries of trans-Atlantic slave trade.[111]
- In 1850, a slave in the Southern United States cost the equivalent of $40,000 today. According to Free the Slaves, a slave today costs an average of $90.
- Approximately two-thirds of today's slaves are in South Asia. Human Rights Watch estimates that in India alone there are as many as 15 million children in bonded slavery.

One could well argue, as we have seen before, a third principle: God's optimum plan was people should have a means of production, and it should not become permanently encumbered by debt. There are well documented cases of people being enslaved in servitude—modern day slavery—for small debts. Coupled with compound interest, these small debts have left people trapped for generations.

A fourth principle from the Jubilee passages: value transactions fairly. "When the years are many, you are to increase the price, and when the years are few, you are to decrease the price, because what he is really selling you is the number of crops. Do not take advantage of each other, but fear your God."[112]

---

111   Disposable People: New Slavery in the Global Economy, Kevin Bales
112   Leviticus 25:16-17

Today there are various Jubilee-related initiatives with a focus on slavery and developing nation (or majority world) debt forgiveness. The Jubilee Act for Responsible Lending and Expanded Debt Cancellation (HR4405) has been introduced to the US House of Representatives but is still in committee.

45. Debt forgiveness requires wisdom

"Forgive us our debts, as we forgive our debtors." The phrase is ingrained into anyone who has prayed The Lord's Prayer. But is debt forgiveness the answer to all debt? This is another area where blanket, but shallow, pronouncements can be dangerous. It sounds altruistic and noble to say all debt should be forgiven, but it is not a universal truth that should be blindly applied.

> What's striking about the Biblical concept of forgiveness is that it is never understood unconditionally. God's love is unconditional, and individuals are exhorted to love one another in that manner as well. But forgiveness is always linked to repentance and the restoration of right relationships between the parties involved. As one source puts it, forgiveness requires " . . . the repentant response which receives love, re-appropriates relationship, and experiences restoration" (Atkinson & Field). Likewise the jubilee concept—the release of slaves from debt—has at its core the concept of restoration of right relationships—among families, and between families and the land—rather than redistribution for its own sake (Atkinson & Field). Crucially, the debt remission implicit in jubilee restores proper relationships among all households, not just between (formerly) enslaved families and (former) masters.[113]

Before one advocates wholesale debt forgiveness one must address why the debt was incurred or mismanaged in the first place. I have a real concern that the behaviors of banks in the US (that led to the accumulation of toxic assets) have not changed since the bailout. This bailout is not just debt forgiveness, but forgiveness of bad management. At the international level,

---

113   Christian Ethics and the Forgiveness of Third World Debt, Stephen L. S. Smith, Gordon College (MA). Faith & Economic #35 Spring 2000

the IMF claims victories in Sub-Saharan Africa where the impact of the global recession has been less than in many other parts of the globe. It appears, however, that those nations most integrated into the global economy, such as South Africa, were harder hit.

One way to avoid crippling interest on foreign debt is to stay out of debt. But Dominique Strauss-Kahn, managing director of the International Monetary Fund (IMF) pointed out in an interview:

> It would be totally unreasonable to believe that poor countries like Democratic Republic of Congo can develop without foreign aid and foreign aid may be foreign loans providing that these loans are very concessional. And that's why in the IMF, using the proceeds of the gold sale from the IMF that we made, which was the property of the membership, we created a new facility, which is a facility where the interest rate is just zero; we couldn't go below. We were asked to be as concessional as possible. We went to the lower boundary, which is zero. So now until the end of 2011—and we will see what happens for the years after—we are lending to countries like DRC at zero interest rate.[114]

Having said lending will still be required in the future, there is a recognized need for concessional plans from lenders and donors. The question is how debt forgiveness fits into a broader national plan to create jobs, boost exports, and improve economic disciplines. People of faith should be cautious about promoting debt forgiveness without simultaneously encouraging transparency, accountability, rule of law and thorough due diligence on projects (i.e., wise investments). These are all biblical financial principles.

46. Spend less than you earn

The commonsense answer to personal and national debt is simple: spend less than you earn. Do not promise to pay for things with money that you do not have. Do not use credit unwisely, cut expenditures when income decreases, as it will from time to time, and set aside money for investments

---

114   March 12, 2010 interview with Charlayne Hunter-Gault of AllAfrica.com

and famines. Don't encumber your personal assets as collateral and ensure that the return on capital assets outweighs the associated debt. It is not rocket science, but it needs to be said.

Western readers: while you are at it, revisit your "needs" with an eye to eliminating frivolous items. Try also to peg your standard of living so that it does not float as soon as you earn more.

47. Honor your word

This should go without saying, but we too often justify vague terms, slight of hand, and lack of follow through on commitments. Jesus said, "Let your 'Yes' be yes, and your 'No' be no."[115] Character, trust and love are currencies of FBF economies. There are no exceptions for people of "other" class, creed, color or capital base. Lying is not an option.

48. Be transparent

Jesus told his followers that their secret conversations will be broadcast one day. His disciple, John, urged believers to "walk in the light, as he is in the light."[116] If trust is the underpinning of contracts, it is all the more essential we have a values-based moral mooring to our economies.

49. Have the same standard for everyone

The Apostle James urged people to not show favoritism to wealthy people. Jesus went so far as to urge his followers to love their enemies. There is, in Christian scripture, no basis for treating someone outside of the faith poorly. This should be a universal constant but is sadly not true for all faiths.

50. Love God and man through your money

The first commandment is to have only one God. When Jesus was asked what the greatest commandment was he summarized things: love God and

---

115   Matthew 5:37
116   1 John 1:7

love your fellow man. When we see money as a means to love God and others, we are on safer ground.

6

The Promised

Land

Good friends asked me to write a book on The Promised Land. I asked them why, and they replied, "Because we feel like we are in The Promised Land, but we are still fighting battles." Since I had no plans to write such a book, I declined. A little later that day we sat having tea and I said, "Hand me your iPhone... it is going to be an audio book. I will record it for you." While this was a fun conversation between friends, fortunately, I still have the recording, and I believe the topic is relevant to those who would be involved in contemplating the economics of the Promised Land.

> I said, "The essence of your question is, 'Where is your fight, or what are you fighting?' This will give you an indication of where you are living."

I went on to tell them, "In Egypt, your focus is on, 'How do I get away from a bad boss? How do I escape from someone who is holding me captive?'"

"In the desert, you are fighting circumstances. Too much sun, too much heat, not enough water, what about food..."

"Also, in the desert, you are fighting other people. 'I don't like Moses, I don't like Aaron.' So, the desert is survival, and being inwardly focused, and fighting other people. Much of the Church is in the desert and spends their time battling each other in disunity."

They agreed.

"The privilege of being in the Promised Land is that you get to fight giants, and you are actually tackling something meaningful: giants can be false religions, the old economies of Egypt and the Desert, and they can be a demonic force, or systems that have set themselves up against the knowledge of God. So, when you are fighting to change an industry, deal with a principality, or disrupt a structure that has been in place for a long time, then you are in the Promised Land."

This little interchange brought to mind some of the misconceptions regarding the Promised Land, and it is worth considering some features of the "ideal" place.

The Promised Land has present inhabitants

Where did we get the notion from that the Promised Land was like an Air BnB where someone laid out a nice little welcome treat, then disappeared into the background, leaving the place all to us? No battle, no fuss... just an easy little transition into a weekend away from the desert? The "evil report" of the 10 spies was not technically incorrect. There were giants, the cities were fortified; it was not an uninhabited paradise.

You must take possession of something in the Promised Land, even though it was a given inheritance from God. In today's world, we are used to getting an inheritance passively. A grandfather or father leaves you money; you collect it from the trust attorneys, and you are done. This is not the way it worked in scripture. The place where God wants you to extend the workings of his kingdom already has occupants. In the world of the New Testament, our goal is not to get rid of them, but to be among them and rid them of things that bind and hinder them from reaching their full potential. Post-

Jesus, we are the salt and light. We are the yeast. So we get in there, and we make a positive difference.

God owns key resources

Before anyone received anything, God made clear which resources belonged to him, and which were up for grabs. Interestingly, the land was his. Everyone except the priests received (post-battles) a piece of property to steward. While they held the title deeds, they knew it really belonged to the Father. Preservation and then growth of capital is a principal inherent to the Promised Land. You can live hand-to-mouth in the desert and manna can drop from the sky each day. Once you cross the Jordan, you must plant, water, harvest, store and bake.

Everyone has capital

To have a functioning society where God was the main thing, and not some appointed monarchy, God designed that everyone be a capital owner. No one should have had a pauper or serf mentality. Now, to be sure, God anticipated that some would be better at growing their capital, so he even made provision for a return of certain types of assets every 7th year.

One cannot leave the topic of biblical principles for finance without addressing the matter of the Jubilee year and the principles surrounding it. The fiftieth year was the year of Jubilee, and in that year certain lands and properties were to be returned to their original owners. The properties in question were generally agricultural land. Houses in cities were usually exempt from the 50-year Jubilee program. There were several premises behind this Jubilee stipulation, the first being that the Israelites did not own the land: God owned the land. "The land must not be sold permanently, because the land is mine and you are but aliens and my tenants. Throughout the country that you hold as a possession, you must provide for the redemption of the land."[117] The same premise underpinned the instruction to not permanently enslave people: "Even if he is not redeemed in any of these ways, he and his children are to be

---

117   Leviticus 25:23-24

released in the Year of Jubilee, for the Israelites belong to me as servants. They are my servants, whom I brought out of Egypt. I am the Lord your God."[118] The takeaway is clear: Israelites were to regard themselves as stewards of that which God owned. They were to grow, increase wealth, make improvements, but at the end of the day, God owned the land...and no-one owned people.

Another principle, which is perhaps greater than ownership and stewardship, is redemption. What was contained in the Old Testament was not a prohibition against property ownership but an illustration of redemption. Christians believe that this foreshadowed the fact that people themselves would be redeemed, set free from slavery by the sacrifice of Jesus Christ. This re-established his rightful ownership of man and was the ultimate Jubilee.[119]

So, in the Promised Land, we are entrusted with capital, are charged with stewarding it, and yet, between us and God, it is his. One reason he gives us "the ability to create wealth" is so that we can fund the fight against giants and increase occupation of areas not yet tackled.

It takes faith to live in the Promised Land

The economies of Egypt and the Desert required little faith; the provision was constant. I have covered the different economic models in detail in the book, Repurposing Capital. By way of recap:

Once the nation of Israel had miraculously exited Egypt, taking a trove of jewelry and spoils with them, they found themselves in a nomadic cycle where their certain supply was gone. In fact, they had to depend on God for miraculous provision of daily necessities, such as water. They lived in tents, had no fixed address, and could not build dams or granaries. They lived from hand to mouth. Many people of faith think this is the ultimate economic model—one of total dependence on God. They embrace the idea of only having enough for today in order to stay dependent on God. There is no doubt that for specific seasons of life—and for some people, their entire lives—this Desert Model is a chosen path. The sad reality is that many

118   Leviticus 25:54-55
119   Repurposing Capital, Brett Johnson - page 245

people live with the mind-set of Desert Economics simply because they do not understand the third alternative: The Promised Land Model.

The Promised Land had elements of Egypt and the Desert, but it was different from both of them. People were allocated land and had a capital base for wealth creation. This was similar to Egypt in "the good old days" when they were still treated with favor. The catch, however, was that there was no River Nile. "But the land you are crossing the Jordan to take possession of is a land of mountains and valleys that drinks rain from heaven. It is a land the Lord your God cares for; the eyes of the Lord your God are continually on it from the beginning of the year to its end." The good news: you have land. The bad news: unless God sends the rain, you have a drought. Scripture then lays out the conditions upon which God would water the land.

So if you faithfully obey the commands I am giving you today—to love the Lord your God and to serve him with all your heart and with all your soul—then I will send rain on your land in its season, both autumn and spring rains, so that you may gather in your grain, new wine and oil. I will provide grass in the fields for your cattle, and you will eat and be satisfied.[120]

You will note that the Promised Land was a blend of capital and faith (in contrast to Egypt, which was capital and no faith, and the Desert, which was no capital and faith).

In summary, the Promised Land carries a greater onus to blend capital and faith such that one is not seduced by the growth of capital, and not tempted to scheme to avoid a dependence on God. This is not an easy blend as it is as much about our hearts as our minds and hands.

The Promised Land still has giants

The platitudes about the Promised Land sketch a scene where everyone is at peace, sitting "under their own vine" and enjoying bug-free harvests. In

---

120   Deuteronomy 11:13-15

reality, warfare was a way of life until King Solomon took over from his dad, the fighting king. Judges chapter 3 has an interesting passage:

———————

¹ These are the nations the LORD left to test all those Israelites who had not experienced any of the wars in Canaan ² (he did this only to teach warfare to the descendants of the Israelites who had not had previous battle experience): ³ the five rulers of the Philistines, all the Canaanites, the Sidonians, and the Hivites living in the Lebanon mountains from Mount Baal Hermon to Lebo Hamath. ⁴ They were left to test the Israelites to see whether they would obey the LORD's commands, which he had given their ancestors through Moses.[121]

Don't miss the key principle tucked away in parentheses: (he did this only to teach warfare to the descendants of the Israelites who had not had previous battle experience).

In other words, battle experience is a pre-requisite to living in the Promised Land. Certainly it is essential to being engaged in societal transformation and fulfilling the Great Commission.

What you are fighting indicates where you are living

Going back to the conversation with my friends: they were in the Promised Land, and they were fighting battles. This is normal. Our problem is that we have been duped into believing that battles are assignments against us from the devil rather than commissions for us from God. You will be in a fight, of that there is no question. You must choose the level at which you want to engage:

- You can burn up your ammunition on your boss, your career, your getting (or not getting) ahead, or
- You can step away from the white picket fence and become a desert wanderer, fighting the battles of daily survival and round-in-circles living, or

———————

121 Judges 3:1-4 NIV

- You can set those things behind you and ask God what is on his agenda, and then willingly go to war with him.

I was chatting with a friend who is about 60 years old recently. His adult children had been to visit for a week or two; some of them had their own children. When there was some sibling "goings on" between the grown children his wife asked him, "What are you going to do?" He replied, "I think I will have some coffee." Later I shared with him that this is, in my view, an illustration of choosing, not your battles, but your battle ground. Grandfathers should not fight their kid's battles. It is not their job to sort out squabbles; they are to save their ammunition for giants. If people are still preoccupied with whose church is better, which doctrine is purer, and what you are going to have for Sunday lunch, figuratively, they are not ready for Promised Land fights. If people are talking Promised Land, but it is just a ruse for have the predictable life of Egypt, then beware: the world is happy to keep you happy as long as you are not a threat to the entrenched kingdom(s) of darkness. I am very grateful, however, for the battle scarred, little-to-lose post-60-year-olds who are winding up for the next big battle. It is time.

Extraordinary courage is essential for kingdom living

Since being in the Promised Land is living a life of meaningful battle, courage will be needed. Living in the Kingdom of God is not for cowards.

When they saw the courage of Peter and John and realized that they were unschooled, ordinary men, they were astonished and they took note that these men had been with Jesus.[122]

From the days of John the Baptist until now, the kingdom of heaven has been subjected to violence, and violent people have been raiding it.[123]

---

122   Acts 4:13
123   Matthew 11:12

Boldness is an attribute of any who want to make a difference and stay the course. The kingdom of God is not for sissies; it is under constant siege.

———

Now, Lord, consider their threats and enable your servants to speak your word with great boldness. Stretch out your hand to heal and perform signs and wonders through the name of your holy servant Jesus."

After they prayed, the place where they were meeting was shaken. And they were all filled with the Holy Spirit and spoke the word of God boldly.[124]

The New Testament response to a threat was a prayer for greater boldness. The opportunities and opposition in the world today demand the same Holy Spirit-inspired courage.

"Christianity is a battle, not a dream:"

Wendell Phillips, American abolitionist

I recommend you read the chapter in Transforming Society that deals with the capital required to make a difference.

- The difficult job of finding Kingdom Capitalists
- Historical examples of Capital for Transformation
- The Journey to being a Transformer
- Common mistakes in skipping steps on the journey
- Repurposing Industries, Sectors, Spheres
- Building a War Chest the size of Texas
- Capital options - Repurposing Capital
- Ways to invest along the value chain

---

124   Acts 4:29-31

- How to become a Societal Capitalist
- The Global Giants Foundation

There are several diagrams that help explain the typical journey from being an employee to entrepreneur to kingdom capitalist to transformer.

I will not reiterate this section but recommend you understand it as you craft your own forward journey. I do want to summarize some key points on the overall theme of Kingdom Economics.

Promised Land Principles are not for those living in Egypt

It is true that universal principles apply universally. Natural laws, such as gravity, do apply to all. Gravity does not apply on the moon, however. Principles have a context, and we can choose our economic context. If you are a person of faith you still have freedom of choice: we have a choice to live in the economic land of our choosing. It is true that you didn't have a choice about which system you were born into, but IF you have been born again THEN you have a choice concerning your economic residency. You can decide to live in Egypt, the Desert or the Promised Land from an economic or financial perspective.

Don't be tempted to cherry pick these 50 principles yet decide in your heart that you are more comfortable living in Egypt or content to stay in the Desert. My experience working with thousands of God-fearing businesspeople is clear: one can learn principles from the Kingdom of God but make the choice to do business as usual.

Imagine if the Israelites had just asked God to help them cope better in Egypt and not implored him to return them to their homeland. Once they had crossed the Jordan, belatedly it turns out, they were instructed to not go back to Egypt, a place of their former slavery. It took a generation for the Israelites to unlearn the ways of Egypt. By the time Solomon reigned as king in Israel there was a booming economy, but did it last?

7

Putting Faith and
Capital back together

Capitalism has a bad name in some circles because it is mistaken for unbridled materialism, wealth at any cost. In the economy taught in scripture sustainable capital was always married to obedience to the principles of God. Further, it was understood that one could not stray far from the presence of God and still hope to live out his principles since these truths flow from God's heart. Later we will dig into the story of King Solomon, a man of enormous wealth.

The acquiring and multiplying of capital is not meant to take us away from God, but it carries that inherent risk.

¹³ and when your herds and flocks grow large and your silver and gold increase and all you have is multiplied, 14 then your heart will become proud and you will forget the Lord your God, who brought you out of Egypt, out of the land of slavery. ¹⁵ He led you through the vast and dreadful wilderness, that thirsty and waterless land, with its venomous snakes and scorpions. He brought you water out of hard rock. ¹⁶ He gave you manna to eat in the wilderness, something your ancestors had never known, to humble and test you so that in the end it might go well with you. ¹⁷ You may say to yourself, "My power and the strength of my hands have produced this wealth for me." ¹⁸ But remember the Lord your God, for it is he who gives you the ability to produce wealth, and so confirms his covenant, which he swore to your ancestors, as it is today.[125]

The Israelites were reminded that they were stewards of capital. "The land is mine… the people are mine… the ability to produce wealth is from me…remember!" In Egypt the River Nile was an ever-present source of water and many looked to it as the source of wealth. The Promised Land economy was set up with a built-in dependence on God. It is as if God were saying, "You can have capital (land) but you will have to have faith to go with it, otherwise there will be no rain. This takes obedience and faith."

¹⁰ The land you are entering to take over is not like the land of Egypt, from which you have come, where you planted your seed and irrigated it by foot as in a vegetable garden. ¹¹ But the land you are crossing the Jordan to take possession of is a land of mountains and valleys that drinks rain from heaven. ¹² It is a land the Lord your God cares for; the eyes of the Lord your God are continually on it from the beginning of the year to its end.

¹³ So if you faithfully obey the commands I am giving you today—to love the Lord your God and to serve him with all your heart and with all your soul— ¹⁴ then I will send rain on your land in its season, both autumn and spring rains,

125 Deuteronomy 8:13-18

so that you may gather in your grain, new wine and olive oil. ¹⁵ I will provide grass in the fields for your cattle, and you will eat and be satisfied.

¹⁶ Be careful, or you will be enticed to turn away and worship other gods and bow down to them. ¹⁷ Then the Lord's anger will burn against you, and he will shut up the heavens so that it will not rain and the ground will yield no produce, and you will soon perish from the good land the Lord is giving you. ¹⁸ Fix these words of mine in your hearts and minds; tie them as symbols on your hands and bind them on your foreheads. ¹⁹ Teach them to your children, talking about them when you sit at home and when you walk along the road, when you lie down and when you get up. ²⁰ Write them on the doorframes of your houses and on your gates, ²¹ so that your days and the days of your children may be many in the land the Lord swore to give your ancestors, as many as the days that the heavens are above the earth.[126]

I have quoted this section at length because it describes the framework of the new economy and its terms and conditions. "If you do this, then I will do that. If you do not, then there will be consequences." It is wonderful that we are not living under the Jewish religious laws today with their many formalities which might be hard to keep. We are, however, still living in a world where God is the source of capital, its rightful owner and beneficiary, and we are asset managers with a mandate to productively grown his capital for the good of mankind. Why is this so hard to grasp? One reason is this: we are way too religious.

Don't get confused by the "priest" language: Remember Melchizedek

When the nation of Israel learned a new religious and economic system 11 of the 12 tribes were economically endowed and the Levites were set up to mostly live off donations. For the most part, their job was to do the work of keeping the religious system up and running, and the others would give tithes and offerings to support them.

---

¹²⁶ Deuteronomy 11:10-21

In the New Testament we see an amazing thing happen. No longer are only some people priests who have access to God and doing the "spiritual work." Now all of us have become ministers of God. This "priesthood of all believers" means that it is not just the priests, pastors, bishops, superintendents and popes (to name just some of the labels that are out there) who get to "do ministry." All of us are now ministers. That's the good news. The bad news is worse: we are often perpetuating the wrong priesthood. We think God opened up the work of the tribe of Levi to the rest of us, minus all the sacrifices of course. With that understanding we inherited a poverty mindset with some sneaking suspicion that the priests did not own property. They had God, so they did not need capital. They had meaning, so they did not need money. Wrong thinking!

Long before there was Moses and the principles he introduced on God's behalf, there was Abram. He was the one with a handful of great promises but an old wife and no kids. He did have a nephew, Lot, and when young Lot got into trouble Abram (and his fighting force) went to help him out by retrieving what had been plundered. Genesis 14 carries the story:

14 When Abram heard that his relative had been taken captive, he called out the 318 trained men born in his household and went in pursuit as far as Dan. 15 During the night Abram divided his men to attack them and he routed them, pursuing them as far as Hobah, north of Damascus. 16 He recovered all the goods and brought back his relative Lot and his possessions, together with the women and the other people.

Two kings meet him on his way back from the battle: one is good news; the other is bad news. One came to bless him, the other to ensnare him in godless systems.

17 After Abram returned from defeating Kedorlaomer and the kings allied with him, the king of Sodom came out to meet him in the Valley of Shaveh (that is, the King's Valley).

18 Then Melchizedek king of Salem brought out bread and wine. He was priest of God Most High, 19 and he blessed Abram, saying,

"Blessed be Abram by God Most High,

   Creator of heaven and earth.

20 And praise be to God Most High,

   who delivered your enemies into your hand."

Then Abram gave him a tenth of everything.

21 The king of Sodom said to Abram, "Give me the people and keep the goods for yourself."

22 But Abram said to the king of Sodom, "With raised hand I have sworn an oath to the Lord, God Most High, Creator of heaven and earth, 23 that I will accept nothing belonging to you, not even a thread or the strap of a sandal, so that you will never be able to say, 'I made Abram rich.'

Dr. Francis Myles gives a clear explanation of the spiritual and economic dynamics at work.

While Abram was returning from the slaughter of the kings from the East, news of his glorious victory reached the ears of the king of sodom. The king of Sodom drove in his royal chariot to intercept Abraham on his victorious return. The "king of Sodom" represents a demonic system that wants to corrupt every businessman and women in the marketplace. Abraham did not know that the king of Sodom was riding ferociously towards him, but the Lord did. The setting of the time and timing God chose to introduce Abram to the priestly order of Melchizedek is very significant indeed. The perfect spiritual timing of Melchizedek's appearance in Abraham's life will shed light on the awesome power of this priestly order. It was no coincidence that God in his infinite wisdom chose to intercept Abram's life just before the king of Sodom reached him. God was determined to touch Abram before the devil's greatest agent had a chance to do so.[127]

---

127 The Order of Melchizedek, Dr Francis Myles

So, seemingly out of nowhere, a King who is also a priest appears on the scene with bread and wine. He blesses Abram who gives him a tenth of the spoils. Psalm 110 draws the curtain back on a dialogue in heaven between Father and Son.

The Lord has sworn and will not change his mind: "You are a priest forever, in the order of Melchizedek."

The priestly work of Jesus derives from Melchizedek, not from Levi. Hebrews 5 explains further:

[5] In the same way, Christ did not take on himself the glory of becoming a high priest. But God said to him,

"You are my Son;

today I have become your Father."

[6] And he says in another place,

"You are a priest forever,

in the order of Melchizedek."

[7] During the days of Jesus' life on earth, he offered up prayers and petitions with fervent cries and tears to the one who could save him from death, and he was heard because of his reverent submission. [8] Son though he was, he learned obedience from what he suffered [9] and, once made perfect, he became the source of eternal salvation for all who obey him [10] and was designated by God to be high priest in the order of Melchizedek.[128]

Yes, we too are priests, but we are king-priests. Kings have a sphere of influence that touches every aspect of society. Their reach is to every corner of a kingdom. We have been brought into the kingdom of God with a king+priest mandate that is not either-or, but both-and. As kings we can

---

128 Hebrews 5:5-10

earn money. As kings we can build and deploy capital for the good of the kingdom. As kings we are not confined to living off tithes and offerings. As kings we can give like royalty. Kings do not have poverty mindsets.

---

5. To Him who loved us and washed us from our sins in His own blood, 6 and has made us kings and priests to His God and Father, to Him be glory and dominion forever and ever. Amen.[129]

As the king+priest combinators we serve on behalf of people, and we stand in the gap between God and man reflecting the King to his world and interceding for the people who are rightfully part of the Kingdom of God.

Remember Melchizedek. Jesus is from his order; so are you. We must also rethink the matter of tithing in the Kingdom Economy. The question is not whether one should tithe, give and be generous. The better question, it seems, is "Are we tithing under the Levitical system to support the clergy, or are we tithing under the Abrahamic/Melchizedekian accord?"

Abraham gave tithes to a king and not just to a priest. Since every king has a Kingdom it is safe to assume that Abraham's tithes were used to support a "Kingdom." Everything that is given to a king becomes part of his royal estate. This means that the Abrahamic tithing model is a Kingdom driven and Kingdom minded tithing model. This is why it is the highest form and level of tithing mentioned in the scriptures. Under the Levitical priesthood, tithes were given to support the priesthood (the clergy) whereas under the order of Melchizedek, tithes are given to support and sustain the advancement of God's Kingdom on earth.[130]

---

129   Revelation 1:5-6
130 The Order of Melchizedek, Dr Francis Myles

Different kingdom, different priesthood, different economy

Imagine waking up one day and realizing you are living in a foreign country, but you are an ambassador. You realize you have had thought the rules of the land were your rules, but you find out you are from another kingdom that has different frameworks, leadership structures and economic foundations... even a different currency. You then realize, not only are you not from the land where you have been living, you are the official ambassador to the country where you woke up. As such you have both diplomatic immunity and you have a responsibility to embody the culture and causes of your own kingdom while being gracious to your hosts. But there's more. You log into your bank account and find you have been paid in your kingdom's currency and it is worth a lot more than you thought. You have been paid in gold while the local currency is cow dung. (Don't laugh... this used to be a currency.)

Far too many of us live like paupers on earth waiting to get evacuated to heaven where we will not have to worry about money and maintenance ever again.

────────

And he said to him, 'Well done, good servant; because you were faithful in a very little, have authority over ten cities.'[131]

Running a city is bigger than managing your family budget or your company financials. It involves planning, infrastructure, growth, order and possibly even maintenance (although there is no rust or degradation in heaven). We know well that our mandate is to pray and see "as it is in heaven" happening here on earth. People will want to go to heaven if they have seen greater glimpses of it on earth. As I indicated at the outset of this book, God's people have abdicated the world of capital, finance, money and wealth. We have thought we are doing God a favor by being financially illiterate and economically challenged. We have elevated poverty to a badge of honor to

───────────────

131   Luke 19:17

the point that we don't have much "good news for the poor." And when our hurting world is looking for answers they seldom think, "Let me go to the Church for economic wisdom." We have been told, "As shoes for your feet put on whatever will make you ready to proclaim the gospel of peace." (Ephesians 6:14 NRSV) So often, however, our desires to proclaim the gospel of peace have been disconnected from our mandate to fruitfulness, multiplication, wealth creation and nation discipling. We have shot ourselves in the foot and wondered why we struggle to run the race.

Reclaiming the Storehouse

In my book, Repurposing Capital, I have expanded on the theme that God wanted to create a culture of generosity in the Promised Land. Many forms of giving would lead to the addressing of the needs of the people so that, in God's ideal world, there would be no poor in the nation. There was a healthy recognition that some would be better at generating wealth than others, so safeguards were built in that would encourage the upskilling of people in the nation so that each became a productive citizen. I therefore have no argument against biblical generosity in its many forms, including tithing. I do want to point out, however, that some have misinterpreted Malachi chapter 3 verse 10. No matter which translation one chooses, the message is the same:

> Bring all the tithes (the whole tenth of your income) into the storehouse, that there may be food in My house, and prove Me now by it, says the Lord of hosts, if I will not open the windows of heaven for you and pour you out a blessing, that there shall not be room enough to receive it. (AMPC)

> "Begin by being honest. Do honest people rob God? But you rob me day after day. "You ask, 'How have we robbed you?' "The tithe and the offering—that's how! And now you're under a curse—the whole lot of you—because you're robbing me. Bring your full tithe to the Temple treasury so there will be ample provisions in my Temple. Test me in this and see if I don't open up heaven itself to you and pour out blessings beyond your wildest dreams. For my part, I will defend you against marauders, protect your wheat fields and vegetable gardens against plunderers." The Message of God-of-the-Angel-Armies. (The Message)

So far, so good. My question is not about tithing—including before or after-tax conversations—but the Storehouse. I have been in churches where preachers have extrapolated on this verse. Their reasoning goes as follows:

> "Bring your tithes to the storehouse. *The storehouse is where you get fed. You get fed at your local church. So bring your tithes to the local church*. Then God will then open the windows of heaven and bless you."

The phrases in red/italics are conjecture. The storehouse in the Old Testament was not the local church coffers. Yes, God did want the Old Testament priests to be supported so that they could dedicate themselves to their responsibilities. The tithe was part of the inheritance for the Levites. But the storehouse went beyond meeting the needs of what today would be the local church.

People of the Christian faith have all but lost the notion of a central storehouse funding initiatives consistent with their faith. Muslims and Jews are much better informed and coordinated in this regard. Part of this is the flabby, if not misleading, teaching that equates the local church to the storehouse, overly spiritualizing what was intended to be a practical topic. Another issue could be lack of planning. A further obstacle to implementing the storehouse principal could be rugged individualism. Whatever the reason, FBF should include the establishment of storehouse-equivalent investment funds.

The building of the tabernacle and the temple are examples, but we ignore them because they are "religious" in nature. The rebuilding of Jerusalem goes beyond a "religious" project and is an example of a Public Private Partnership that used funds from multiple sources, including a foreign government, and promptly reinstated the storehouse in Jerusalem.

I am not suggesting for a moment that local pastors manage the money in the storehouse. They may or may not have the skills to do so. Spiritual leaders could be part of the management team, bringing a needed perspective, but they will most likely not be effective money managers on their own. Even the early Church apostles delegated financial management to suitably qualified deacons.[132]

Few want to tackle the topic of tithing, and this is understandable. Some preachers avoid it for fear of offending their congregations. Translocal ministers (those who are five-fold ministers whose work is largely outside one local church, itinerant preachers, evangelists and the like) do not want to appear to be going against local pastors. Non-profit (often mislabeled "para-church") leaders likewise do not want to run foul of local church leaders and be branded anti-church.

If we reclaimed the meaning of the storehouse and did not focus our funds on building better local churches, then perhaps God would indeed open the floodgates of heaven because he could trust us with money. What if we said a combination of these things?

- We do not really need 10% to run our local church. We can control our expenses in many ways, not least of which is empowering non-church-staff to do the ministry.
- We do, however, need 10% and more to make a difference in the world. There are vast needs and we, God's people, could help address them.
- So, let's set up a fund, managed by people who have a track record in asset management, and put anything above 2% into the kingdom-advancing storehouse-type fund.
- The storehouse funds would be local, city-wide and perhaps national and international
  - o Deuteronomy 14 gave the tithe-distribution task to business leaders, heads of household, not the priests
  - o Every third year the corporate celebration was to be held at home and was to include the widows, orphans, foreigners and priests/Levites. This was an example of local management.
  - o The building of a temple or city... these were national and city-wide projects

132 Repurposing Capital, by Brett Johnson (Indaba Publishing, 2010) – Page 242

There are many options for how this could be done. My point here is simple: we have hamstrung the advancement of God's kingdom by focusing on one slice of generosity (the tithe) and then, to make matters worse, we have tucked it under the wrong priesthood (the Levitical mindset) and not extended the rhetoric of "the priesthood of all believers" to encompass the are of finances and capital.

The Generosity Prism

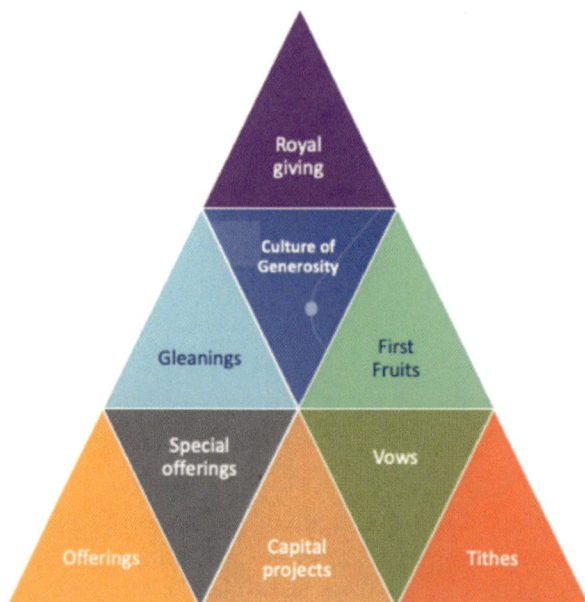

A Culture of Generosity is the norm in the Kingdom Economy. There were many forms of giving, voluntary and mandated, that formed part of the daily, weekly and annual cycles of the newly formed nation of Israel. The goal was not to set up impossible standards and catch offenders. The intent was to reveal the generosity, kindness, faithfulness and creative nature of God so that other nations would say, "their God is amazing." I have sketched this "Generosity Prism" so we can see how these things all work together to bless those in and outside the household of faith. I will not expand on each one, but do want to list them so we can see the heft of the goodness of God:

- Tithes: 10% of everything
  - Sometimes going to priests

- o Sometimes administered by heads of households/businesses
- Offerings
  - o Over and above the tithe
- Special offerings
  - o For special needs, occasions
- Capital projects
  - o Freewill offerings for projects
  - o An example is the building of the temple (and its rebuilding from time to time)
- Vows
  - o When people made a vow to give something for whatever reason
- Gleanings
  - o Items left at the edges of fields or on trees that allowed widows and the disadvantaged to easily get something to eat but with the dignity of work, not the demeaning nature of handouts
- First fruits
  - o The first of any produce: livestock, fields, fruit
  - o This was given before you knew what your harvest was
  - o Some have likened it to crop insurance because it is given in faith out the outset
  - o Sometimes it went to priests, and sometimes to the source of one's blessing (like a referral fee or commission)
  - o The amount varied by commodity
- Royal giving
  - o Given in honor, by royalty, to royalty, not based on need
  - o It reflects the status and standing of the giver as well as the receiver
  - o I cover this topic more later in the book.

You may well identify other forms of giving, like giving out of need (the widow who fed the prophet first), or dedicating property to the Lord. This is not an exhaustive list but an attempt to show the kaleidoscope of generosity our good God reveals.

8

Before there was Ethereum
was there Ethereal?

[Note to readers:

A relatively small group of people have had experiences in finance that are not what we would call "orthodox." It has to do with "seeing" or perceiving things in heaven regarding finance that have an impact on what happens on earth. You will probably not find these in university textbooks, nor hear them preached at mainstream churches. That said, this book would not be complete without a consideration of this aspect of Kingdom Economics. I will break the chapter into three topics: scripture, experiences, principles. Feel free to skip this chapter if the topic seems too ethereal.]

Scriptural constructs: the Mysteries of God

There are passages in scripture I tend to skip over and say, "That's nice, but it seems to be one man's experience and is not relevant today." This is a dangerous stance because it leaves me open to the selective application of scripture. As I look through scripture and must accept that people from Old Testament prophets to kings, to unnamed servants of leaders to New Testament people saw God, experienced his presence in many ways, conversed with angels and took trips to heaven, one might say.

The Apostle Paul alludes to this in his writings to the Corinthians.

> Though it is not profitable, I will go on to visions and revelations from the Lord. I know a man in Christ who fourteen years ago (whether in the body or out of the body I do not know, God knows) was caught up to the third heaven. And I know that this man (whether in the body or apart from the body I do not know, God knows) was caught up into paradise and heard things too sacred to be put into words, things that a person is not permitted to speak. On behalf of such an individual I will boast, but on my own behalf I will not boast, except about my weaknesses.[133]

I have read stories of people who died on operating tables, pilots who crashed and went to heaven, then returned to their bodies and more. I have spoken with some of these people personally. I have listened to preachers and authors talk about their experiences of heaven. I have friends whose children say they regularly take trips to heaven. But what about businesspeople? What about practical finance people? What about investors and bankers and accountants? While Paul said he heard things "too sacred to be put into words" I am taking the chance of asking reputable people in the world of business, finance and capital to share their own experiences of heaven in regard to finance.

---

[133] Corinthians 12:2-5 (NET)

Stories of heaven

We live in a time when there are no shortages of movies and books about people with supernatural experiences. Children, adults, sinners, Saints tell of their stories of going to heaven, meeting angelic beings, and returning to earth. In the emerging generation these stories may be viewed with skepticism, but they are not unusual. To the older generation they do seem strange, perhaps. The delineation however is not in my experience a factor of age but of different theological, philosophical or religious streams. I will share some of these stories not so that you can judge the efficacy of this story but simply to point out that there are growing number of people who claimed to have some insights on finance based upon there experience of heaven, or the theological belief that there are different layers in the heavenlies.

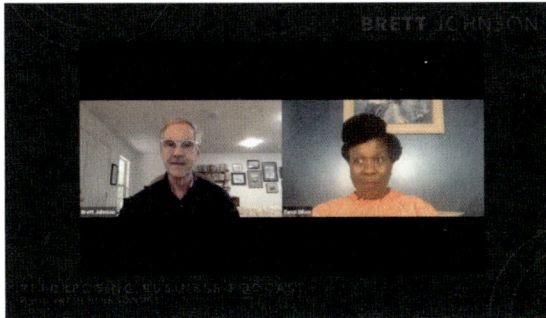

Zienzi Dillon is CEO of Carmel Global Capital in New York and hails from Zimbabwe. She worked at the Reserve Bank of Zimbabwe, and has functioned in local, regional and global banking levels. She also worked in corporate and investment banking. In a recent podcast interview[134] she shared how God spoke to her. "I want you to look at where you have come from and come out of there. You said you want to work with me to build kingdom banking systems..." He challenged her to think through topics such as credit risk models, enterprise-wide risk management frameworks, and interest rates and how they are set up to exploit people and nations, all at the expense of people. "One thing I have learned, Brett, is that you cannot regulate the heart."

---

[134] https://www.youtube.com/watch?v=Q820JAwV0n4&list=PLjLRWI_y1Hg1J4N3DcXa-s3Dk2nOaU7tX&index=3

"I had the opportunity one day of ascending in the heavens. I was introduced to my angel. I have a number of them: one is a personal assistant. I've got a mandate angel; I call him my Chief of Staff. I was introduced to an angel, The Banker, he was huge."

"There are books and books on banking in heaven. The scrolls are there. There are books and books for nations. They are there. How can we then ascend into the heavens in his presence? We cannot be kingdom citizens if we don't know what's happening [in heaven]. If we are ambassadors, we do not have our own narrative; we have the narrative of the sending government."

"That banking experience as for you to know the wicked side of it, but there is another side of it." I am not saying everything is wicked, but the spirit behind it... and why it was developed..." is of consequence.

Zienzi then went on to talk about developing "new wineskin" banking models and how we are being deployed from the presence of God so that we can bring the kingdom of God here on earth. We talked about how the present banking systems are programmed to create the losers, "There have to be losers, and it is just so sad that most of the losers are the ones at the bottom of the pyramid. So how do we then shout out, "Restore, restore!"? We therefore have to come out of the Babylonian way of thinking into the Kingdom way of thinking. It is really about substance over form. Faith is the substance of things hoped for. The Father has the substance. It is sitting waiting for us to appear at the table."

Zienzi and I went on to discuss different forms of capital and the emphasis placed in scripture on human capital and the trustworthiness of people with finances. "When I worked in finance the Central Bank always had to approve all executive appointments and the list [of characteristics] can be tracked back to the Word of God. Trust and Goodwill are another [form of] capital that is linked to me."

Shawn Bolz begins his book, Keys to Heaven's Economy, with a description of an angelic visitation.

The Lord's audible voice filled the room, introducing the angel standing before me: "Welcome the Minister of Finance for the Kingdom."[135]

If you're skeptical about angels and heaven, this book might not be for you. If you are curious, however, about whether Paul's seeing of things "in the third heaven" is meant to influence howe we approach life, check out the book. (You can easily find his interviews in YouTube to hear more of what he experienced.) His book is not a treatise on economics or finance but does give a glimpse behind the curtain of what might be going on in heaven around finance and resources. Like Zienzi, Shawn suggests there are resource accessible to those doing assignments for God.[136] Despite the rather dramatic angelic encounter, the topics from another of his books, Keys to Kingdom Resources, are down to earth:

- Giving and Generosity
- Finance, resources and time can be used to solve society's big problems
- Favor, relationships and influence are tied to wisdom
- Hard work should be a way of life
- Creativity: be filled with the Spirit, be creative when it comes to solutions that bless others
- Education: keep learning
- Risk and faith
- Intimacy with God: "Part of developing intimacy will cause you to fall in love with those God is in love with, and that will cause you to have a different result in your stewarding of God's economy."

The worst thing we can do in life is to have a relationship with God that brings nothing to this world. That would be a shallow relationship indeed." AW Tozer

_____

[135] Keys to Heaven's Economy: An Angelic Visitation from the Minister of Finance, by Shawn Bolz
[136] I read the book 10 years ago and checked out the book's ratings on Amazon, especially the bad reviews. 96% are 4-5-stars, by the way, but there are detractors.

Bolz's point is to link resources to the assignment we have been given on the premise that God is good and will not withhold what is needed to get the job done. Don't dismiss his insights because of the "weird and wonderful" angelic encounter or Zienzi's trip to heaven. This has nothing to do with "name and it claim it" and everything to do with discovering what's out of line with earth's economy and reconciling it to heaven's, with accessing the vaults of heaven so God can accomplish all that's on his heart through us.

Observations on heaven and finance

The longer we walk with God the more we realized that there are many things which are a mystery to us. The Christian life is not about having pet answers to complex issues, and the challenges that face us on this planet are indeed significant. Since God is it turn off, invisible, knows all, and sees the beginning from the end, is it not possible that there are still things that we have to learn from him in the realm of finance and economics? Is it not possible that he has a view of capital in all its forms that is higher than our understanding? So we approach these conversations with open hearts and minds keen to learn from the Holy Spirit.

My first observation, to echo what I highlighted above, is that God wants us to learn how to access resources which he has allocated to the assignments which he has given us. I understand full well that there are instances in scripture when the impossible was accomplished with the minimum. 5,000 people who are fed with five loaves and two fishes. Huge armies were defeated when singers want out ahead of Israel's troops. There are, however, instances where God pre-planned that leaders not yet born would provide capital for the rebuilding of the temple. This was a case with Cyrus who learned that 70 years prior to his rein it was prophesied that he himself would be instrumental in accomplishing God's purposes. This is miraculous. Nehemiah then accessed the many forms of capital needed to accomplish the rebuilding of the worlds of Jerusalem. When it comes to the mandate given to us by Jesus to go and make disciples of all nations we have to admit that the likelihood of success is radically increased when we properly harness capital in all its forms.

My second observation is that there is often opposition against the assignments which God has given you. It is not uncommon for the hindrances that we face to come in the form of lack of money or capital. Part of this is our own fault. For centuries Christians abdicated the world of finance and failed to embrace principles made clear by God in scripture. We over spiritualized and were left undercapitalized. We therefore need to come to grips with the essence of Kingdom economics.

Principles

I have already covered 50 principles of faith-based financing elsewhere in this book but want to take a moment to underline some areas that may be worth repeating.

1. Capital is multifaceted. Someone has suggested capital is material, mental and spiritual.
    a. Material: money for its own sake, a goal, meeting our needs, some a "god"
    b. Mental: a pre-occupation, taking up mental space, bringing joy or creating a sense of happiness
    c. Spiritual: the unseen preceding the seen, the substance in heaven—the shadow in earth. It enables us to live from heaven toward earth.
2. There is a power in seeing and praying differently. We can either see what we already have, whether we see with the eye of faith based on revelation in scripture, or whether we are among the few who actually see things in heaven. There is a difference between thanking God for what he has already provided and begging him to provide. I will share a story on this in a moment.
3. The third principle is that I see a parallel between three areas of life all of which where addressed in the death and resurrection of Jesus Christ. We are quick to embrace the first, slower the second, and reluctant the third.
    a. The first is the area of how we come to have a relationship with God through believing in the completed work of Jesus Christ on the cross. Everything that we need to obtain a right relationship with God, a legal standing, has been accomplished already. Our response is to accept this, believe in Jesus, and place our trust in him for our eternal salvation. There is no work that we need to do and nothing that we can add: it is through faith by grace alone.
    b. The second area is that of physical healing. Scripture says "by his stripes we are healed" and speaks of it as

something that was already accomplished through the suffering death and resurrection of Christ. Once again, there is nothing we can do to accomplish our own healing yet there is a part for us to play. We have to appropriate the healing and perhaps call for others too pray for us to be healed on the basis of the completed work of Christ. There is no debate about whether God is good, whether God has the power to heal, and the holdup often seems to be at my end of the equation. There is no additional thing that God has to do to make healing a possibility for me.

c. The third area is finances or resources in whatever form. The basis upon which we receive what we need is no different. Yes, there is a part for us to play just as there is in us accepting Christ and taking a step of faith regarding our salvation, or in us asking for prayer or declaring our own healing. But there is a supernatural element to financial provision as well and this comes down to issues of favor, blessing, co-laboring with God, sowing and reaping with God smiling on our efforts. You might well say that whatever the practical outcomes are on earth are a consequence of that which is already in the mind of God in heaven. I will set aside the argument about God speaking and creating the universe and then setting up natural laws by which it operates; even in making this statement we must acknowledge that so called natural laws have their source in the supernatural.

I was recently reading my grandfather's memoirs and there was a passage in which he described the situation where a church he was leading at Lewes in the Sussex Down needed a new building. Before they could obtain a new property they had to sell an existing site.

"But there was a slump in the property market. All efforts to sell the older property seemed unavailing. The time for the option on the more suitable building was ready to expire. I felt constrained to engage in a special season of personal single prayer. Before breakfast one morning I went forth for a walk on the Downs overlooking the town. My prayer rose on the morning air. It was autumn; a footpath ran through the stubble where the corn had been cut and harvested. Suddenly a lark started up from the stubble. It sang as it soared. Cascades of thrilling music ripple down from the skies. As it floated on the wings and its lyrics filled the air, it seemed that heaven was opened to my prayer and the rising desires of the heart were answered by the rapturous assurance from above. It was as if the skies were alert and the angels of God ascending and descending, as they did for Jacob, with promises of preservation and provision. There came the conviction that prayer was answered. That evening a prayer meeting had been called to seek God's guidance and resolve whether or not to proceed with the project. Before the presentation commenced I made a daring announcement. "Friends," I said, "I had an unforgettable experience this morning," and I described the exquisite communion with its positive conviction. "I trust you will not think it presumption or foolhardy but instead of praying for the old building to be sold I want you to give thanks that it will be sold." For a few moments there was an awed silence. Then, as if the sky lark were trilling again there arose an ecstasy of prayer which was answered by an exuberance of confidence. By the end of the week the old building was sold."[137]

No one can accuse JL Green, a Baptist minister, of being a "name it and claim it" preacher. He was a relatively conservative pastor from an earlier century, but he understood the power of proclamation consistent with what we have seen God do in the spirit.

We must deal with loopholes before strongholds

There are passages of scripture that seem to be apexes, pinnacle paragraphs. One such collection of truths is found in Paul's 2nd letter to the Church in Corinth.

The tools of our trade aren't for marketing or manipulation, but they are for demolishing that entire massively corrupt culture. We use our powerful God-tools for smashing warped philosophies, tearing down barriers erected against

---

[137] JL Green, His Story. (Unpublished)

the truth of God, fitting every loose thought and emotion and impulse into the structure of life shaped by Christ.

Our tools are ready at hand for clearing the ground of every obstruction and building lives of obedience into maturity.[138]

There is a "massively corrupt culture" in the world of banking and finance. It is fraught with "warped philosophies" as Zienzi and others have alluded to. They have deployed combine harvesters in the fields of working people that suck up the best of the harvest for themselves and leave the scarps for the true creators of value. We have the weapons to expose them, remove them, blow them up. There is a catch, however. You don't get to 2 Corinthians 10 without going through the prior 9 chapters. Or, as David Lloyd George said, "You can't cross a chasm in two quick jumps." The premise of being power-filled people of 2 Corinthians 10 is a journeying through the laundromat of the earlier chapters.

Ch	Theme	Reflection	Obstacle
1	Suffering so that we can comfort others; reliance on God.	What part of your suffering could be a comfort to others?	Pain: it can cause us to get stuck, or cause us to empathize, then heal others.
2	A new type of minister with a new economic model - "we do not peddle the Word of God for profit."	Do you fully believe you are a minister? If not, why? Where are you in understanding the strategic importance of not peddling the gospel for profit in reaching the nations?	Compromise: we can adopt the world's economic models which might disqualify us from bringing about something new. Poverty Mindset: choosing to not "peddle the Word for profit" is different from having a poverty mindset. It is a place of strength in God.

[138] 2 Corinthians 10 (The Message)

Ch	Theme	Reflection	Obstacle
			Driven: being propelled by economics, not obedience.
3	A new type of competence—ministers of the Spirit. "*we are not competent in ourselves...our competence comes from God.*"	Do you know you're competent in God? Or do you depend on natural gifts, education and skills?	Self-perception: we have to see ourselves as citizens of heaven, ambassadors of a different way of doing things, with a different competency.
4	A new set of measures— "*pressed in, crushed, perplexed, persecuted, abandoned...*"	How have you changed your definition of success? Not only do we need to measure returns beyond ROI, we must change our definition of success.	Performance Orientation: This will trap us in the measures of our bosses, neighbors, even Christian friends. We need new scorecards.
5	All things are new, and we have a ministry of reconciliation, bringing everything into alignment with Christ, including businesses, finance, capital, money.	"My ministry of reconciliation is to..." (complete the sentence) If your answer is only "my neighbor" then you are probably not ready to be a kingdom economist. God wants his economy on earth so that people from every tongue, tribe and nation are impacted positively, whether they have come to you, or you have gone to them.	In the book, Transforming Society, I outline "3 Bad Fixes" to the brokenness of the world. Isolation, Defeatism, Evangelism. We need to believe it is possible for all things, the cosmos, to be reconciled to God through Christ. We must also know this is the work of all of God's children, not just some of them.
6	There are costs involved in pioneering—the marks of an apostle. Commending	Are you totally sold on right positioning, not posturing? Are you prepared to pay the price of pioneering?	Comfort, ease, leisure: Tearing down strongholds is not a hobby but a battle. Paul pointed out that battle scars were his credentials, not a comfy

Ch	Theme	Reflection	Obstacle
	ourselves because of tough experiences, not puffed-up appearances.		chair on a big stage in front of a large audience.
7	Don't be touchy, love those who have hurt you, and let Godly sorrow produce a soft heart, not a bitter root.	Have you let an offense block your path to being used effectively by God?	Offense: This is a killer. If you go to battle against bad economic systems chances are you might get shot once or twice by your colleagues who are on the same side as you. Get over it. Develop a thick skin because snowflakes will melt in the heat of battle.
8	We need to give ourselves: "*But they gave themselves, first to the Lord, and then to us*"	Do you feel that giving is a burden, a guilt-trip, or a grace?	Privacy: Being an introvert, a private person, or separated from others by your money (this happens) does not cut it if you hope to tackle giants.
9	We need to decide how we will give, and do so liberally, knowing God gives seed for sowing (capital) and for eating (working capital).	How would you characterize your giving? Held back, or hilarious? What's your understanding of seed?	Tight-fistedness: if you are still holding onto money there is no space in your hand to hold a weapon that tears down strongholds. Greed: If you are not a cheerful giver you will probably be a miserable soldier. Failure to distinguish capital (sowing) and working capital (bread). I believe I have covered this elsewhere.

Ch	Theme	Reflection	Obstacle
10	We have weapons to tear down strongholds; opposing the "*your kingdom come*" Jesus prayed for.	Where's the battle? What are your weapons? How much did 2 Corinthians 1 through 9 do its work in you...how confident do you feel about tearing down strongholds?	Mindset: The strongholds are in the minds. We must have our thinking renewed so that we can "take every thought captive to the obedience of Christ."

On August 31, 2021 The US troops pulled out of Afghanistan. Moments later the Taliban were on TV wearing the uniforms and carrying the weapons of the US and allied forces. Many weapons, helicopters and armored vehicles were left behind. Former enemies were now armed to the teeth and defied the US or others to try to come back and reclaim territory. This is a picture of what has happened in the world of capital. The early church was actively involved in banking and had a wide financial operation. Historical records indicate that the church in Antioch supported 50,000 widows and orphans. This took some means. There are historical records of slaves who were believers working their way out of slavery through banking. And, of course, the Jews had been and remained involved in the world of capital and finance. After the Council of Nicaea in AD324 the church distanced itself from the Jews and walked away from the world of finance. If someone was involved in charging interest, for example, they would not be buried in a Christian cemetery. This "holier than thou" attitude toward the finances left a gaping hole in the arsenal of Kingdom advancers. (This is not to say that the church was not gaining in wealth and property during the next 1000 years. That is another conversation.)

The world system has imposed its tools of fractional reserve banking, Fiat currencies, the production of money out of debt, inflation, end departure from real assets on the world. Systems that were meant to bless people so that they could be a blessing to others, create wealth so that there would be no poor, and add value through genuine work done in collaboration with each other and with God... These systems were hijacked and replaced with diabolical counterfeits. Whether we arrive at new financial systems through studies, through creativity, through inspired innovations, or through angelic encounters and heavenly revelations, we need better answers and we need them soon. The battlements built "against the knowledge of God" must be torn down first in our hearts, and in our own minds, and then in the battlefield of the marketplace.

Warning to those who criticize the rich

We need capital to transform society. I have met many people who have felt that God has told them one way or another that they will handle large sums of money. A gentleman came to me in South Africa and said he had a prophetic word that millions of Rands would go through his hands, "but it has been five years and nothing has happened yet." I laughed. "Only five years?" He looked a little shocked so I recommended he go and read my book, Convergence, so that he could understand the patterns of God's dealings with us. If you need a lot of money to fulfill your assignment, then don't bemoan the people that do have money. If you want to be rich, stop slandering the wealthy. You cannot disciple what you do not love. You cannot impact what does not touch your heart. You cannot reach influencers if you are still influenced by envy or inferiority. In this whole realm of wealth and finance, know who you are. You are wealthy because you have the God of wealth. He has given you all riches in Christ Jesus. You have been blessed with every blessing in heavenly places: now, some of you are saying that you would like some of those blessings in earthly places... Remember that we need to see them, if only in our godly imaginations, in heavenly places before we see them on earth.

Finally, if you truly believe that God is your source then you will not be looking to man and your nose will not be out of joint if wealthy people do not get behind your latest initiative. Some say there is "the law of the draw" where the favor of God in your life draws people to you. History is full of people, including the apostle Paul, who had to bear the cross of not being recognized or rewarded buy those he can't serve. Our scorecard is not just on earth.

Warning to the rich

If you are rich, heed the cautions of scripture. We tend to rely on God when we are in need and forget him when we have plenty. This is the message of Deuteronomy 8: 18. Fast forward to the book of James chapter One and you will see the affirmation for those of humble means and the caution for those of wealth.

> If you are a brother of humble means, celebrate the fact that God has raised you up. If you are rich and seemingly invincible, savor the humble reality that you are a mere mortal who will vanish like a flower that withers in the field. The sun rises with a blazing heat that dries the earth and causes the flower to wither and fall to the ground and its beauty to fade and die. In the same way, the rich will fall and die in the midst of their busy lives.[139]

Some people have a great deal of money yet it does not stick to them. "It's just a resource." They are not enamored by it, nor impressed with themselves. Others fear that if they let the "have nots" near them they will, sooner or later, ask for money. To shield themselves they spend their time with other wealthy people and congregate in their bubbles. This is just as true for Christians, by the way, and we even set up "clubs" to cater for the elite. This is not the pattern of the New Testament church, however, nor of the Old Testament. If "the poor" do not have working exposure to "the rich" how are they expected to learn? The Principle of Jubilee was there to incentivize the rich to upskill the poor for the good of all concerned. Favoring the rich or separating them from the poor causes isolation, loneliness, concentration of wealth and, at worst, arrogance. One day one might wake up thinking one has all these resources because of who one is, not despite who one is.

It's a mystery

> No one can deny that this religion of ours is a tremendous mystery, resting as it does on the one who showed himself as a human being, and met, as such, every demand of the Spirit in the sight of angels as well as of men. Then, after his restoration to the Heaven from whence he came, he has been proclaimed among men of different nationalities and believed in all parts of the world.[140]

---

[139] James 1:9-11 (The Voice)
[140] 1 Timothy 3:16 (Phillips)

My brothers and sisters, I did not pose as an expert with all the answers. I did not pretend to explain the mystery of God with eloquent speech and human wisdom.[141]

Some might find these concepts too ethereal yet have no problem buying Ethereum. What I mean is, we may scoff at the notion that there are heavenly answers to economic problems, currencies, trading and finance, yet off we go and invest in things we barely understand. When we strip economics of the supernatural power of God we decrease the likelihood of exponential blessing. When we do due diligence for an investment we rightly have 101 questions. Since we are spiritual beings who have the Spirit of the Living God inside of us, shouldn't our due diligence extend to a deeper set of issues? Was the business leader called by God? Was the product inspired? Does it meet a need God cares about? Is it positioned for God's blessing? Is the presence of God evident and tangible in the company? Are they partnering with spiritually aligned companies? Is this good soil for an eternal return? What would Jesus say about this investment? Would he want me to risk his capital here? What will my reward be if he says "invest" and I say "but I am withholding capital because I am being a good steward"?

141 1 Corinthians 2:1 (The Voice)

9

What did Jesus say about

Capital, Economics, Money?

Jesus spoke about money, the challenges of wealth, and generosity. He demonstrated how to live with and without a regular income, and how to receive support from wealthy patrons. He challenged the wealthy, and he enjoyed their company. He seemed to move freely in social circles, yet he was not caught up with the personal trappings of wealth. He spoke about giving, and he paid taxes. And prior to starting his three years of public ministry, he was, let's remember, a businessman who made money from his work.

Was Jesus quiet on purpose?

When it came to the subject of "Do's and Don'ts of Investing" he did not appear to say too much... at least at first glance. Reflect on the focus of his teaching and you will see that Jesus did, in fact, teach a lot about the broader context of finance, namely, the kingdom of God. Why is it that he did not host a Kingdom Economics Forum, or publish Ten Tips for Financial Freedom? Perhaps he knew if he emphasized the "how to" of investing we would zero-in on the mechanics and forget the "why" of finances. I am reminded of a Proverb, one of my favorites, that says:

It is the glory of God to conceal a matter; to search out a matter is the glory of kings.[142]

It is logical: Jesus taught extensively about the kingdom of God knowing, if our focus was there, then we could be trusted with temporary assets. He put it this way, and I paraphrase, "Don't spend your time worrying about money, clothing or food. Go after my kingdom first and foremost, then all of these things will be taken care of."[143]

Was Jesus quiet on purpose? Was he deliberately avoiding the mechanics of making money? I think it is fair to say when people asked him for rules, he pointed them to a greater reality. When they asked him for formulas, he taught them faith. When they asked for religion, he gave them relationship. When people asked about how to get, he showed them how to give. He lifted them to a higher plain, namely, the kingdom of God. He met their needs on earth, whether the challenge was healing or hunger, and he continuously exhorted them to look to God as their source. He emphasized the purpose of business, rather than the legalities of business.

The overriding principle is this: if we are looking for the rules of God on finance we will inevitably end up in realm of religious legalism. Since

---

142   Proverbs 25:2

143   Matthew 6:33

scripture will not cover every permutation, we will have to add man's rules to God's rules. The Jews have the Oral Law; the Muslims have the hadith; and the Christians are no less legalistic when they look for the formulas of God instead of the face of God. When Jesus was chatting with some grumbling Jews about who he was, he said, in effect, 'If you claim God as Father, that is good; but make sure that you listen to him.'

In John 6:45 Jesus made this statement which is risky for anyone wanting to know Father God's heart on finances, or life, for that matter:

Everyone who listens to the Father and learns from him comes to me.

Jews and Muslims and Christians all claim God as father; I urge us all to listen to Him. We need to seek the heart behind the principles or else we will end up with rules, and we will miss the bigger picture, namely, intimacy with God. When we grasp the kingdom of God we are positioned to grasp kingdom economics. Until then, we are looking for a fix from God instead of the face of God. I think Jesus knew this, and therefore taught on the kingdom of God, within which the realm of FBF is contained. He focused less on the specifics of financing (in terms of funding mechanisms, etc.) and more on the spirit of financing.

Having summarized some of the pertinent principles broadly related to the topic of finance, the question remains whether we are ready for financial institutions and products that are based on God's economy and principles.

Should kingdom investors settle for less?

Some make the argument that investors must accept lesser returns on investments made for the sake of the kingdom. Others argue that biblically responsible investing (BRI) produces returns that are as good as market returns... if not better. Robert Netzly has a good article on this topic.

Don't get me wrong, I believe and have experienced that Christians are not required to accept lower investment returns in order to invest biblically responsibly. But even if that was the case, or even if it somehow became the case in the future, does it matter? Would we reject the call of God because we are unwilling to give up performance potential? Or would we immediately drop our investments and follow Him? [144]

When is enough enough?

Isn't there a danger that an accumulation of wealth will torpedo our calling? Scripture has already affirmed this danger, yet God is still willing to take the risk that a people will rise up whose hearts are fully his and whose bank accounts, stock portfolios and earthly assets are dull in comparison to his glory in and through them. How much do you need to fund your calling? What resources are needed to fulfill your mandate? How much would need to flow through you and me to meet the needs of those in our sphere of influence? What capital and resources are needed to turn unjust systems on their heads and replace them with righteous, godly alternatives?

We sing "He's more than enough, more than enough" and we are right to do so. Let's apply that to our own contentment, of course, and extend to the millions who don't yet know his enoughness.

Economics of Mutuality

Thankfully we are well beyond the belief that the purpose of business is to maximize returns to shareholders. Corporations have been contemplating how they can transform their business models to sustainably achieve solid returns while positively impacting the communities in which they operate. One such company is the Mars Corporation that began by asking, "How much profit is enough?" Bruno Roche and Jay Jakub outline the crux of their thesis.

▬▬▬▬

Our approach is based on the simple assumption that most business sustainability issues can be solved effectively and durably, not through ad hoc CSR initiatives or philanthropy, but through innovative but business model

[144] https://www.faithdriveninvestor.org/blog/should-christian-investors-risk-lower-returns-to-invest-biblically

approaches that have the ability to drive both social and environmental performance while also delivering strong financial performance.[145]

Their work builds on the notion that it takes many forms of capital to make something successful and sustainable including human capital, social capital and more. An interesting piece of their work contemplates how the different capital sources should be remunerated. They do not cover all forms of capital, but focus on social, human, environmental and financial. (I believe we need to recognize all forms of capital mentioned earlier, but still like their attempt at tackling the four that they do. I concur with the notion of avoiding measuring only monetary returns.) Roche and Jakub lay out guiding principles before getting into the specifics of remuneration:

1. First principle—The Sabbatical. They link sustainability to the biblical construct of rest for people, for communities, and for nature.
2. Second principle—Remunerate on a like-for-like basis. The authors advocate the contributions capital can make to those elements that are driving business results. This includes programs to build up employees and communities and ensuring that there is a net positive return to the other forms of capital. "Because natural capital measurement essentially comprises five meta variables (water, air, soil, and organic and inorganic material), remunerating it is essentially about ensuring that for every unit of natural capital taken from the planet, a unit of similar or higher quality is returned to the environment, creating a positive return."
3. Third principle—To further decipher and document links between the types of capital. Since the different forms of capital are interdependent, they argue that understanding the linkages and remunerating fairly will heal rifts and further sustainability.
4. Fourth principle—Being intentional and determined to find the "right" level of profit. They argued that profits have been determined by shareholders and not stakeholders, and without regard to the health of the overall ecosystem. "Hence, we assert that to a large extent the level of profit of most firms is not real."

While they book, Completing Capitalism, is not written expressly from a biblical perspective their observations echo the injunctions of scripture to create and economic climate built on righteousness, justice, concern for the

---

[145] Completing Capitalism, Bruno Rocje and Jay Jakub

poor, protection of property, reward for hard work, and faith. Why faith? Embedded in their first principle, the sabbatical, is a reliance on God to produce a good return even when we do not work 24 x 7. The so-called highly efficient and optimized systems of this world do not stop churning. In the Kingdom of God work is preceded by rest, and we ceased from our own works and entered the rest of God. (Hebrews 4). In the Kingdom of God the environment also rests. Animals have a day of rest. Employees have a day of rest. Implicit in this model is trusting God for provision while people and the environment and productive assets rest. Elevating returns on financial capital above human and societal flourishing he's not only unproductive, it is also unbiblical.

Should "above and beyond" be dedicated to expanding the Kingdom of God?

I have seen an interesting phenomenon over the last 20 years: God had given businesspeople and social entrepreneurs inspired innovations which could have a positive impact on society. The problem, however, is that these "inventors" often do not have the financial capital to create the products, solutions or business is needed to bring their idea to market. At the same time, I have seen an upswell in the number of followers of Jesus (genuine Christians) who have capital in their hands and are looking for worthwhile investments. The inventors cling to their ideas particularly since they believe the idea came from God; the investors bring a traditional investing lens to their activities and have expectations of returns, term sheets, and timelines that reflect the thinking of Babylon, not the promised land.

You might say, "Brett, the simple answer would be to get the investors and inventors in the same room, agree on fair returns for each party, and agreed that any excess returns (which come about from the favor of God, perhaps) get set aside for the expansion of the Kingdom of God." I have seldom seen this work in practice however probably because of two factors: first, the financing infrastructure is built on the systems that we see in Angel investing, private equity, bank financing, venture capital etc., etc. Term sheets and deal structures look pretty much the way they do in "the world". A second reason is simple: greed. either the investors want too great a return, or the investees see the success and want more of the pie for themselves. If we ought to be serious about Kingdom Economics we should recognize that there is a spirit behind greed, namely, Mammon. Mammon is like an aggressive cancer in the world of money and finance, and Christians are not exempt from its influence. We can rightfully expect that God wants to give his people and abundance, and such blessing is full of the extension of his Kingdom. To counter the effects of and insidious nature of Mammon (greed deified), we have to be very intentional about how blessing is to be funneled.

Many years ago I took a team of Kingdom business people to a developing nation and we conducted a 10-day consultation with various businesses. We agreed upfront that we would not charge their businesses for our services, but if their business grew beyond their planned growth, then 3% of the excess would be contributed to Kingdom efforts. One of the businesses began to grow rapidly as a result of implementing the biblical principles we taught and because of the expertise we had brought to the table, and the owner of the business was soon begging to get out of the financial agreement.

Clear terms up front

Most of the issues arise because expectations are not aligned or contractual terms are not stated clearly and upfront. It is not right to expect that Christian investor will forego normal returns unless you have addressed this in your prospectus or contracts. It is, however, perfectly acceptable to agree on a fair return for investor and investee with an up-front agreement the returns exceeding this agreed threshold will go into an agreed fund or towards a particular purpose. (Again, set this purpose in advance, and put it in writing.)

The Ananias and Saphira principles of investing are quite clear. Insofar as the Apostles were concerned, the property and the proceeds belonged to Ananias and his wife, Saphira. Acts 5 has the story:

Now a man named Ananias, together with his wife Sapphira, also sold a piece of property. 2 With his wife's full knowledge he kept back part of the money for himself, but brought the rest and put it at the apostles' feet.

3 Then Peter said, "Ananias, how is it that Satan has so filled your heart that you have lied to the Holy Spirit and have kept for yourself some of the money you received for the land? 4 Didn't it belong to you before it was sold? And after

it was sold, wasn't the money at your disposal? What made you think of doing such a thing? You have not lied just to human beings but to God."

As far as God was concerned, it belonged to Him, and when they lied about what they were giving there were deadly consequences. A friend made an investment on behalf of her clients and all agreed, in writing, that a small percentage would go to a "gleanings fund" to bless local people in the nation where the investment took place. When the deal matured, however, the investors wanted to wiggle out of the contract. Had it not been in writing they would certainly have done so.

10

Where is

Kingdom Economics today?

In a recent conversation with Paul Cuny, author of Secrets of the Kingdom Economy, I asked him how he felt we are progressing towards a stated premise of his book:

The Kingdom economy will soon be the dominant economic system on the earth. Even now, the Lord is preparing his representatives in the marketplace for this time. In the days ahead, those who will succeed in this economy will be his servants who understand this principle. It is the Lord who gives his prophetic insight, ability, sound judgment, wisdom and the understanding of complex financial issues to generate this kind of income. It is because of him, not our own personal genius.[146]

As indicated elsewhere, Paul felt we were well underway to seeing the beginnings of this becoming a reality. As I reflected on this I remembered how often Jesus had to point out the kingdom to people who could not see it, even when it was right under their nose.

From that time on Jesus began to preach, "Repent, for the kingdom of heaven has come near." Matthew 4:17

Jesus went through all the towns and villages, teaching in their synagogues, proclaiming the good news of the kingdom and healing every disease and sickness. Matthew 9:35

As you go, proclaim this message: 'The kingdom of heaven has come near.' Matthew 10:7

When Jesus saw that he had answered wisely, he said to him, "You are not far from the kingdom of God." Mark 12:34

Heal the sick who are there and tell them, 'The kingdom of God has come near to you.' Luke 10:9

In his book, Like a Mighty Wind, Mel Tari spoke of the revival in East Timor.[147] His second book, The Gentle Breeze of Jesus, adds to the stories of revival but points out that, if one was not alert, one might miss seeing what was going on. I feel we are at a similar juncture with Kingdom Economics today. We might be closer than we think, but we are not going to get where we need to go on a whim and a prayer. If I were to take a crack at answering the

---

146 Secrets of the Kingdom Economy, Paul L. Cuny

147 In the mid-1960s thru the 1970s, the islands of Indonesia experienced what some feel was one of the greatest revivals in the 20th century, which has led to millions coming to Christ. A young man of just 18 when this period of revival began, Mel Tari witnessed amazing miracles like those written in the Bible within the remote communities of Indonesia. Tari became a well-known evangelist and missionary to the world from Timor, authoring the bestselling book, Like a Mighty Wind, which documents the amazing events of this spiritual revival in Asia.

question I asked Paul Cuny I would suggest we examine this on a more granular level.

- The growth of Biblically Responsible Investing as an asset class
- The growth of Faith-driven Investing as an investment group with a clear focus
- The increase in faith-driven generosity

If I were to rate these three areas I would say that things have improved tremendously through the work of people such add as Robert Netzley at Inspire Investing who has made tremendous strides on the biblically responsible investing (BRI) front with close to $2 billion under management.[148]

Henry Kaestner and the team at Faith Driven Investor have created platforms for qualified investors to make direct investments in entities, be they businesses or social entrepreneurial ventures or charities.[149] They have launched a marketplace where investors and entrepreneurs can find each other.

Daryl Heald at Generosity Path[150] is inspiring people on journeys of generosity, whether they have little or much. Since generosity is often a leading indicator of whether the kingdom of God is advancing, I believe good progress is being made. I say this even though I am aware that too many followers of Jesus still live in a two-pocket economy: they have one pocket for what is theirs and another for what is given to God and/or charity. Jesus said, "Where your treasure is, there will your heart be also." When generosity increases—no matter how many pockets we start with—it ends up pulling our hearts towards the kingdom.

These are just some examples of people who have taken something that was not visible and brought it into the mainstream. Hats off to them.

The state of the world's economy

There are many who recognize that existing systems are unjust, inefficient, murky and manipulative. Levels of national and corporate debt are off the

---

148 https://www.inspireinvesting.com
149 https://www.faithdriveninvestor.org
150 https://www.generositypath.org/daryl-heald

charts. Stimulus money that was pumped into banks in 2008 with the intent that they make capital available to grow businesses was hoarded by financial institutions who reinvested in already precarious markets. When many large corporations received capital they engaged in stock buybacks. While the stock market performance has looked good, for the most part, they underlying fundamentals were never fixed. There are therefore plenty of economists who think a correction, if not a reset, is inevitable.

Added to this financial situation is what Kotlikoff and Burns call "The Coming Generational Storm" where the ratio of working to retired people becomes unworkable.

In 2030, as 77 million baby boomers hobble into old age, walkers will outnumber strollers; there will be twice as many retirees as there are today but only 18 percent more workers. How will America handle this demographic overload? How will Social Security and Medicare function with fewer working taxpayers to support these programs? ... if our government continues on the course it has set, we'll see skyrocketing tax rates, drastically lower retirement and health benefits, high inflation, a rapidly depreciating dollar, unemployment, and political instability. The government has lost its compass... and the current administration is heading straight into the coming generational storm.[151]

The questions is, where to next? And, for people of faith, will we be in any position to offer an alternative system? (For those who have not read Repurposing Capital, when the crisis happened in 2008 some Islamic Finance proponents said, 'if you had our economic system you would have averted the crisis.')

----

[151] The Coming Generational Storm: What you need to know about America's economic future, Laurence J. Kotlikoff and Scott Burns

Three unworkable responses: Materialism, Isolationism, Interventionism

When I published Repurposing Capital in 2010 I saw three responses to the financial crisis.

1. Materialism: prop up existing systems with debt; leave motivations or mechanisms intact; keep capital markets vibrant.
   a. The basis is greed; the driver— materialism, touted as capitalism
2. Isolationism: insulate group based on religious affiliation, or a cause such as Zionism, Islamization or Dominionism.
   a. The basis is fear; the fruit is radicalization and dualism (decrying the systems they rely on).
3. Interventionism: intervene with funding, regulation and/or government control; cap gains and redistribute wealth.
   a. The belief: few (usually government) know better than many.

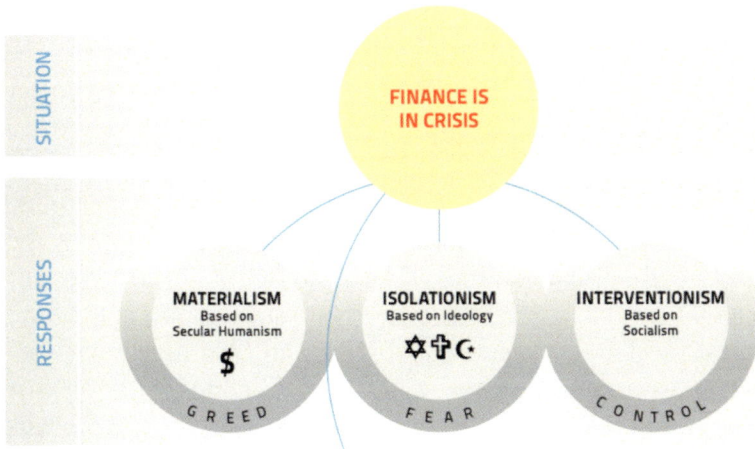

In the past 10 years these three responses have been accentuated. Free market proponents have continued to pour money into the stock markets, wealth has grown in aggregate, and greed has not been neutered, to say the least. The Materialism bubble has produced for those at the top of the pyramid, however, but left the masses with stagnant purchasing power and costs of some essentials, like housing, healthcare and education, increasing dramatically. In the USA the Trump years had a sub-theme: 'You may not like me, but the market do, and your 401k is better than ever.'

Moving to Interventionism: under the Biden administration there has been massive intervention in the economy with the Covid pandemic giving governments around the world an excuse to deploy interventionist policies. This leads to greater dependence on government since people are more incentivized to stay home than go to work. It is hard for shipping companies to find truck drivers since they are paid more to stay at home than go to work. With looming tax increases, this will worsen. Biden's $6 Trillion spending plan is most likely going to create more free-government-money addicts.

This brings me to the middle scenario, and this is where it gets tricky for people of faith. I see a regular slew of proposals about how to create alternative economic systems. Some of them are based on hope and faith. Others are based on fear. The fear-based approaches inevitably lead to Isolationism which simply does not work. The financial systems that are presently active in the world are hugely interconnected. Not only is it possible to do business globally with relatively few barriers, it is also impossible to isolate ones nation or economy from other nations. Central banks are interconnected and there is relatively little autonomy at the national level. Having a critical mass is essential to a viable alternative system, and isolationism based on ideology (and driven by fear) is not a viable option.

Coming out of the World's System

The Kingdom of God is full of paradoxes. We are "in the world, but not of the world." We have an address on this planet, but our real life is hidden with Christ in God. One day we will see Jesus face to face and today we can experience his presence. As indicated before, the Kingdom of God is here and not yet. What, then, does it mean to come out of the world's economic system?

> "To come out of the world's system does not mean to stop functioning within
> the system. It means, do not trust or look to it as your source because, when
> you do, it becomes your God"[152]

The progression of the people of Israel from the world in which they lived in
Egypt—physical, cultural, economic and more—to a new world shaped by
God is quite something to behold. In my book, rēStart, I outline 50 principles
on how to reset foundations after a crisis. What I do not unpack fully in that
book is some of the capital dynamics that are taking place.

One of the levers God used to get the Jews out of Egypt (along with quite a
few others) was the economic pressure that accompanied many of the
plagues. Some of the catastrophes happened only to the Egyptians; others
befell the Egyptians and the Israelites. Sometimes the Israelites were
protected simply because they lived in the land of Goshen. In Exodus 9 we
see the plague on livestock decimating the Egyptians and not touching the
Israelites. The Jews did nothing; God gave them special treatment.

> And the next day the Lord did it: All the livestock of the Egyptians died, but not
> one animal belonging to the Israelites died. Pharaoh investigated and found
> that not even one of the animals of the Israelites had died.[153]

Scripture does not say it, but who controlled the prices on the cattle market
the following day? Is this not a form of wealth transfer?

In the case of the plague of hail, however, the Israelites had an act of
obedience to benefit from a coming financial crisis. They had to move their
cattle indoors or to a safe place. Their economic preservation depended upon
their asset management strategy in today's terms. It is also interesting to
note that those Egyptians who followed the asset management strategies
of the Israelites also preserved their capital.

---

[152] Money and Wealth in the New Millennium, Norm Franz
[153] Exodus 9:6-7

18 Therefore, at this time tomorrow I will send the worst hailstorm that has ever fallen on Egypt, from the day it was founded till now. **19** Give an order now to bring your livestock and everything you have in the field to a place of shelter, because the hail will fall on every person and animal that has not been brought in and is still out in the field, and they will die.'"

20 Those officials of Pharaoh who feared the word of the Lord hurried to bring their slaves and their livestock inside. **21** But those who ignored the word of the Lord left their slaves and livestock in the field.

22 Then the Lord said to Moses, "Stretch out your hand toward the sky so that hail will fall all over Egypt—on people and animals and on everything growing in the fields of Egypt." **23** When Moses stretched out his staff toward the sky, the Lord sent thunder and hail, and lightning flashed down to the ground. So the Lord rained hail on the land of Egypt; **24** hail fell and lightning flashed back and forth. It was the worst storm in all the land of Egypt since it had become a nation. **25** Throughout Egypt hail struck everything in the fields—both people and animals; it beat down everything growing in the fields and stripped every tree. **26** The only place it did not hail was the land of Goshen, where the Israelites were.[154]

If the Israelites had left their livestock in an Egyptian field they would have lost the livestock. They had to take a step of obedience to protect their assets. Are you dependent on an ever-rising stock market, or are you diversifying wisely? What assets do you think will survive an economic shaking?

━━━━━━

As I have already pointed out, neither debt-based paper investments nor artificially inflated profits survive any type of serious financial shaking. In fact, their ultimate destiny is total destruction. Only the values of righteous tangible assets will survive the financial shakings in the days ahead. Therefore, holding

---

[154] Exodus 9:22-26

righteous investments, at righteous prices, under righteous terms is the only way we can hope to participate in the end time transfer of wealth.[155]

Kingdom Economics is therefore apparent today in the lives of people whose heart is in the right place and whose dependence is not on the economic systems of this world, even though they still have investments and assets in the world. They may have positions or investments that depend upon the day-to-day systems that exists, but their hope is not in Wall Street or their wallet. Where they do have investments, they have considered carefully whether such investments are invested in a biblically responsible manner, and whether the returns being produced would please God.

Buy Banks, or Start "Christian" banks

"The way to repurpose a company is to acquire it." So said a man to me many years ago. I know of a number of groups who are staying within the existing banking systems and hoping to properly purpose or repurpose banks. Why would they stay in the system? If you have ever been involved in trying to transfer large sums of money internationally you will know you end up being at the mercy of the banks, usually the big banks. Some have concluded "unless we own a bank we will always be blocked." They are therefore involved in acquiring banks.

The second group believes banks are necessary, but they need to operate on a better set of values. My friend, Vince Siciliano, former CEO of a bank in San Francisco, was involved in setting up an organization, Global Alliance for Banking on Values.

The Global Alliance for Banking on Values (GABV) is a network of banking leaders from around the world committed to advancing positive change in the banking sector.

Our collective goal is to change the banking system so that it is more transparent, supports economic, social and environmental sustainability, and

---

[155] Norm Franz

is composed of a diverse range of banking institutions serving the real economy.

Our research also backs up the soundness of the values-based banking model, showing that lending to the real economy delivers better financial returns when compared with the largest banks in the world. As well, we have demonstrated the positive social impact of this model through the activity of our members during decades, their strong capital positions, and their steady financial returns.

The GABV is here to change finance, as it is necessary to finance change and ensure that banking is a healthy force for the advancement of society and the protection of our planet.[156]

A third group is setting up new banks, hoping to build them on the biblical principles. They face the challenge of innovating around financial services products while doing so within existing systems and structures, by which I mean banking regulations that are no faith-based but built on fiat currencies and fractional reserve banking. They will be able to do a certain amount, including set an example to other banks, but only so much until new policies are shaped. They can serve the under-served, have fair products and practices, and be ethical and values-based, and hopefully they will be able to innovate enough within existing frameworks to make a difference; time will tell. They will, however, contribute to the rising tide of those, like the GABV group, who want to see better banking.

New approaches to Capital: New platforms

This is perhaps the most difficult area to evaluate. I am aware of several initiatives that wish to set up banks, trading platforms and alternative economic systems that are quite separate from the world systems. The challenge for all of these is getting to critical mass and achieving a sense of legitimacy. Many years ago there was an attempt by certain Christians to create a worldwide market where products and services could be purchased and sold. They set up the infrastructure but did not attract a critical mass of merchants. It failed. I have the same concerns with local exchange trading

---

[156] https://www.gabv.org/about-us

systems (caps LETS). While some of them have worked on a micro level they failed to gain international exposure or traction.

That said, there has been a fairly rapid increase of enlightened investors who are practicing Biblically Responsible Investing (BRI) and a sanctification, for want of a better word, of Impact Investing to be more kingdom focused. Chris Maclellan shared with me, "At Maclellan Foundation we have fully implemented our BRI strategy so that all of our public equities are screened based on our set of criteria. We have committed over $75 million to Mission Related Investments (MRI- our term for Christian Impact investing) and implemented a low interest PRI fund as well. Our MRI returns are above our initial goal and in the mid teens (IRR) over the last four years."

New approaches to Capital: The gold standard

Some expect us to go back to the gold standard arguing that fiat currencies are about to topple, and money invested in stock markets will disappear overnight. Only those holding tangible stores of value will survive. At the personal level they advocate having a good portion of your holdings in gold and silver coins.

> This is what the Lord Almighty says: 'In a little while I will once more shake the heavens and the earth, the sea and the dry land. I will shake all nations, and what is desired by all nations will come, and I will fill this house with glory,' says the Lord Almighty. 'The silver is mine and the gold is mine,' declares the Lord Almighty. 'The glory of this present house will be greater than the glory of the former house,' says the Lord Almighty. 'And in this place I will grant peace,' declares the Lord Almighty.[157]

Some see a linkage in this passage between the glory of God and silver and gold, and further believe that gold and silver are more unshakeable than other things.

At the national level there are periodic discussions happening about the viability of returning national economies to the gold standard. This is

---

nothing new, but the urgency of such plans has ramped up given the spiraling national debt and the shortcomings of the underlying economic systems have people worried. Many pragmatists believe we cannot go back to the gold standard. There are pockets of people who believe it is not only possible, but imperative, and they believe there will be enough gold underground and mined to make this possible. Will it happen?

———

Yet some investors/historians want to revisit the empires of Rome and the UK and point out how debasement of those currencies led those powers losing their default status as the reserve currency of choice. They also draw parallels with the path the US empire is on today. No argument with me concerning history. That said, it doesn't mean the US, let alone the world, will go back to the gold standard anytime soon. After all, the UK didn't go to the gold standard after the pound lost its position as the world's leading currency. In fact, no country is on the gold standard today, the last being Switzerland which left it two decades ago.

So, it's clear, at least to me, that global finance ministers and the IMF have been tussling with "the problem" for decades now, and the best "solution" they came up with was Special Drawing Rights (SDRs). That is likely to be the case in the future. And if the US loses its status as the world's reserve currency, it is likely its % weighting in the SDR "basket" will fall.

Any investor investing in gold simply for as a "hope and a dream" that the US, or the world in general, will return to the "gold standard" - that stopped working decades ago - will likely be disappointed in that opinion. But they will be happy because they likely hold gold, and that will, I have no doubt, continue to appreciate (especially in US$ terms). In fact, I think the popularity of Bitcoin is a sign that investors not only don't believe a gold standard will return, they believe well-designed digital currencies are the future.[158]

This takes us to a discussion of the next "solution" – digital or crypto currencies.

———

[158] Michael Fitzsimmons, The US Dollar Back on the Gold Standard? Never Happen, August 31, 2020 (seekingalpha.com)

New approaches to Capital: Crypto

The wise king Solomon said there is nothing new under the sun so I'm hesitant to call this "new approaches" but it is worth updating the three responses I saw in 2010. A few things have changed since then.

First, cryptocurrencies have become more mainstream. It is still the Wild West days of crypto currencies and there is huge volatility. That said, corporations are taking Bitcoin to settle transactions, and central banks are minting their own coins to try to avoid being bypassed. In June 2021 El Salvador become the first country in the world to formally adopt bitcoin as legal tender. "It will bring financial inclusion, investment, tourism, innovation and economic development for our country," President Bukele tweeted. China has created its own digital currency, controlled by the central bank. It is positioning the digital yuan for international use, untethered from the US Dollar-dominated global financial system. (It probably also wants its own, controlled crypto since Chinese nationals have been using crypto to move assets out of China.)

When combined with blockchain, proponents of crypto currencies hope to remedy the issue of central controls over the monetary system. Asset-backed crypto is becoming more popular and there are Christian organizations minting their own coins and linking them to minerals, agricultural assets and other "hard assets." Regarding the question "But where can I spend these coins?" some are tying their currencies to online stores. In the world of virtual currencies, proponents believe that the volatility is worth the ride if it frees one from the perceived manipulative controls of the IMF and BIS. Perhaps the sustainable future of cryptocurrencies will ride less on the rails of Dogecoin-type speculators and more on the routine trade and finance being conducted using crypto on the more boring back of blockchain-enabled platforms.

But are crypto currencies biblical? Do they pass the test of Faith-based Financing products? You will recall from Chapter 1 how faith-based products have ten characteristics; the first six are "must haves" and the last four are "to be avoided." I had the opportunity to engage with Mark Moss, a Bitcoin proponent, entrepreneur and investor, on how he thought Bitcoin stacked up against these 10 characteristics.[159] In the podcast Mark said, "The financial

---

[159] https://youtu.be/dNznuzDctbE and https://www.brettjohnson.biz/podcast

system is cracking apart. In 2008 nothing fundamentally changed because it can't. That's the design of the system. The financial system is the root of all problems... the fiat money system, which means by decree, is inherently evil because it is built on a system of theft, lies and deceit. So anything that comes off that system is inherently evil... so that has to change." I recommend you listen to the whole podcast which also discusses how global forces are trying to push digitized information into an app that can be controlled.

What gives the government the power to take [freedoms] away from us, to do lockdowns, to build this technology... it all comes from the money printer. Bitcoin is the only tool that fights back against this... A lot of people think that Bitcoin is like digital gold, like digital cash: it is those things, but it is so much more as we are seeing new technologies being built on the Bitcoin network, a censorship-resistant network that we can build our lives on.[160]

I have summarized some of our conversation in the table below.

Characteristic	Do crypto currencies meet the criteria of FB products?
1. Have a noble purpose and create social value.	Yes, it is open, fair, decentralized and democratizes freedom. "If you are living in a Third World economy, it has lots of value. In the world today, about 2 billion adults do not have access to banking because they don't have permission to join." A key premise of a biblical economy is choice; totalitarianism takes away choice.
2. Have transparency of terms.	Bitcoin is an open ledger so anyone can view anything; it is anonymous, but not private. It is transparent. Because it is code, we know

160 ibid

Characteristic	Do crypto currencies meet the criteria of FB products?
	exactly what the supply schedule is; it is set in code.
3. Clearly articulate the risk for all parties.	"You have to define what risk is: with Bitcoin, there is no company, CEO, term sheet... so I don't know if it checks that box. But because of its openness and transparency, that limits risk if you understand how the network works—there is very little risk that it could be shut down." There is no certainty about the price, however. There is no risk someone could freeze your account.
4. Foster long term positive relationships.	"This point is x 1,000 because it changes the incentive structure. This changes the entire social fabric of the world. The oldest problem we have is someone coming to steal our stuff... Bitcoin gives them a way to store their wealth..." Bitcoin cannot be inflated by the government, cannot be frozen. It brings better incentives for long-term relationships.
5. Grow the pie for all— generate wealth.	People don't get rich by stealing other peoples' money but by meeting needs. When they create wealth, it empowers others to create wealth.
6. Empower all parties.	Bitcoin is a tool that can be used any way. Current systems are subject to selective bias, however, deciding who we can and cannot send money to. Bitcoin enables the free market in that choice and reciprocity are bookends of biblical economics: there is a combination of free will and loving our neighbor.
THE PRODUCT SHOULD AVOID THE FOLLOWING	

Characteristic	Do crypto currencies meet the criteria of FB products?
7. **Invest in questionable industries.**	Not necessarily... Bitcoin is a tool, and some say it can be used for harm (drug smuggling, etc.) "Terrorists also use cars, phones, drink water...." You cannot attach a value to Bitcoin because of who uses it. So, this one is neutral.
8. **Create a negative environmental impact.**	I challenged Mark about the environmental impact of crypto mining since the servers use a lot of electricity. "This has been a hot topic... who are you to decide what a waste is? Uses a lot of energy compared to what? The servers YouTube runs use a lot more energy... It uses 8 times less energy than clothes dryers in the US alone. That still requires a subjective judgement." "The single biggest expense is the electricity... you cannot run a Bitcoin miner in California. Bitcoin is portable, so they can take it and move it wherever there is excess energy that is being wasted." Net: Bitcoin is not having a negative environmental impact.
9. **Entrap the borrower.**	While borrowing is not normally associated with borrowing, like most assets, you can borrow against them. "Currently, I would say Bitcoin pledged as collateral to satisfy a debt is not entrapment because you have to pledge at least 150% of your Bitcoin which forces people to be more conservative when they borrow."
10. **Violate the requirements of appropriate index.**	Borrowers can influence the rate they pay based on the amount of capital they are willing to put up as collateral. There is openness and transparency which encourages price discovery and therefore a greater fairness in interest rates.

Towards the end of our conversation Mark asked whether I thought Bitcoin passed the test. In general, crypto currencies pass muster as vehicles for creating faith-based-compliant products. Beyond that, Mark Moss is clear that crypto currencies (and his preference is Bitcoin) give us the tools to peacefully create an alternative future that is less likely to be squashed by those with nefarious intentions. Furthermore, as the El Salvador "Bitcoin Beach" experience attests, it fosters financial inclusion.

Faith-driven, Impact, Direct Investing

I have covered more direct investing approaches elsewhere, and this is probably where the biggest practical gains will be made. Investing in "real work" earlier in the Societal Value Chain through more direct investments (whether through platforms like the Faith Driven Investor Marketplace or consortiums The Global Giants Foundation, or individually) is where followers of Christ can best place investments in good, albeit still risky, soil. Such investments are going by many names including impact investing, social entrepreneurial investments, missional investing, and more. The bottom line is everyday investors, qualified and unqualified, are choosing to put their money to work for eternal returns in many settings. This trickle needs to become a flood. Mistakes will be made, some money ventured based on expected "Christian" or societal impact will be "lost" but my hope is that the boats will rise with the tide. As of the time of writing (late 2021) many are predicting a market crash. It seems money that one thinks is safely tucked away in traditional investments, only to lose their value, might better be deployed in more direct investments with the hope of an eternal return. Are we in a moment again, like we say in the Dot.com era, when billions sat in the hands of believers but was here today, gone tomorrow? What will future generations say about us as they follow our money trail through the 2020/2021 economic times?

New approaches: Changing banking regulations

Uli Kortsch and his colleagues believe changes in banking regulations can bring about the necessary changes, but he does not believe there will be the political stomach for his before another crash. "Ever since my first book, I have been told that it is just not politically feasible to make the needed changes until another crash comes along. For many years I have not believed that, but sadly I have now come to the same conclusion." That said, he proposes changing the money creation system from debt-based to a value-/equity-based system along the lines of the Chicago Plan of the 1930s.

> When the aggregate money supply is increased through Sovereign Money, the current method of debt-based money creation needs to stop. One way of doing that is to convert the whole banking system to an LPB (Limited Purpose Banking) system at once as described in Chapter 9. What this LPB conversion would do is make the investment side of banks into mutual funds that would then be regulated (in the U.S.) by the Securities and Exchange Commission (or the equivalent in different countries, similarly to the way mutual funds are regulated today).[161]

Will governments go back to business as usual after a future catastrophe (as they did in 2008) or will there be a fundamental shift? Either way, it is incumbent on us to imagine a new future, put on our thinking caps, and prepare for the opportunities that present themselves in a crisis.

Revival, Reformation, Spiritual Renewal

Whatever ingredients combine to make a solution the question remains, "Can this happen without a change of heart?" I do not believe things will change without a concomitant spiritual move that changes the motivations of our hearts. Greed, power and systemic inequities that favor some at the expense of others cannot be regulated away. The answer seldom lies in rules and regulations since an army of loophole specialists will dissect and skirt new rulings before the ink has dried. A new future where Kingdom Economics becomes a reality is premised on a great awakening among God's people and an influx of people into the kingdom of God. Only regeneration by the Holy Spirit can change the appetites and thinking of mankind. Clever financial constructs will not do the job alone, nor will spiritual fervor without wisdom that comes from God. This is not an either/or time in history: "And" is one of the most powerful words in the Old Testament. We need fresh

---

161 The Next Money Crash and a Reconstruction Blueprint, Uli Kortsch

thinking AND we need a powerful move of the Holy Spirit on the earth such that it aligns more closely with heaven.

11

Leaving a legacy:

Money & More

A good friend of mine in Indonesia told the story of his mother-in-law visiting his home for a short while. One day she said, "I'm going home on Tuesday." He asked her whether she had purchased a ticket for the train or airplane, and she replied, "No, I am going home to heaven." When Tuesday came she got up and dressed in her finest clothes, emptied her wallet by giving her money to the servants in the house, sat on her bed with her Bible, closed her eyes and died. Some would regard this as a good way to go.

I remember Bob Buford, author of Half Time, saying he hoped his last check bounced. In other words, his goal was to get rid of everything during his lifetime. Since then I have seen a number of foundations that were formed with the express purpose of giving away all of the assets by a particular sunset date. In practice, however, it seems that the foundation bureaucrats struggle to develop a rhythm of giving and it seems inevitable that they will violate their own charter. (Note: I am not advocating the sunsetting of foundations, funds, investments. I do encourage flow, risk, asset growth, generosity and multi-generational impact.)

There are others who don't want to give it all way but want to leave a legacy, including a financial one, for their offspring. They will cite the verse from Proverbs speaking about leaving an inheritance for one's children, and they take it to mean a financial endowment.

A good person leaves an inheritance for their children's children, but a sinner's wealth is stored up for the righteous.[162]

The Amplified Bible unpacks this a little: "A good man leaves an inheritance [of moral stability and goodness] to his children's children..." The Passion Translation says, "The benevolent man leaves an inheritance that endures to his children's children, but the wealth of the wicked is treasured up for the righteous." Do these translations skirt the leaving of money?

It is interesting to see the vast sums King David handed over to Solomon for the construction of the temple from his personal treasury, this in addition to large quantities he had already dedicated from his conquests.

- About 3,750 tons of gold[163]
- About 37,500 tons of silver
- Then he added from his personal resources:
- Gold: 110 tons of gold[164]
- Silver: 260 tons
- This prompted the leaders to add about 190 tons of gold and about 380 tons of silver, not to mention 675 tons of bronze.

---

162 Proverbs 13:22
163 1 Chronicles 22:14
164 1 Chronicles 29

It is easy to say, "Well, that was a special occasion" and miss the principle that the bequeathing of capital can empower the next generation to achieve their calling. Solomon inherited various things that gave him a jump start, of course: a title or position (there were plenty of brothers who could have been king), great wealth, a kingdom with secure boundaries, and more. All of this was premised on one thing: the Word of the Lord. It was the prophetic word that led David to choose Solomon and give him the assignment.

---

⁵ David said, "My son Solomon is young and inexperienced, and the house to be built for the Lord should be of great magnificence and fame and splendor in the sight of all the nations. Therefore I will make preparations for it." So David made extensive preparations before his death.

⁶ Then he called for his son Solomon and charged him to build a house for the Lord, the God of Israel. ⁷ David said to Solomon: "My son, I had it in my heart to build a house for the Name of the Lord my God. ⁸ But this word of the Lord came to me: 'You have shed much blood and have fought many wars. You are not to build a house for my Name, because you have shed much blood on the earth in my sight. ⁹ But you will have a son who will be a man of peace and rest, and I will give him rest from all his enemies on every side. His name will be Solomon, and I will grant Israel peace and quiet during his reign. ¹⁰ He is the one who will build a house for my Name. He will be my son, and I will be his father. And I will establish the throne of his kingdom over Israel forever.'

¹¹ "Now, my son, the Lord be with you, and may you have success and build the house of the Lord your God, as he said you would. ¹² May the Lord give you discretion and understanding when he puts you in command over Israel, so that you may keep the law of the Lord your God. ¹³ Then you will have success if you are careful to observe the decrees and laws that the Lord gave Moses for Israel.[165]

Solomon built on that platform and his reign was marked by unparalleled prosperity, so much so that gold and silver were as common as stones in the streets.

---

165 1 Chronicles 22: 5-13

> The king made silver and gold as common in Jerusalem as stones, and cedar as plentiful as sycamore-fig trees in the foothills.[166]

Few of us are going to leave tons of gold for our children and, if we could, it might not be wise. Solomon's inheritance was proportional to his assignment. Children who inherit money without a heartfelt call to a proportionate assignment may well be in danger of losing the calling and the cash.

Different perspectives on legacy

Many a movie have been made about large inheritances being passed with provisos: there are lists of things to do, lessons to learn, relationships to reconcile, gifts to give, money to spend and, of course, wives/husbands to be found and married by a deadline. The subtext of the person leaving the bequest is often, 'I was more than just a pile of money; I struggled, I had a life with real emotions, cares and causes… and you need to get in touch with them if you want the inheritance.' The other subtext is, 'I messed up as a parent or grandparent, but this inheritance will right my wrongs and fix what I could not sort out while alive.'

King Solomon was well known for his wisdom. Part of his quest was to discover the meaning of life, or at least explore a variety of things to find out which gave lasting satisfaction. His opening lines are not very encouraging:

> "Meaningless! Meaningless!"
>
> says the Teacher.
>
> "Utterly meaningless!
>
> Everything is meaningless."

---

166 2 Chronicles 1:15

Gold, sex, music, business enterprises, trading, dabbling in foreign religions, great wealth, substance abuse... he tried them all. In addition, he embarked on massive projects: palaces, agriculture, public works.

> I hated all the things I had toiled for under the sun, because I must leave them to the one who comes after me.[167]

What happens when I am gone? I may do fantastic things but there is no guarantee that I will be remembered, and my successors may blow their inheritance. Clearly he was thinking about more than life; he was thinking about legacy. This is not surprising since he had been the participant in not one, but two "passing of the baton" ceremonies with his father, King David.

> 9 "And you, my son Solomon, acknowledge the God of your father, and serve him with wholehearted devotion and with a willing mind, for the Lord searches every heart and understands every desire and every thought. If you seek him, he will be found by you; but if you forsake him, he will reject you forever. 10 Consider now, for the Lord has chosen you to build a house as the sanctuary. Be strong and do the work."[168]

Despite this warning Solomon did not finish well. I Kings 11 has a long description of how Solomon, a smart man who knew better, failed to heed this father's warnings and outright disobeyed the written Word of God. It is a difficult read because it includes foreign wives, foreign gods, and the likely offering of child sacrifices to be severely burned or killed.[169]

> ¹ King Solomon, however, loved many foreign women besides Pharaoh's daughter—Moabites, Ammonites, Edomites, Sidonians and Hittites. ² They

---

167 Ecclesiastes 2:18
168 1 Chronicles 28:9-10
169 https://www.chabad.org/parshah/article_cdo/aid/4372130/jewish/The-Tragic-History-of-Molech-Child-Sacrifice.htm

were from nations about which the Lord had told the Israelites, "You must not intermarry with them, because they will surely turn your hearts after their gods." Nevertheless, Solomon held fast to them in love. ³ He had seven hundred wives of royal birth and three hundred concubines, and his wives led him astray. ⁴ As Solomon grew old, his wives turned his heart after other gods, and his heart was not fully devoted to the Lord his God, as the heart of David his father had been. ⁵ He followed Ashtoreth the goddess of the Sidonians, and Molek the detestable god of the Ammonites. ⁶ So Solomon did evil in the eyes of the Lord; he did not follow the Lord completely, as David his father had done.

⁷ On a hill east of Jerusalem, Solomon built a high place for Chemosh the detestable god of Moab, and for Molek the detestable god of the Ammonites. ⁸ He did the same for all his foreign wives, who burned incense and offered sacrifices to their gods.

⁹ The Lord became angry with Solomon because his heart had turned away from the Lord, the God of Israel, who had appeared to him twice. ¹⁰ Although he had forbidden Solomon to follow other gods, Solomon did not keep the Lord's command. ¹¹ So the Lord said to Solomon, "Since this is your attitude and you have not kept my covenant and my decrees, which I commanded you, I will most certainly tear the kingdom away from you and give it to one of your subordinates. ¹² Nevertheless, for the sake of David your father, I will not do it during your lifetime. I will tear it out of the hand of your son. ¹³ Yet I will not tear the whole kingdom from him, but will give him one tribe for the sake of David my servant and for the sake of Jerusalem, which I have chosen."[170]

There is much to say about what went wrong with Solomon, and over 200 scriptures dealing with inheritance, but for the sake of brevity I am asking, "What are some of the tendencies of the five types of leaders in the LEMON Leadership® model?" Leaving aside spiritual waywardness, how we are wired impacts how we think about legacy and inheritance.

---

170 1 Kings 11:1-13

LEMONs and Legacy

LEMON leadership

Legacy has become a bit of a buzzword among leaders and some have become obsessed with what they leave behind. Inevitably the legacy will leave is tied to our identity and character. In one of my classes, LEMON and Legacy, I explore the tendency of different types of leaders to focus on different forms of inheritance or legacy. LEMON leadership covers five different types of leaders who have a fundamentally different wiring or leadership DNA. We all have some combination of all five slices of the LEMON. That said, my observation has been that we have a primary and secondary slice of leadership which has a huge influence on how we see things. This is also true when it comes to the topic of legacy.

Luminaries and Legacy

Luminaries with means dream about projects, civil construction, building cities that will remain in their honor, great works. Those who may not have as much money get into Causes that are often driven by principles, if not ideologies. "I built this, and it is still here 200 years later."

If they do leave a will—who needs a will when you think you will last forever?—it will be more like foundational principles whereby those who inherit should live their lives for decades to come.

Entrepreneurs and Legacy

Entrepreneurs hope to leave companies, organizations or groups of companies behind. They hope to launch movements that have lasting momentum, critical mass, and scale. "I launched this, and it is still going 50 years later." They may try to hand over to the next CEO while still alive.

Managers and Legacy

Managers want to die with lots of things under their control and the organizational capital secured to keep them going. They leave wills that resemble annual plans.

If the Managers are engineers, they may think of putting problem-solving solutions in place that outlive them. A patent and a plaque would be a bonus.

Organizers and Legacy

Organizers like to go out with a bright flame, or at least a big bang. So bucket lists, traveling to many places, going to many events, making and checking off many lists... a legacy of activity, leaving it all on the field, emptying the tank before they die, setting an example of busyness. They may jettison the frivolous, so they pack light and leave the world at speed. They may be sentimental but prefer to give things away while still alive (rather than passing on heirlooms in their wills).

Networkers and Legacy

Networkers die with their memberships in associations, fraternities and alumni groups still active. If they died while still President of anything it would be a social club or sporting association or bridge club... for three successive terms. (Other members knew they only sure way to replace them was via a funeral.)

Solomon was probably correct in assessing that people will probably not remember you and me when we are gone... in the natural. But the kingdom of God is different. Why? Because in the kingdom of God there is a thin veil between today and eternity and there is a "great cloud of witnesses" cheering us on. Somehow heavenly records are being kept and what we do on earth is not just forgotten but remembered because it prepares us for our work for eternity. We therefore need to consider our bias or bent when it comes to the topic of legacy and reconcile it to a scriptural view of legacy.

Give like a king

Lavish amounts were given for the building of the future temple. Read the account to see King David's clear perspective on wealth.

----

[14] "But who am I, and who are my people, that we should be able to give as generously as this? Everything comes from you, and we have given you only what comes from your hand. [15] We are foreigners and strangers in your sight, as were all our ancestors. Our days on earth are like a shadow, without hope.

¹⁶ *Lord our God, all this abundance that we have provided for building you a temple for your Holy Name comes from your hand, and all of it belongs to you.* ¹⁷ I know, my God, that you test the heart and are pleased with integrity. All these things I have given willingly and with honest intent. And now I have seen with joy how willingly your people who are here have given to you.[171]

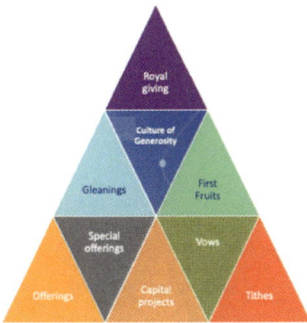

David knew what he had was not his and what had been pledged rightly belonged to God. Royal giving is "next level" giving where we give as a matter of honor, not because of the needs of the recipient. Second, we give because we are royalty, children of the King of Kings. The world has yet to see what could happen if the children of God gave like wealthy heirs-apparent. We had two friends come and visit us when we were living in the San Francisco Bay area. It was clear that one of them had resources and the other was a full-time missionary. Nonetheless again and again the missionary said, "We'll pay for that!" which really meant "my friend will pay for that." We need to become more hilarious in giving away God's money.

More than money

Of the 220 verses mentioning inheritance, only 20 are found in the New Testament, yet they take things to a whole new level. Two such references are in Ephesians 1:

And you also were included in Christ when you heard the message of truth, the gospel of your salvation. When you believed, you were marked in him with a seal, the promised Holy Spirit, *who is a deposit guaranteeing our inheritance* until the redemption of those who are God's possession—to the praise of his glory. For this reason, ever since I heard about your faith in the Lord Jesus and your love for all God's people, I have not stopped giving thanks for you, remembering you in my prayers. I keep asking that the God of our Lord Jesus

[171] 1 Chronicles 29:14-17

Christ, the glorious Father, may give you the Spirit of wisdom and revelation, so that you may know him better. I pray that the eyes of your heart may be enlightened in order that you may know the hope to which he has called you, *the riches of his glorious inheritance* in his holy people, and his incomparably great power for us who believe.[172]

The emphasis has shifted from places and possessions to people. Inheritance in the new era ushered in by Jesus Christ is less about kings and more about kingdoms, especially the kingdom of God. The letter to the Colossians explains:

We continually ask God to fill you with the knowledge of his will through all the wisdom and understanding that the Spirit gives, 10 so that you may live a life worthy of the Lord and please him in every way: bearing fruit in every good work, growing in the knowledge of God, 11 being strengthened with all power according to his glorious might so that you may have great endurance and patience, 12 and giving joyful thanks to the Father, who has qualified you to share in the inheritance of his holy people in the kingdom of light. 13 For he has rescued us from the dominion of darkness and brought us into the kingdom of the Son he loves, 14 in whom we have redemption, the forgiveness of sins.[173]

As such, every follower of Jesus Christ is included in this inheritance which includes forgiveness, redemption, sonship and more. This new inheritance includes something out of this world: eternal life.

For this reason Christ is the mediator of a new covenant, that those who are called may receive the promised eternal inheritance—now that he has died as a ransom to set them free from the sins committed under the first covenant.[174]

---

[172] Ephesians 1:13-19
[173] Colossians 2:9-14
[174] Hebrews 9:15

The Apostle Peter sums it up:

---

3 Praise be to the God and Father of our Lord Jesus Christ! In his great mercy he has given us new birth into a living hope through the resurrection of Jesus Christ from the dead, **4** and into *an inheritance that can never perish, spoil or fade*. This inheritance is kept in heaven for you, **5** who through faith are shielded by God's power until the coming of the salvation that is ready to be revealed in the last time.[175]

Leaving an inheritance of temporary assets—stocks, bonds, cash, land and the like—is of particular value if it propels the recipient to discover and fulfill their God-given assignment(s) on earth. If it causes them to forfeit their eternal inheritance, it is less than worthless.

The final lesson on inheritance and legacy is this: the wise steward traded his master's financial capital for relational capital. If we must choose between maximizing what is stored up on earth (to be destroyed eventually) and increasing the number of people being in perpetual relationship with their Creator for eternity, then it is not even a choice. Legacy must always have an eye on eternity otherwise it becomes unwise hoarding.

---

[175] 1 Peter 1:3-5

12

From Biblical Principles

to Economic Policies

It is one thing to embrace scriptural principles or timeless truths for economics, finance and capital (and it is important that we lay a solid foundation in this regard) but, if we do not help translate these principles into policies that can be instituted at the personal, corporate, local government and central government levels will we ever have faith-based financing? Remember that "the world system" has an expression in the prevailing economic systems, particularly the world of capital. If we are to see the kingdom economy become the best alternative to the flawed and failing systems of this planet then we need to help policy makers write charters that will support Kingdom Economics.

Many years ago I sat around the table with gentlemen who were writing legislation to allow their nation to set up Islamic Banks. When I talked about Faith-based Financing being the broader universe of finance and Islamic, Jewish and Christian banking being a subset, they agreed with me. One even recommended that we have legislation that enshrined faith-based banking and allowed each faith to have their own flavor of banking within the broader framework. Inevitably, however, if one asks for a banking charter specifically for "Christian banking" you will hear one of three responses:

1. Why can Christians not just operate within current legislation: why do you need your own policies?
2. We know Islamic Banking, but where in the world has Christian banking been practiced?
3. Which country is using these Christian (or Kingdom Economic) principles you want us to legislate?

Even within the so-called Christian world people wonder, "Why would you need separate policies that encourage Kingdom Economics or Faith-based Financing?" If we are still asking this question we have not grasped that there are two opposing kingdoms and each has its own economy. The world was designed to operate on the platform of God's economic principles and policies but it got hijacked. A usurping platform that seeks to undermine the ways and magnificence of God has been instilled as the "norm" and we generally do not have the policies in place that enable us to fight it. The legal basis for biblical finance has been systematically stripped from the public record or, if it remains, it is defined in secularist terms. (Now, I am all for avoiding religious jargon, but I am not for the neutering of truth.) We must there learn to recapture the art and science of writing good policies in appropriate language based on eternal principles.

During 2020 I met with leaders from South Africa on a Zoom call where I outlined a rough flow that touched on the role of policy as one of the steppingstones in efforts to foster societal change.

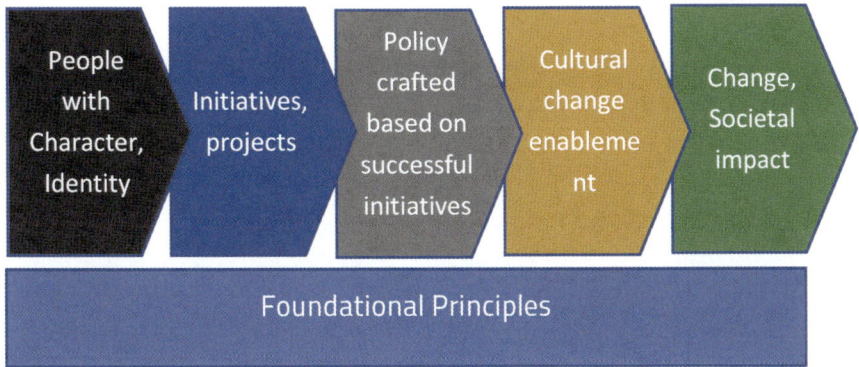

The role of older-generation leaders (whom we equated to grandfathers and grandmothers) is to:

1. Recognize existing leaders who are already doing good work.
2. Endorse leaders and projects and network them to likeminded leaders and projects to get critical mass.
3. Draft policy based on successful projects. Dr. Clyde Rivers has helped me see this connection. Policy does not just come from thin air or ideology but from existing success stories. Clyde makes the point that, when a policy is drafted, a handful celebrate but it puts a stake in the ground that allows others to launch new products, services, organizations and initiatives that bring about societal improvement.
4. We can then figure out culture-shaping strategies, including the use of relevant media, that build on the platform created by the new policies.
5. This then helps to bring about lasting societal transformation.

All of the above are built on Foundational Principles which are timeless truths about how society, including economics, actually works. The laws given by Moses are an example of such principles.

Policies

In my conversation with Uli Kortsch[176] (on the When Capital meets Eternity podcast series) he points out that the legal basis of the current system needs to change. He does not subscribe to a conspiracy theory about the operations of the Federal Reserve Bank, for example, but says that their actions are an inevitable outcome of their policies. Unless the underpinnings of debt and fiat currencies are addressed—and unless the change becomes policy—nothing will change. It is policies that allow some of the evils of "the world system" such as:

- Usury, excessive interest on consumption debt
- Debt, including credit card debt with usurious interest rates
- Lack of capital for productive endeavors. (In many countries it is easier to get a loan for a Mercedes than machinery.)
- Inflation and its wealth-destroying effects
- Deficit spending and its "hidden confiscation of wealth" as Alan Greenspan called it.

Central bankers rationalize away the role of faith in matters of financial policy. In a speech by Professor Otmar Issing, Member of the Executive Board of the European Central Bank, at St. Edmund's College Millennium Year Lecture in Cambridge on 26 October 2000 he said:

> Fundamentally, money represents a promise. It requires trust by the users of money in the issuer of money to honour this promise. Money is built on trust, but in turn trust must be built on solid foundations. The promise must be made credible and this - at least in relatively modern times - is the job of central bankers.
>
> There is today a broad consensus that stable money is too important to be left to the day-to-day political process, which inevitably will always have to balance different objectives, conflicting interests and short-term pressures. If stable money is regarded as a common good for the benefit of all and if it is seen as a precondition for long-term prosperity and social justice, then it

[176] https://youtu.be/BdNM49L8_Aw

makes sense for society to create an independent institution that stands above the fray of day-to-day politics and can pursue this objective with minimum distraction. This is the basis for central bank independence.[177]

Central bankers don't necessarily know better, he argues, but if they are kept on a short leash with a defined purpose, they may add value. Professor Issing goes on to say:

An independent central bank thus pre-supposes a broad consensus on the "quasi-constitutional" nature of the common good of price stability. Assigning the central bank a clear overriding objective also imposes limits on its discretionary exercise of power and makes it easier for the public to hold the central bank accountable for its mandate. This is important to keep in mind if we entertain the possibility that while, yes, "money is too important to be left to the politicians" one could similarly concur with Poincaré that "money is too important to be left to central bankers" (as quoted by Milton Friedman in his 1962 essay on "Should there be an independent monetary authority?"). In other words, why should one trust central bankers more than politicians?

The problem with the professor's argument is this: he sees only two players at the table, namely, central banking institutions and mere-mortal politicians (who come and go). The faith community has no voice at his table. Since capital always has an agenda, should there not be a moral voice at the table as well (not to say politicians and bankers are immoral, but they advocate being closer to amoral)?

Central banks are a given and, in the case of the European Central Bank at least, they argue they should be constrained by a narrow purpose. The question is, can their purpose become one that is more noble than simple "stable money"? Does this not take us back to topic of the purpose of money and the creation of wealth?

---

[177] https://www.ecb.europa.eu/press/key/date/2000/html/sp001026_2.en.html

The Purpose of Wealth: a reminder

The creation of wealth through value-adding work reflects the nature of God. The better we do it, the more we can grow the pie. But why? And for whom? A core principle comes from the God-Abram interchange in Genesis 12 and is summed up as "blessed to be a blessing."

I will not reiterate all the scriptures and principles, but inherent in this mandate is the just creation of wealth, fair treatment of employees and customers, righteous business practices, and the avoidance of enslaving people through business or financial shenanigans. Generosity was a hallmark of the Promised Land economy with the byproduct of poverty elimination. There was a capital allocation for each household and a serious discouragement of asset degradation. Provision was made for upskilling fellow-citizens and asset redemption. God came before money; money was not a god.

At the same time there were property rights, rewards for industriousness and warnings against government excess in the form of taxes and a bloated governing class. The Israelites were to avoid slavery in its many forms, including the bondage of debt and interest.

The world system says, "we will keep the currency stable" and the details will take care of themselves. The biblical aspiration for kingdom capitalists is much higher. Capital is not just a neutral measure of natural giftedness or privilege: if you have it you get more. Kingdom Capital is a means of blessing people, growing their capacities, funding improvements in business, cities and nations and tackling persistent problems that plague our world. In the world the rich get richer; in the kingdom the gaps grow smaller, not through tax and redistribution, but through the elevating of humankind from net consumers to producers. Why? Because they are made in the image of God to work like God, for God and for the good of their fellow inhabitants of his planet. Central banks should be chastised if their policies and practices increase the concentration of capital in fewer hands while the plight of the many is not improved... whether there is stable money or not.

Policies that underpin Purpose

It is easier to give the objectives of policies rather than chapter and verse simply because the circumstances where policies are to be deployed vary so much. The context of city governments differs somewhat from banks in their city. The modus operandi of banks is different from private equity firms. Investment houses and credit card companies and central banks all have a context. It would take workshops or taskforces in each of these to begin to craft something meaningful. They would all tested against the high standard of purpose.

As a test of the 50 Principles covered earlier, I started to consider the complexion of policies that would see these 50 Principles become reality. It is a work in progress, but I have included my noodling thus far in the Appendices. I have copied the first five principles below to get your creative juices going.

#	Principle / Concept	Policy ideas	World system
1	Principles, not laws	Policies ensure there is fairness and righteousness with everyone having the opportunity to benefit equally.	Policies ensure that the rich get richer through the unjust scales of fractional reserve banking (FRB), controlled access to capital, debt and interest.
2	There are 3 different systems intellectually, and two practically: Egypt and the Promised Land	Policies in the kingdom should be linked to property ownership, real assets, being debt-free, managed interest and asset-backed currencies.	The world runs on the systems of Babylon / Egypt with unjust scales.
3	Foundational Principles	Appeal to universal laws	
	SOURCES		
4	God is the source	Since God is the source, policies and systems should encourage dependence on God, with delayed gratification, if need be, and not dependence on banks or man.	Lures people into debt which enslaves them to its system.

#	Principle / Concept	Policy ideas	World system
5	God is not limited to any one source	Policies should encourage diversification of income streams: salary, property rentals, trading, online business, investing, etc.	Governments depend on "tax and spend" rather than creating environments that foster creativity, ownership, entrepreneurship and wealth creation.

For years we have helped businesses keep scorecards that track their movement to becoming biblically based, kingdom-purposed entities that impact society. There are currently many attempts to measure impact that goes beyond the bottom line; this is wonderful. The Inspire Impact Score is a good example of a faith-based ESG security selection methodology that helps find best companies to invest in.[178]

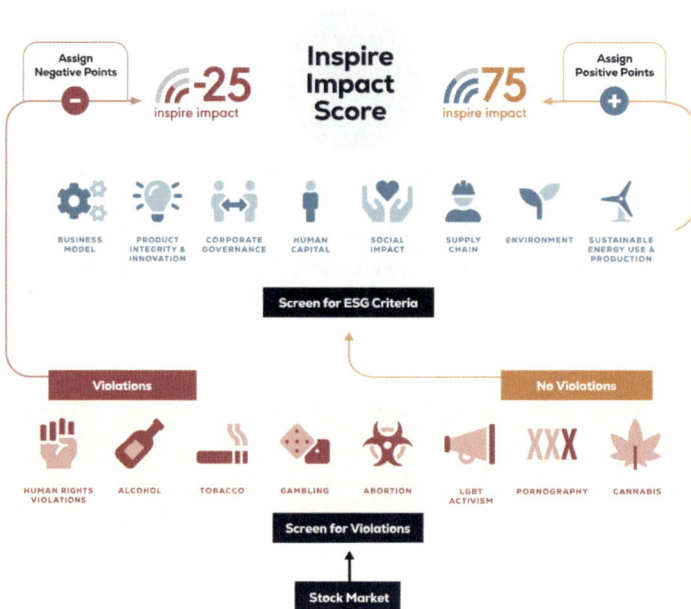

[178] https://www.inspireinvesting.com

In addition to these efforts (and not taking away from them at all) I believe we need to conduct a spiritual audit of the economic policies of nations, cities and corporations to evaluate their compliance with biblical truth.

These Policy Ideas are broad by their very nature. I have therefore also included in the appendices the guidelines for non-interest banking from the Federal Republic of Nigeria.

The Premise behind the Purpose

In the kingdom of God everything is his: "The land is mine, the people are mine, the gold and silver are mine" – to cite just a few specific mentions. We are entrusted with portions of his wealth to use for his purposes. God expects us to risk, to act, to collaborate with the Godhead and our fellow humans in the use of money and capital in all its forms. Our use of money should give Jesus a Return in Investment. His logic is counter intuitive and goes something like this: "If you forget about yourself and focus on doing what I tell you to do then I will not just take care of you, but I will give you a better return than you expect. And, if you give to the poor, you lend to me."

Some people are better at growing capital than others; God knows this. Others are better at social entrepreneurship and others at education, arts or street preaching. Those with financial capital are not better or worse than those with spiritual, intellectual or relational capital, but they do have a particular responsibility to get money out of the worlds system and into God's system. Not 10% of it, or 23%... *all* of it. Money must be redeemed repurposed, and redeployed. Think about our "spiritual" life. We strive as a matter of urgency to see the spiritually enslaved escape hell and be assured of heaven. It is life or death. Our methods may be blatant or subtle, but we don't wish eternal separation from God on anyone. Why are we content to leave capital in the clutches of God's sworn enemy? Why are we so smug when a miniscule 10% is snuck away from Mammon and donated to charity? Would we be happy if our farm manager reported that only 10% of our field produced a harvest or 10% of our vineyards bore grapes or 1 in 10 hens laid eggs? Should we be happy if the bulk of "our" assets are invested in index funds and hedge funds and private equities so that 5% or whatever of growth on capital can be allocated to charitable causes or noble endeavors?

Kingdom Economics has a very personal application

We all need to discover our calling—know our purpose in life—and at some stage ask, "What capital is needed for this high calling to be fulfilled?" We do not wait until we have all the capital we need, but like Nehemiah, we back our revelation with calculation; to hard work we add petitions for favor. God will start with what is already in our hand, move us onto a journey of generosity to ensure fear and greed are not future traveling companions, and restore his image within us so that we reflect him fully, whether in plenty or in lack, with money in the bank and in flat -pocket seasons.

Each of us can ask ourselves a series of questions, starting with "Am I a person of faith?" and then exploring whether and how our faith informs our finances. This decision chart (borrowed from the Repurposing Capital book) helps us through the logic:

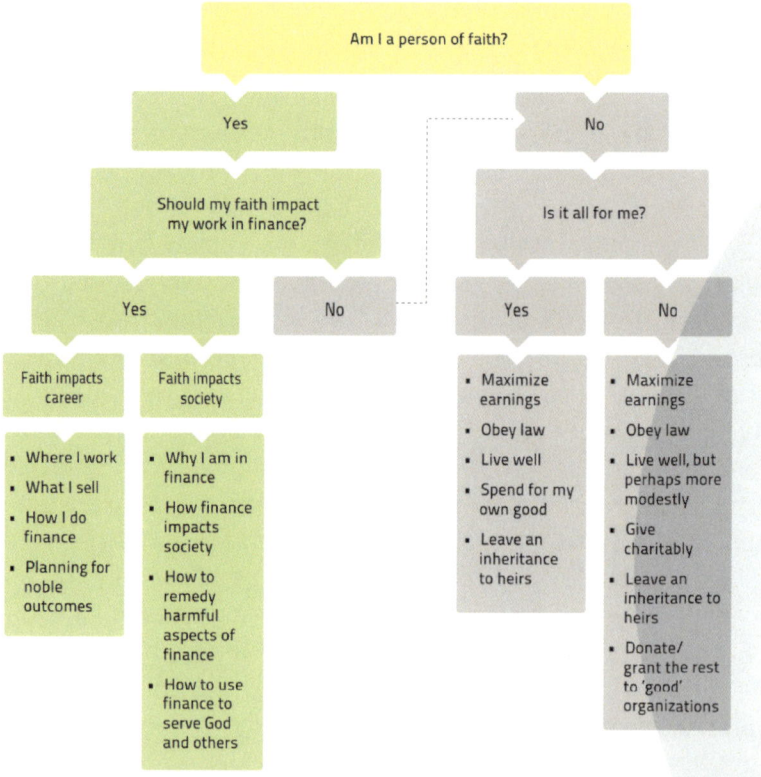

Since we have a mandate to go and make disciples of all nations scripture does not leave us with the option of just applying our faith / finance principles to just our personal lives. We have and imperative to go beyond their personal to the corporate application.

Kingdom Economics has a corporate application

Followers of Jesus Christ cannot hide behind the corporate veil. We cannot say, "We only invest in first world companies and always keep X% in indexed funds" without ascertaining whether our investments are furthering the kingdom of darkness or the kingdom of light. After a friend listened to my conversation with Robert Netzly of Inspire he then checked the details of where his Vanguard Fund was investing. "We were shocked that the Vanguard MF investment we looked at deals with 287 companies. 58 of those invested in or supported LGBT, porn, abortion, preborn stem cell and/or ru486. We are in shock... next week we will change our investments. Thanks for your effort, concern, insight and caring about Christian biblical responsible investing." What soldier would go to war and send checks to fund his enemy? If your businesses financial or investment policies are bad, change them: don't hide behind them.

Perhaps you do not invest in stock portfolios or the markets. What is the corporate application in your case? Norm Franz makes the point that investments in privately held companies can't produce a better return and you, as an investor, can have a more direct influence on what happens in the business. Someone has said "capital is stored energy." if you have a business or enterprise that is simply storing capital you should be thinking about where to deploy it to produce a better return for the Kingdom of God. The unprofitable servant (in the parable of the talents) was lambasted for not risking the capital. Under the guise of "stewardship" many Christians bury their talents under beautifully framed investment strategy guidelines, and behind the shield of investment committees and bureaucratic processes. The Pharisees had perfected the art of keeping things for themselves and not meeting the needs of God's people. We must avoid being 20th Century financial Pharisees.

Kingdom Economics has a national and global application

I do not know the mechanisms God will use to make his economy the dominant economy. Will it be the democratization of capital using blockchain and crypto currencies? Some believe this to be the case as crypto has the potential to de-fang central banks. (Yes, the central banks are looking at their own crypto currencies to stay in the game.)

Others expect a return to a gold standard believing that gold and silver are the only tangible assets frequently mentioned in scripture as a form of enduring value. Some have told me, "Gold is God's currency." Yet others believe God has placed assets in every community to not only meet their needs, but to form a basis of trade and wealth creation. Decency and fairness dictate that such assets should (a) not be colonized, and (b) be priced fairly. Uli Kortsch has proposed that a metric valuing a nation's GDP can be calculated and adjusted, much like exchange rates are adjusted. The standard is the local economy, however, not the US Dollar.

I hesitate to mention the concept of "wealth transfer" as it has connotations of sitting in our easy chairs waiting for large sums to be transferred into our bank accounts. It is worth noting however that there were several wealth transfers that took place in the history of nations. I have already pointed out that there was a wealth transfer from Egypt to Israel during the Exodus plagues. When the Egyptians were eager to get rid of the Israelites they gave them gold, jewelry and other precious items. This was another part of the wealth transfer.

When Solomon was king many nations brought tribute to him. In addition, his trading vessels and activities filled the national coffers. He used the wealth left by his father and gathered through various military conquests to lavishly build the temple and stock it with an inventory of solid gold and gold plated items. There was untold wealth... but it did not last.

Successive kings refused to follow the instructions of God wholeheartedly and the nation of Israel slid from its material pinnacle. 2 Chronicles chapter 36 records the resulting demise:

But they mocked God's messengers, despised his words and scoffed at his prophets until the wrath of God was aroused against his people and there was no remedy. He brought up against them the king of the Babylonians, who killed their young men with the sword in the sanctuary, and spared neither young man nor young woman, old man or aged. God handed all of them over to Nebuchadnezzar. He carried to Babylon all the articles from the temple of God, both large and small, and the treasures of the Lord's temple and the treasures of the king and his officials.[179]

This is a reverse wealth transfer: the treasuries of Israel were emptied and shipped to Babylon. The country's economy was decimated. The temple and palaces were burned, the walls torn down: "they destroyed everything of value there." Hundreds of years before this event Moses had given this promise and warning which we do well to heed:

---

[17] You may say to yourself, "My power and the strength of my hands have produced this wealth for me." [18] But remember the Lord your God, for it is he who gives you the ability to produce wealth, and so confirms his covenant, which he swore to your ancestors, as it is today.

[19] If you ever forget the Lord your God and follow other gods and worship and bow down to them, I testify against you today that you will surely be destroyed. [20] Like the nations the Lord destroyed before you, so you will be destroyed for not obeying the Lord your God.[180]

In Completing Capitalism, Roche and Jakub have as their first principle the concept of Sabbath. God ordained a day of rest each week and a year of rest every 7th. At the end of the books of Chronicles we see Zedekiah, like many other kings before him, doing "evil in the sight of the Lord his God... He became stiff-necked and hardened his heart and would not turn to the Lord." The land of Israel—God's land—had endured hundreds of years of leaders, both political and religious, who failed to fully do what was instructed through Moses. Eventually "there was no remedy" and the accumulated wealth was transferred to Babylon. Then there is this amazing verse:

---

[179] 2 Chronicles 36:16–18
[180] Deuteronomy 8:17–20

> The land enjoyed its sabbath rests; all the time of its desolation it rested, until the seventy years were completed in fulfillment of the word of the Lord spoken by Jeremiah.[181]

It is as if God said, "Enough is enough. I have had it with these people and their disobedience. I would rather the land be fallow than see them continue with abhorrent practices." The Message translation put it this way: "This is exactly the message of God that Jeremiah had preached: the desolate land put to an extended sabbath rest, a seventy-year Sabbath rest making up for all the unkept Sabbaths."

Don't you wonder how God feels when he looks at the earth he created, the nations he formed for his glory?

---

181 2 Chronicles 36:21

13

A call to

Kingdom Capitalists

Do you have the feeling that the world is at an inflection point? Does it seem like the shenanigans of mankind have left us with no remedy? Are we at a crossroads where we as God's people could either wholeheartedly follow His ways (when it comes to money, finance, capital, property, assets, generosity, sowing and reaping, etc.) or we could be left to our own devices, reaping what we have sown? Is it not true that most Christians have sown their economic seed in the fields of Egypt rather than in the Promised Land? We have placed our trust in the predictable returns of pension funds and indexed funds rather than in the eternal endeavors of God. Our trust is in the bulls of Wall Street and the mechanisms of fiat currencies, unjust weights/scales that make the rich richer and the poor poorer.

Even those who claim to "live by faith" have essentially been practicing Desert Economics, living from hand to mouth without growing capital. They have been aided and abetted by well-meaning Christians who donate monies to charities and outsource their ministry to non-profits rather than think through how their own work/business can be a ministry in and of itself. These are the early-stagers who still earn into one pocket and give from another pocket thereby perpetuating the secular-sacred dichotomy.

Thankfully I see a rising cadre of people of faith who are listening to the direction of the Holy Spirit, tilting their ears towards heaven, and risking their capital (in all its forms) in new ways. They are investing directly, starting new funds, forming collectives, sharing learnings and asking better questions of themselves and others. They are seeing that the abundance they have is not for themselves. They, like Abram before them, are grasping the promise: "I will bless you, and you will be a blessing to all nations." Among these are the platform-reformers who don't know all the answers but are seeking a better system. They are asking God for better ways to earn, better ways to measure returns, better ways to identify needs and add value, better ways to grow capital, and better ways to get temporal and eternal returns. I therefore end this book with hope. Why? This rising army of people who are trading normal for exciting, predictable for purposeful, and temporal for eternal, they have destiny at their fingertips. Let's explore this in more depth.

The Opportunity: Believers with Kingdom Economics have answers at Fingertips | B

| Holistic Capitalization | Repurposed Businesses: In God's Business | Households: Broad Stakeholders & Shareholders | 10-P Scorecard: Metrics for Today & Eternity | Giants toppled, Society Transformed | Nations Discipled |

You don't get a Nobel Prize for recognizing that the world is not a peaceful place. Geopolitics, pandemics, economics, migration, demographics, emerging technologies, artificial intelligence, failures of intelligence, crypto currencies, space travel... there are lots of wild things happening. Sometimes, when it looks as if things are on their last legs, new things rise from the ashes. Are we not in Divine-exchange season when need to trade-up?

God sent me to announce the year of his grace—

a celebration of God's destruction of our enemies—

and to comfort all who mourn,

To care for the needs of all who mourn in Zion,

give them bouquets of roses instead of ashes,

Messages of joy instead of news of doom,

a praising heart instead of a languid spirit.[182]

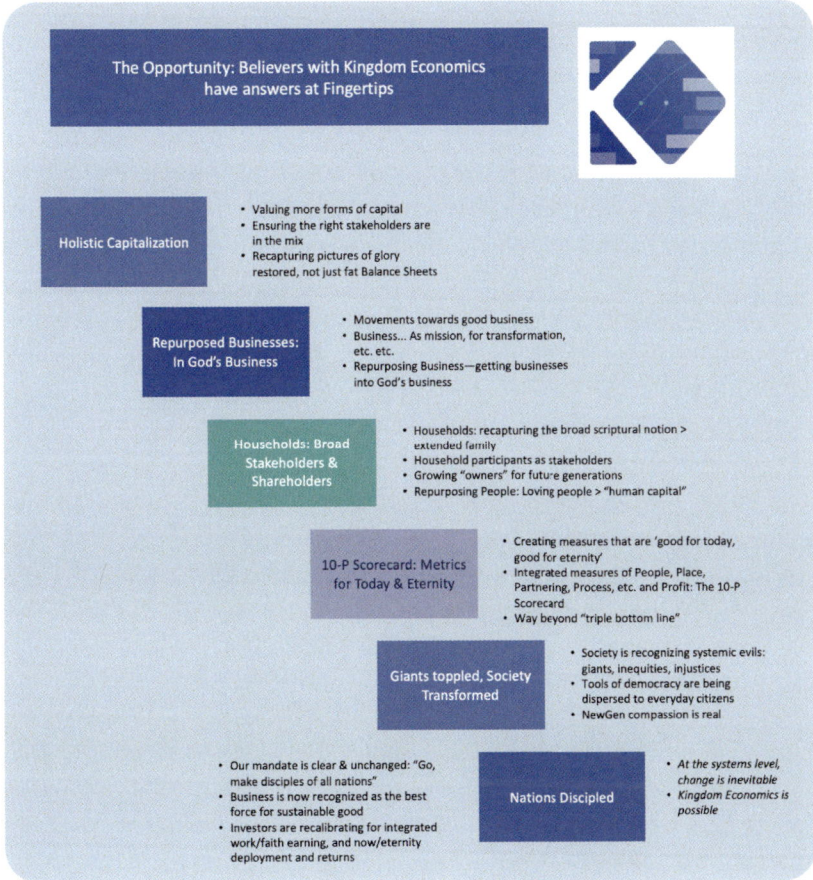

The Opportunity: Believers with Kingdom Economics have answers at Fingertips

Holistic Capitalization
- Valuing more forms of capital
- Ensuring the right stakeholders are in the mix
- Recapturing pictures of glory restored, not just fat Balance Sheets

Repurposed Businesses: In God's Business
- Movements towards good business
- Business... As mission, for transformation, etc. etc.
- Repurposing Business—getting businesses into God's business

Households: Broad Stakeholders & Shareholders
- Households: recapturing the broad scriptural notion > extended family
- Household participants as stakeholders
- Growing "owners" for future generations
- Repurposing People: Loving people > "human capital"

10-P Scorecard: Metrics for Today & Eternity
- Creating measures that are 'good for today, good for eternity'
- Integrated measures of People, Place, Partnering, Process, etc. and Profit: The 10-P Scorecard
- Way beyond "triple bottom line"

Giants toppled, Society Transformed
- Society is recognizing systemic evils: giants, inequities, injustices
- Tools of democracy are being dispersed to everyday citizens
- NewGen compassion is real

- Our mandate is clear & unchanged: "Go, make disciples of all nations"
- Business is now recognized as the best force for sustainable good
- Investors are recalibrating for integrated work/faith earning, and now/eternity deployment and returns

Nations Discipled
- At the systems level, change is inevitable
- Kingdom Economics is possible

[182] Isaiah 61 extract (The Message)

Capital can be redefined, businesses can be repurposed, rationale can graduate beyond shareholders-or-nothing, and new metrics can be imagined and inculcated.

Holistic Capitalization

Holistic Capitalization	• Valuing more forms of capital • Ensuring the right stakeholders are in the mix • Recapturing pictures of glory restored, not just fat Balance Sheets

The world is waking up to the fact that we are whole people and we have to live in concert with others while we become better stewards of everything on the planet, all forms of capital, from the environment, to human beings created equally in the image of God, to digital capital, to generational capital, to social capital, to intellectual capital (not just tech IP, but the reverence of truth), to spiritual capital AND financial capital. We will still have to fight Asset Colonization and single-minded people who still pursue shareholder value exclusively... but they will be a dying breed. Of course there are risks that ESG, and other quasi-kingdom metrics, will try to coopt this movement towards good, but the people of God—those who know his Name—are beginning to use godly imagination to see a world restored to its intended glory. Kingdom accountants are seeing a new kind of reconciliation and glimpsing the Balance Sheets of heaven.

18 And all these things are from God who reconciled us to himself through Christ, and who has given us the ministry of reconciliation. 19 In other words, in Christ God was reconciling the world [cosmos] to himself, not counting people's trespasses against them, and he has given us the message of reconciliation. 20 Therefore we are ambassadors for Christ, as though God were making his plea through us. We plead with you on Christ's behalf, "Be reconciled to God!"183

183 2 Corinthians 5:18-20 (TEV)

We are waking up to what the world already sees: God's work of reconciling "the world" to himself, through Christ and his ambassadors, is not just about people: it covers the whole cosmos... which is hugely bigger than triple-bottom lines and ESG. We have these truths at our fingertips.

> In my opinion whatever we may have to go through now is less than nothing compared with the magnificent future God has planned for us. The whole creation is on tiptoe to see the wonderful sight of the sons of God coming into their own. The world of creation cannot as yet see reality, not because it chooses to be blind, but because in God's purpose it has been so limited—yet it has been given hope. And the hope is that in the end the whole of created life will be rescued from the tyranny of change and decay, and have its share in that magnificent liberty which can only belong to the children of God![184]

Business is getting into God's business

I started down my personal path of work-faith integration over forty years ago when I found myself doing three things at once: working in business at Price Waterhouse, leading a local church, and consulting to mission organizations. Some time later (1987) God told me we should start a new kind of organization that fuses business, local church and missions. The concepts seemed strange to most people as B Corporations, Social Enterprises, Business as Missions, Holistic Entrepreneurship, etc. etc. did not exist. (There were marketplace ministry efforts focused mainly on evangelism, and some early pioneers who signed over their businesses to God, like Stanley Tam and Le Tourneau.) Today, however, there are millions of Christians who have woken up to the notion that they can do more with their careers and companies.

---

[184] Romans 8:19 JB Phillips

Repurposed Businesses: In God's Business	• Movements towards good business • Business... As mission, for transformation, etc. etc. • Repurposing Business—getting businesses into God's business

The work we do with the rēp Community[185] (Repurposing Business®) is a small part of this. Our goal is not to get God into business, but to get businesses into God's business by finding their true purpose then aligning (reconciling) every aspect of the organization behind that purpose.

Households

I will save an in-depth discussion of households for another book except to point out here that the world is waking up to the biblical construct of Household but have not quite put their finger on it. As they broaden the focus from shareholders to stakeholders they are getting closer, but can they ever go all the way?

Households: Broad Stakeholders & Shareholders	• Households: recapturing the broad scriptural notion > extended family • Household participants as stakeholders • Growing "owners" for future generations • Repurposing People: Loving people > "human capital"

A household is not just an extended family. There are 162 instances of household in scripture from which we can glean that it included multi-generational extended families, employees, servants, co-workers, and people influenced by the business or work. What was the 2nd miracle Jesus performed? We all know the first one: Jesus turned water into good wine at a wedding.

---

[185] http://repurposing.biz

49 The royal official said, "Sir, come down before my child dies."

50 "Go," Jesus replied, "your son will live."

The man took Jesus at his word and departed. 51 While he was still on the way, his servants met him with the news that his boy was living. 52 When he inquired as to the time when his son got better, they said to him, "Yesterday, at one in the afternoon, the fever left him."

53 Then the father realized that this was the exact time at which Jesus had said to him, "Your son will live." *So he and his whole household believed.*

54 *This was the second sign Jesus performed* after coming from Judea to Galilee.[186]

In scripture there are at least six incidences where an entire household— today, a whole business or corporation—got saved... all at once! You can add the metaphorical (though real) Noah's ark (built for the salvation of his house) and you get the picture. Kingdom businesspeople are not looking out for "stakeholders": they are the fathers and mothers of households who carry their household in their hearts. They have been transformed by an encounter with Jesus and their hearts have been stretched as they realize their realm of responsibility includes co-workers, families of employees, suppliers, customers, bankers, lawyers and auditors. They care about their household's living conditions, whether their children are eating nutritious food and getting educated. They care about the wellbeing of the communities in which their businesses operate. The monitor the spiritual climate at their workplace and in their communities. They practice the presence of Jesus in offices, call centers and service vehicles eager to carry the fragrance of Christ wherever they go. These businesspeople know they are the pastors of their household, whether the people know Jesus or not, and they are the priests that represent God to them, and them to God. This takes a heart change, not a Corporate Social Responsibility brochure. Punitive and agenda-laden ESG measures can never inspire the care given by heads of households, women and men who know their identity and calling in Christ. This is not about "human capital" but loving people.

---

186 John 4:49-54 (emphasis added)

¹² My command is this: Love each other as I have loved you. ¹³ Greater love has no one than this: to lay down one's life for one's friends. ¹⁴ You are my friends if you do what I command. ¹⁵ I no longer call you servants, because a servant does not know his master's business. Instead, I have called you friends, for everything that I learned from my Father I have made known to you. ¹⁶ You did not choose me, but I chose you and appointed you so that you might go and bear fruit—fruit that will last—and so that whatever you ask in my name the Father will give you. ¹⁷ This is my command: Love each other.¹⁸⁷

Love each other—including all in our household—and do his business. If we do not understand his Father's business we are not his friends. This extends to the economic model of his Father's business, would you not say?

Metrics for Today & Eternity

What if heaven has an Accounting Department that tracks business performance? What might they deem important? What metrics do they celebrate? I applaud people who are looking for better measures. "What's measured improves," said Peter Drucker, and my brother, Doug, says "People don't do what's directed, the do what's inspected." There are lots of smart people trying to figure out the right metrics to get better results for all.

10-P Scorecard: Metrics for Today & Eternity	<ul><li>Creating measures that are 'good for today, good for eternity'</li><li>Integrated measures of People, Place, Partnering, Process, etc. and Profit: The 10-P Scorecard</li><li>Way beyond "triple bottom line"</li></ul>

We had a group of very smart people around the table in 2003 discussing a "kingdom scorecard" for a business. Since then we have worked with over 400 companies around the world helping them create scorecards that, we hope, are "good for today and good for eternity." I like what has been

---

¹⁸⁷ John 15:12-17

proposed to put metrics around people and planet to complement profitability measures.

I recommend you listen to my interview with Kristos Makridis where we discuss these questions who has researched policy, management sciences and economics.[188] "Just because a company has articulated certain ESG goals does not mean they have aligned their culture behind it... When we do know our identity, what we are saying 'Yes' to, then it is easier to create metrics. A lot of corporations are being pushed to support a particular narrative..." and the push is often just a public relations exercise, not identity driven. "When you do things with the wrong motives you might get more traction in the short run, but is this actually good...?"

In the podcast Makridis asks three practical questions which we unpack in the podcast:

1. How are we defining value, which could be spiritual, or could solve a specific problem? Once we start measuring the metrics improve. This helps you avoid getting hijacked by "proxy" causes.
2. What is the time horizon you have chosen? "Way too many businesses are short term focused, and as Christians we should have an eternal focus." Be clear.
3. What positive externalities are you contributing to? We must define things that lead to positive outcomes and not get caught on the woke side of the cause of the day. "Is this having a direct effect, or a third-party effect that has an impact generations later?"

I would add some areas that should be measured:

- Societal assets and how they are stewarded: one of the key challenges at the city and nation level is the under-stewardship of assets. This is a Genesis mandate that has been dribbled away to petty politics and unbridled greed.
- Spheres of society, and how healthy they are. We cannot proclaim the health of a city or nation unless we begin to monitor its vital statistics. Every sphere of society can make a distinct contribution to the surround sound symphony of God's goodness... if the spheres are healthy. If not, they can become cancerous and suck the life from the rest of a community.

---

[188] https://www.youtube.com/watch?v=_D7KBQis1xg&list=PLjLRWI_y1Hg1J4N3DcXa-s3Dk2nOaU7tX&index=6

- Key Performance Indicators (KPIs) that cover more than people, plant and profit. When we started The Institute in 1996 we identified 10 Drivers of Corporate Impact that apply to any organization of any kind. I happened upon this as I noticed the centuries-long impact of the Church in Europe where topography and skylines are dotted with steeples. I began to see Place as a driver of organizational impact. (I had already seen people, processes, products and partnering, to name just some.) I codified The 10-P Model® and it has stood the test of time. When it comes to the impact of an organization, particularly a business or investee, we should consider KPIs across all of The 10-Ps.[189]
  - Purpose
  - Product
  - Positioning
  - Presence
  - Partnering
  - Process
  - People
  - Planning
  - Place
  - Profit

---

[189] Email me if you would like to take a free Kingdom Business Assessment

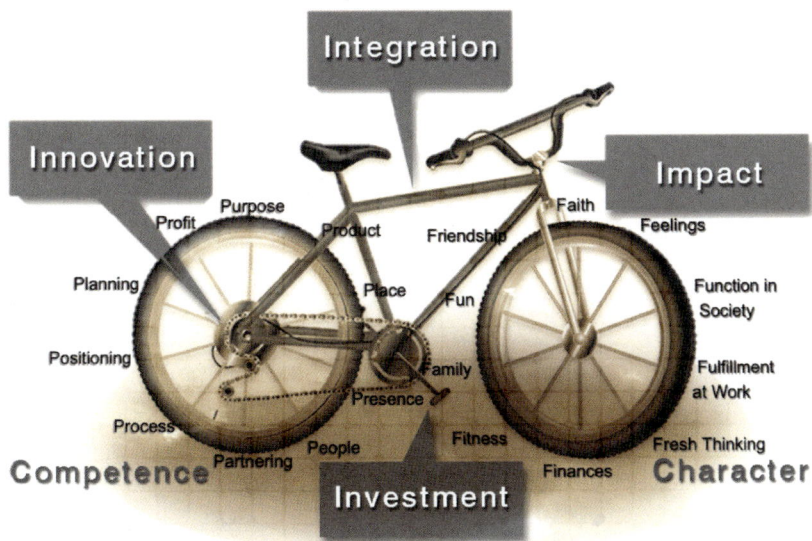

The 10-F Model® looks at 10 drivers of personal impact. These are like the front wheel of the bicycle. What we have found in work with communities is that the felt needs of communities can be discovered through the lens of The 10-Fs. Societal giants are also readily apparent in this framework.

- Corporate KPIs that are linked to Giants or societal ills: dichotomy is still alive and well when companies make money then throw the money over the wall to social enterprises, be they non-profits, churches or others, to fix problems or meet needs. An integrated life means doing business without creating societal problems in the first place and meeting genuine needs (adding real value) through the business' products and processes. The 10-P Scorecard gives you the ability to link your organization's KPIs to spheres of society and to giants. (You can use whatever tool you like, but making the linkage is invaluable.)

Which brings us to the topic of Giants.

Giants

Since I have written at length about giants in Transforming Society I will not elaborate on examples. The Sustainable Development Goals are an example of an international effort to take down big giants. In the lifecycle of leaders as the progress in their journeys many become giant fighters. Look at the latter years of Bill Gates, Richard Branson, Nelson Mandela, and Marc Benioff, to name a few. They are focused on using their capital—financial, political, organization, etc.—to not just make a difference, but to tackle what they perceive to be giants.

Millions of cause-conscious NewGeners armed with mobile phones (with video capabilities) are quick to shine a light on what they perceive to be injustices, inequities, crimes against their sensibilities or acts of kindness. About 10 years ago we talked about the role of technology in the Arab Spring. Today we hear mainstream newscasters frequently say, "...as reported on social media." Some tools of grassroots democracy are in the hands of everyday citizens. We have learned this last year that posting a video seldom changes the world when the corporations hosting such videos have the power to delete said video. You might ask what gives them the right, and they will point to "our internal policies." Setting aside whether this is right or wrong, this is a good analogy for what is happening in the world of finance. Your ATM is neither your best weapon nor the real enemy: there are systems and policies of entrenched players that wield control of capital and economies. That said, every now and then a viral video gets through and it sets a ball rolling. In the world of economics we are now in a season when giants can topple, entrenched players can become unseated, and emerging technologies can help democratize the world of finance and capital.

Giants toppled, Society Transformed	• Society is recognizing systemic evils: giants, inequities, injustices • Tools of democracy are being dispersed to everyday citizens • NewGen compassion is real

Completing the mandate

There have been many efforts to transform nations by missions and humanitarian groups. I am not sure any have succeeded. One of the key reasons is the lack of an economic engine to bring about sustained change. Said another way, transformation initiatives have been disconnected from capital. Today, however, business is widely recognized as a vehicle that can bring about positive transformation.

> Business, in our view, is much more likely to move the world from aspirational to the practical in terms of transformational lasting change, provided business leaders are convinced that a new way is available to them to "do good, and do well" at scale.[190]

Part of the "new way" is returning to the ancient paths of biblical economics. We cannot relegate the instructions of scripture to the annuls of quaint historical writings. They contain powerful principles still applicable today. Financial products of today are incredibly complex. That said, the remedies of faith-based financing are straightforward. If investors, bankers and other financiers—good people with their hearts in the right place—change the measures used, adjust time horizons to include eternity, and truly embrace integration, then we have an unprecedented opportunity.

- If we learn that all forms of capital are important, not just financial capital...
- If we see results from God's perspective...
- If we adjust our aspirations from return on our investments to giving Jesus a return on his ultimate investment...
- If we ask less whether we are stewarding our capital well and rather ask how well we are discipling nations...
- If we dedicate resources to help shape the metrics of the future, and
- If we apply creativity, urgency and resolve to create new systems that are rid of the unrighteousness of the world's system...
- Then we can complete the Great Commission.

Yes, there is more to this than money. I have a written extensively about the Why's and How To's in the book, Transforming Society. Yet capital, finance, money and economics are key elements, so we have to make the radical journey from Babylonian to Biblical Economics. I have much more to learn on this topic, there are depths yet to plumb, yet I am hopeful.

---

[190] Completing Capitalism, Roche and Jakub

I am hopeful because I see bankers starting new banks, faith driven investors collaborating and sharing their hearts and resources with each other, main street investors creating options for biblically responsible investing. I am hopeful because thousands of entrepreneurs are starting worthwhile businesses that meet real needs and advance God's purposes on earth. When I meet with believers creating asset-backed crypto currencies aimed at generating wealth for many and creating means of exchange for future commerce, I get a shot in the arm. (Wait... perhaps that's not such a good phrase nowadays.) When I see serious efforts to tie currencies to things that reflect the real value of work, I am encouraged. When I see crowd funders get behind passionate product creators, I say "Yes!" All of these things are happening today.

• Our mandate is clear & unchanged: "Go, make disciples of all nations" • Business is now recognized as the best force for sustainable good • Investors are recalibrating for integrated work/faith earning, and now/eternity deployment and returns	**Nations Discipled**	• *At the systems level, change is inevitable* • *Kingdom Economics is possible*

Become a Kingdom Capitalist

Sir Winston Churchill said, "The inherent vice of capitalism is the unequal sharing of blessings; the inherent vice of socialism is the equal sharing of miseries." When we grown beyond confusing capitalism with greed we see that capital comes in many forms. If you pray, you can build spiritual capital. If you think, you can build intellectual capital. If you can start a business or build a company, you can grow organizational capital. If you are an analyst or technologist you can build digital capital. Each of us has some form of capital because God is fair; we all have something in our hands. How well are we shifting our capital from the world's system? How radical will we be in seizing the opportunity at this critical juncture in history?

Societal Value-Chains focus on Real Work

You do not have to be an accredited investor to begin investing. You can invest sweat-equity, you can participate in crowd funding, buy crypto currencies, or make direct investments (structured in writing, with a disciple-making element) in businesses. In the early stages you can invest in your own side hustle; it might become a legitimate business. You can look more closely at what you have in your hand and ask whether it is invested sufficiently in the front-end of the Societal Value Chain; if not, why not?

You might remember the life journey diagram from chapter 2: this is an expanded form. In the Transforming Society book I expand on the journey and highlight the common mistakes we make. I also outline some of the tools that can help.

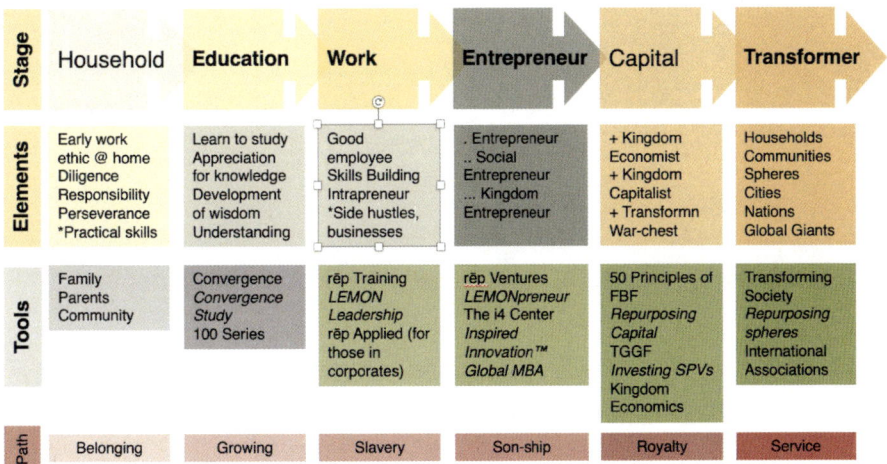

Stage	Household	Education	Work	Entrepreneur	Capital	Transformer
Elements	Early work ethic @ home Diligence Responsibility Perseverance *Practical skills	Learn to study Appreciation for knowledge Development of wisdom Understanding	Good employee Skills Building Intrapreneur *Side hustles, businesses	. Entrepreneur .. Social Entrepreneur ... Kingdom Entrepreneur	+ Kingdom Economist + Kingdom Capitalist + Transformn War-chest	Households Communities Spheres Cities Nations Global Giants
Tools	Family Parents Community	Convergence *Convergence Study* 100 Series	rēp Training *LEMON Leadership* rēp Applied (for those in corporates)	rēp Ventures *LEMONpreneur* The i4 Center *Inspired Innovation™ Global MBA*	50 Principles of FBF *Repurposing Capital* TGGF *Investing SPVs* Kingdom Economics	Transforming Society *Repurposing spheres* International Associations
Path	Belonging	Growing	Slavery	Son-ship	Royalty	Service

191

Kingdom Economics is an attempt to sketch the outlines of the economy of the Kingdom of God as opposed to the kingdom of this world. It is also a call to action. Become a kingdom capitalist. Use all you can to align with all of the opportunities afforded you at this moment in time.

---

191 Transforming Society, by Brett Johnson – Part 12: Transformation and Capital

We know that we will never see every aspect of economics fully reconciled to God's original intent before the return of Christ. This should not stop is fulfilling our "ministry of reconciliation" where we do all we can to bring the areas of the world (cosmos) that our hands touch into greater alignment with His design. It will happen eventually, and we can start the job today.

———

The seventh angel sounded his trumpet, and there were loud voices in heaven, which said: "The kingdom of the world has become the kingdom of our Lord and of his Messiah, and he will reign for ever and ever."

Revelation 11:15

About the Author

Brett Johnson founded The Institute for Innovation, Integration & Impact, Inc. in 1996. His writings complement his work in tackling societal issues counter to the principles and practices of the Kingdom of God. He is passionate about the abolition of dichotomy-—eradicating the false barriers between facets of life, especially the so-called secular and sacred.

Brett has over forty years experience with leading public accounting and management consulting firms, helping corporations from global multi-nationals through to business start-ups and social sector organizations. Brett was a Partner at KPMG Peat Marwick and at Computer Sciences Corporation. He spent fourteen years at Price Waterhouse working in South Africa in the United States.

Brett and the community around The Institute (and Repurposing Business/rēp) have repurposed hundreds of corporations, working extensively with executive teams helping them envision new futures, and aligning such teams around a common purpose. These include businesses, NGOs and international charities. The Institute has developed intellectual property and frameworks to rapidly analyze corporations and help them discover a fresh purpose that radically increases their focus, alignment and impact.

Brett is a Chartered Accountant and holds a bachelor's degree in commerce from the University of Cape Town. (BCom, CA (SA)) He and his wife, Lyn have four grown children: Fay, James and his wife, Jessica; and Davey.

Other Books by the Author

Convergence
Integrating your Career, Community, Creativity and Calling (2000, 2010)

LEMON Leadership®
Radically fresh leadership (2005, 2010, 2016)

I-Operations: the Impact of the Internet on Operating Models
with Gary Daichendt, the former EVP of Worldwide Operations at Cisco (2000). The second edition is titled I-Operations: How the Internet can transform your Operating Model (2003).

Repurposing Capital
Rediscovering Faith-based Financing (2010)

CYCLES
A journey to Purpose (2010)

Transforming Society
A framework for fixing a broken world (2010, 2016)

X-Ordinary
The miraculous story of ordinary people in God's business (2013)

The Availability Index
What men wished women knew about the signals they send (2016)

The Initiative Index
What women wished men knew about the signals they send (2016)

50 Principles of Faith-based Financing

This Land is your land, This Land is my land
The next land grab in South Africa (Land expropriation without compensation) (2017) (2nd Edition, 2018)

LEMON for Lovers
Refreshing the love of your life (2018, 2nd Edition 2020)

LEMONpreneur
A Fresh Generation on the Entrepreneurial Journey (2021)

rēStart
How to reset your Foundations for a Fresh Future (2020)

10 Steps to Restoration
Does God have a process whereby he Restores? (2020)

Work like God in 31 Ways
(2021)

Contact Information

http://brettjohnson.biz

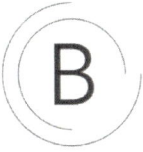

You can listen to podcasts at https://www.brettjohnson.biz/podcast

Brett's blogs can be found at https://www.brettjohnson.biz/blog

His books and classes can be accessed at
https://www.brettjohnson.biz/resources

Trademarks of The Institute for Innovation, Integration & Impact, Inc.

A partial list of trademarks includes:

Bizcipleship®
Convergence™
Head of a think thank, hands of a business, heart of philanthropy®
Heartistry®
Inspired Innovation™
i-Operations®
LEMON Leadership®
LEMONpreneur™
Partnering with leaders to maximize Impact®
rēp®
Repurposing Business—Transforming Society®
The 10-P Model®
The 10-F Model®
The i4 Center™
The i4 Methodology®

Where these have been referenced in this book they have been done so with permission.

Appendix 1: Kingdom Economics Class

One of the reviewers of Kingdom Economics asked for practical application questions and exercises. These are contained in the Kingdom Economics Class. While the class is not just a teaching through this book, it is an opportunity to think through personal mindsets and practical strategies to put Kingdom Economics into practice. You can either join a live class or go through it at your own pace. The details can be found at:

http://brettjohnson.biz/kingdomeconomics

0   Webinar introducing Kingdom Economics

1   Capital - A missing Sphere in Society

2   Why Money Matters & Forms of Capital

3   The Purpose of Money: Is it important?

4   Three Economic Systems: Egypt, Desert & Promised Land

5   Where are you in terms to the 3 Economic Systems? Source,
     location,
     operation

6   Debt & Interest: Trap or Triumph?

7   Generosity: The Barometer of the Heart of Kingdom Economics

8   Stewardship of Permanent Assets, Pivoting Investments

9   Where is Kingdom Economics today?

10   The Path to becoming a Kingdom Capitalist

11   A Fund to tackle Global Giants

Each lesson has a presentation, Applied Learning exercises and a Zoom recording from the first Kingdom Economics class in 2021.

Again, you can check out the latest class offerings on
http://brettjohnson.biz

Appendix 2: Kingdom Investor Self-Assessment

Over the years I have developed assessments that have helped organizations, leaders and investors ascertain where they are today and where they aspire to be. The Kingdom Business Assessment is useful for those who have/want to have a business that is in God's business. The Kingdom Investor Assessment helps investors determined how aligned their investment focus and practices are with the economy of God. Many of our assessment use The 10-P Model® which is a framework for analyzing the 10 Drivers of Corporate Impact.

These are statements in four of ten categories one evaluates in The Kingdom Investor Self-Assessment.

10-Ps	Investor characteristics
Purpose	Our heart's desire is to use capital to establish the Kingdom of God.
	We are resetting the foundations of capital on biblical foundations.
	We deliberately overcome the negatives of traditional capital approaches.
	Our timelines and deal terms have one eye on eternity.
Products	We define capital broadly: includes intellectual, relational, organizational, spiritual and financial (at least)
	The ensure the products/services of our investees meet genuine
	We assess whether investee products/services have been inspired by God.
	Our own investment products have all 10 characteristics of Faith-based financing (FBF) products.
Positioning	Our leadership team has built spiritual capital together.
	We understand how Mammon works and we work in an opposite spirit.
	We have positioned our fund to contributes to God's work on earth.
	The fund partners/owners are fully aligned around a corporate calling.
Presence	We make the connection between capital, trade and kingdom expansion.
	Our approach to capital attracts the Presence of God.
	Our investment approach blends principle and presence.
	Our business is marked by the miraculous.

If you take this self-assessment and would like to see your results in a chart form, please email me at brett@inst.net   I will then send you a spider diagram reflecting your results. It will look something like the chart below.

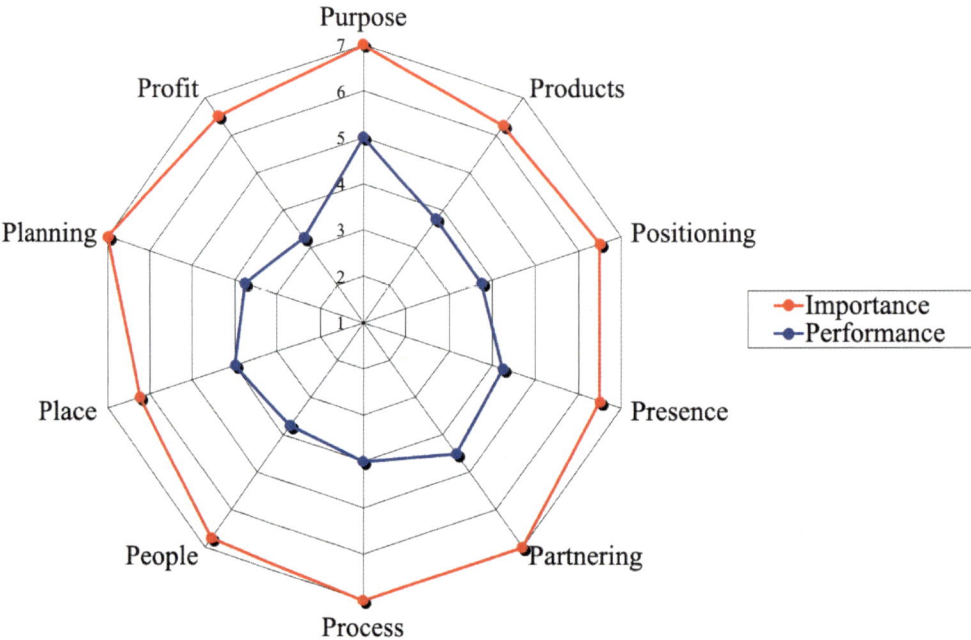

Appendix 3: Kingdom Economic Policy Ideas

#	Principle / Concept	Policy ideas	World system
1	Principles, not laws	Policies ensure there is fairness and righteousness with everyone having the opportunity to benefit equally.	Policies ensure that the rich get richer through the unjust scales of fractional reserve banking (FRB), controlled access to capital, debt and interest.
2	There are 3 different systems intellectually, and two practically: Egypt and the Promised Land	Policies in the kingdom should be linked to property ownership, real assets, being debt-free, managed interest and asset-backed currencies.	The world runs on the systems of Babylon / Egypt with unjust scales.
3	Foundational Principles	Appeal to universal laws that empower	Appeal to rules and regulations
	SOURCES		
4	God is the source	Since God is the source, policies and systems should encourage dependence on God, with delayed gratification, if need be, and not dependence on banks or man.	Lures people into debt which enslaves them to its system.
5	God is not limited to any one source	Policies should encourage diversification of income streams: salary, property rentals, trading, online business, investing, etc.	Governments depend on "tax and spend" rather than creating environments that foster creativity, ownership,

#	Principle / Concept	Policy ideas	World system
			entrepreneurship and wealth creation.
6	Faith leads to action	Action based on hearing God. Policies that reward risk-taking, tax breaks for investments that create positive social change.	Action based on calculation. Encourages entitlement as this leads to dependence on government (hoping to secure votes, loyalty)
7	Resources are not necessarily scarce	Start with what one has, and what is possible with God. Create entry-level access to financial systems ("financial inclusion") without collateral so that the "underbanked" can participate. Policies that place a value on multiple forms of capital, not just financial. (Education, arts, culture, intellect, environment, etc.)	Resources are scarce; they have to be rationed. Access to financial systems is dependent on credit worthiness and / or collateral.
8	God rewards initiative	Reward those who work. Work for benefits. Disincentivize laziness.	Governments create dependency handing out money to people who do not work (in the name of 'compassion')
9	Business risk can be an expression of faith	Reward risk-taking by favoring the provision of loans, capital, investments for production loans far above consumption debt. Discouragement of consumption debt, which	

#	Principle / Concept	Policy ideas	World system
		includes most credit card debt. Policies and plans to help people get out of consumption debt.	
10	Hard work creates value	Build education into financial products (which is what they Year of Jubilee concept included) so that people can work themselves up the ladder.	Capital produces capital. Taxes and interest on debt move wealth towards governments and the wealthy.
11	You reap what you sow	Guide people towards smart "sowing" where they reap a present and eternal return on investments. Underscore the "cause and effect" nature of finances.	In socialist settings, you reap what other people sow.
	USES		
12	Money is a tool, not a goal	Reward the deployment, not the hoarding, of money. Placing the money in the bank was the least commendable use of funds (in the parable of the talents)	Make money a goal, an idol
13	Money must serve the right purposes	Provide incentives for noble uses of capital. Create positive metrics for things such as the SDGs.	Money is its own purpose

#	Principle / Concept	Policy ideas	World system
14	Financial capital is not king	Financial capital is just a resource that is used alongside other forms of capital to achieve a purpose.	Capital is used (by those who have it) to control those who need it, or do not have it.
15	Capital and working capital are different	Restrict borrowing to meet temporal needs such as pay-day loans. If allowed, curtail interest to make it unattractive for the lenders. Restrict borrowing on short term platforms (such as credit cards) that are punitive for long-term needs (such as capital for a business).	Create an over-emphasis on working capital with easy access to consumer debt. This yields the highest interest rates and returns.
16	Wealth creation is normal	Policies that foster entrepreneurship and discourage entitlement, mediocrity and laziness. Encourage second incomes, side hustles and an ownership rather than employment mindset. "I must start a business" rather than "I want a job"	Wealth creation is an evil that should be frowned upon and taxed.
17	Finances grow people	Institute policies that encourage a healthy relationship between people and money, assets, capital. This includes the ability to work, earn, save, invest, own property and develop passive income.	Keep people financially illiterate so that they are dependent on government, or, fill them with greed so that money is a god, not a tool.

#	Principle / Concept	Policy ideas	World system
18	Be careful when using collateral	Enter into financing relationships based on shared risk not mortgaged collateral. Avoid lender/borrower dynamics.	Ensure collateral is bigger than the loan. Lend to the hilt knowing lenders have little to lose. Do not share risk.
19	"The bottom line" is not the bottom line	Foster conversations, metrics, celebrations that acknowledge and reward those who have gone beyond "the bottom line" and "the triple bottom line" to broader good-for-society metrics. New metrics for banks and fintech companies that give visibility into how they actually make money, how much, sources, etc.	SDGs are broad goals at the societal level. BUT... ESG is being captured by radicals. Banks and financial institutions are still opaque as to how they earn their money. Greater accountability is needed.
20	Be content	Place "governors" on financial services products that stimulate greed and financial overreach. e.g., limit extent of credit card interest, consumer debt.	Be greedy.
21	Have Integrity: honest weights and measures	Remove dishonest scales from the economic system such as Fractional Reserve Banking, usury.	Fractional reserve banking devalues money, as does inflation, and is a hidden tax on everyday people. It is a form of dishonest scales.

#	Principle / Concept	Policy ideas	World system
22	Gainful employment	Craft policies that foster the creation of gainful employment.	Encourage dependence and entitlement.
23	Ignorance can lead to poverty	Promote financial literacy, teaching people to think like owners, not slaves. Decrease dependence on handouts and "finished goods" – teach the possibilities in raw materials + work. Make city, state, national resources more readily available to those who will work. Should one limit imports? Stimulate more robust and well-rounded local economies.	The Egypt mindset keeps people as financial slaves, not thinking like "owners." People are hopeful of long-term employment (but it is unlikely)
	STEWARDSHIP & SPENDING		
24	Stewardship supersedes ownership	Tackle the giant of failure to steward local and national assets ~ reframe. Instill policies such as the development of city/national registries of assets with measurements of the effectiveness of their stewardship.	Failure to see assets. Failure to steward assets. Plundering of assets.
25	Save to invest	Encourage delayed gratification and saving.	Spend now, pay later

#	Principle / Concept	Policy ideas	World system
		Policies that encourage personal savings.	
		Matching of investment capital.	
		Policies that push banks to stop sitting on cash (and investing it in markets and stock buybacks) and get it into circulation for PRODUCTION loans (capital, not working capital)	
26	Exercise personal freedom with societal responsibility	Look for opportunities to reduce legislation that hinders work, job creation, wealth creation and capital building AND ensures rights of individuals, cities and communities are not subjugated to the rights of corporation and central government.	Get the populous hooked on handouts: Quantitative Easing, Stimulus packages, Infrastructure bills... trillions of dollars of debt irresponsibly loaded on future generations.

#	Principle / Concept	Policy ideas	World system
27	Distinguish between self-interest and selfishness	Encourage generosity through "double entry theology" – blessed to be a blessing. Make policies that allow the industrious to be blessed AND encourage them to be generous to the less advantaged. Foster not only handouts (by the more prosperous) but hand-ups by giving tax incentives to those who invest in positive enterprises not just those who give to charities.	Use identity politics to label anyone who wants to better themselves as entitled, privileged and/or colonizers... not to mention racist. Encourage people to think of themselves as victims.
28	Respect property rights	Enshrine the protection of property rights into law while recognizing local customs (such as communal land being owned by chiefs for the good of communities). Prohibit government overreach where land is expropriated and then mis-stewarded by bulging government land holdings or redistribution to interested parties. Pass laws prohibit anyone in the household of a government member (or bank, if it is doing the confiscating) to receive, acquire or otherwise have any interest in expropriated property.	Encourage encroachments on property, squatting, looting, burning: victim rights above owner rights.

#	Principle / Concept	Policy ideas	World system
		(See the 20 Foundational Principles of Land and Property in "This land is your land, this land is my land."	
29	Foster freedom of exchange	Since free markets are premised on a willing buyer and willing seller, ensure that barriers to such exchange are removed. (examples include excessive transfer duties on sales of productive assets, real estate, etc.)	Create trade barriers (internal and external), support monopolies, protect big business against upstarts.
30	Avoid certain types of debt	Distinguish policies for consumption debt and production debt. Prohibit excessive interest on consumption debt (e.g., credit cars, automobiles, etc) which ultimately prevents people from building capital that could go into productive assets. What about a tax on excessive interest earned by financial institutions?	The system is premised on debt as borrowings from banks become assets on their books and they then leverage these assets to create money out of thin air. Also, in many nations it is easier to get money to buy a car than business assets, a personal house than a business facility (factory, farm, office).
31	Be cautious with interest	Campaigns to expose the dark underbelly of interest and debt. Prohibit slavery through debt; outlaw it. Penalize offenders.	Let interest run amok.

#	Principle / Concept	Policy ideas	World system
		Put caps/parameters on different categories of interest (see The Appropriate Interest Index).	
	GENEROSITY		
32	Give to God first	Provide tax deductions for gifts to churches and other legitimate religious organizations.	Take away tax incentives for generosity.
33	Giving is a given	Provide tax incentives for charitable contributions at the personal and corporate levels. Prohibit the government from attaching strings to deductions for charitable contributions which could lead to the politicization of charity. Empower citizens to give directly.	Tax and spend (as opposed to earn and be generous). Government is better at giving than empowered citizens.
34	Sowing and reaping: Giving and gaining	Too often sowing and reaping is associated with charity work. Create policies that encourage businesses of all sorts to invest in worthy businesses that can, intern, produce a return for that community. Create new measures that track returns on all forms of capital that are "balanced" and for the good of society. Remove lopsided measures of returns for	Taxes curtail the enjoyment of the rewards for one's labors. Take the rewards from the workers and give them, involuntarily, to the non-workers.

#	Principle / Concept	Policy ideas	World system
		shareholders (at the expense of all stakeholders).	
35	Care for the poor	In Deuteronomy 14 local businesses gave back to their local communities every three years out of the business profits. There were designated recipients: widows, orphans, poor, resident aliens.	Today, central (state, federal/national governments) collect the lion's share of revenues in most countries. Could more be done to empower local businesses to deploy gains wisely in their local communities?
	INVESTING		
36	Expand with God	Some countries are overly bureaucratic and have the legal structure of a first world nation but the economy of a third world nation. One of the reasons for this is historic legal frameworks that are not suitable for the now independent nations. Review existing policies to ensure that they are trimmed back or aligned with the underlying realities in the economy.	View all expansion as bad and squash it using tools such as environmental legislation, land appropriation, imminent domain, population control and taxation.
37	Avoid financial schemes	Ensure policies give favorable treatment for actual goods, services and work rather than schemes which do not involve the real creation of value and are not expressed in practical work.	Allow banking and financial services organizations to create nefarious financial activities that usually just make money for the financial services sector at the expense of everyday people. (Example: derivates,

#	Principle / Concept	Policy ideas	World system
			repackaged debt, subprime mortgages, lax lending, foreclosures, etc.)
38	Create communal funds for capital projects	Examine policies that would keep capital closer to the place where it is needed and we're local interested stewards can put it to best use. Empower people to "build and protect their own section of the wall" (in the Nehemiah analogy). For example, in some countries the national road infrastructure is controlled by the government but when it passes through the states or provinces the roads are not well managed but the local economies no longer have their monies to steward the assets because it has been sucked back to then national treasuries.	Centralize. A handful of politicians and central bankers know better than a nation of people.
39	Foster Self-governance	The intention of scripture is that people would be self governing under the leading of the Holy Spirit. This should reflect in financial policies that shorten the gap between where taxes are collected, for example, and where such tax revenues are administered. This could have the effect of fostering self governance.	Create dependence on corporations and/or government. Once the central government has tasted revenues from states, provinces or cities, it is hard for them to give up such income streams. But people generally do not desire to have "a king" over them and do better when they are

#	Principle / Concept	Policy ideas	World system
			empowered to look after their own affairs.
40	Treat relationships as covenants	Under the law, a verbal agreement is off and a binding contract. The shielding of personal liability through the vehicle of corporations may have led to a decrease in trust and transparency. Re evaluate whether such laws are resulting in D violation of what could be considered covenants post op for example, recently a man who is a well-known Christian borrowed money from poor people who could ill afford it, and then refused to repay it on time. When they pressed him for the return of the loan he pointed to clauses in the legal agreements which gave him a way out. There are many such examples. There are sometimes broken covenants at the city level as well and these need to be examined to see what loopholes allow them to come about: such loopholes need to be closed.	Hide behind legal structures. (How many people went to jail because of the subprime mortgage scandal of 2008 that destroyed the wealth of millions of people?)
41	Engage in multi-generational thinking	Ensure policies allow multi-generational businesses without prohibitive generation taxes.	Burden future generations rather than deal with issues today.

#	Principle / Concept	Policy ideas	World system
		Celebrate family businesses that go beyond one generation.	
42	Plan to leave an Inheritance	See above.	Transfer wealth to the government when people die.
	REMEDIATION		
43	Restitution, where economic harm was done	Create policies where a culture of restitution is driven by justice and fairness rather than guilt and identity politics.	Encourage victims, create bureaucracies to support victims.
44	Jubilee: Avoid financial captivity	Create policies that avoid the simplistic side of jubilee and recognize the more nuanced aspects of perpetual property ownership whereby people have income producing assets, the upscaling of the less equipped by the better equipped citizens, and the avoidance of long-term debt, slavery, etc.	Provide government handouts that keep people in a perpetual state of dependence.
45	Debt forgiveness requires wisdom	Where lenders have created economic indebtedness through sleight of hand, or appealing to greed or exploiting dire circumstances of recipients of loans/credit, then such lenders should share responsibility for accumulated debt. In essence, they have to self insure against debt write	

#	Principle / Concept	Policy ideas	World system
		offs and manage their investment portfolio wisely so that they do not get stuck with the debt. In other words, there should be accountability on the part of the lenders if they have made credit available too readily. They should share risk.	
46	Spend less than you earn	Policies that encourage delayed gratification and discourage excessive use of credit.	Spend before you earn.
47	Honor your word	Should there be a score for corporations that have not kept their word just as there is a credit score for individuals? If lending institutions have entrapped borrowers, should they not be some indication of this? Likewise, where lenders have behaved honorably, there could be a similar positive ranking.	Truth is relative.
48	Be transparent	Require clear, transparent terms in financial products and contracts. Create negative incentives for obfuscated Terms and Conditions.	
49	Have the same standard for everyone	The concept of fairness, justice and righteousness translates to having the	In the world system, things are set up so that those with capital increase their capital and

#	Principle / Concept	Policy ideas	World system
		same standards for everyone.	those without increased their debt. This is a constant wealth transfer from the have nots to the haves.
50	Love God and man through your money	One of the purposes of money is to give God the return to achieve is entitled. Between you and God, all of the money is his. There is a difference between loving money and expressing once love for God and once fellow man through the deliberate deployment of money. Jesus said one cannot have two masters; we either serve him always serve mammon. There is no in between.	Love money.

Appendix 4: Banking Guidelines

Nigeria is a country that has a secular constitution and still makes provision for a multi-religion environment where traditionalists, Christians and Muslims can co-exist. They have a population over 200 million that is set to reach 750 million by 2050. Financial inclusion is a major issue in Nigeria and they are attempting to find ways to include the unbanked and under-banked in their systems. This was one of the reasons behind their decision to offer guidelines on "non-interest banking" which is perceived to be Islamic Banking by many. There has been some controversy around this, but we can learn lessons as we examine their guidelines.

GUIDELINES FOR THE REGULATION AND SUPERVISION OF INSTITUTIONS OFFERING NON-INTEREST FINANCIAL SERVICES IN NIGERIA

1.0 PREAMBLE Whereas:

The Central Bank of Nigeria, (CBN) New Banking Model authorizes the establishment of the following banking structures as defined under the Banks and Other Financial Institutions Act (BOFIA) 1991 as amended:

1. (i) Commercial Banks;
2. (ii) Merchant Banks; and
3. (iii) Specialised Banks.

Specialised Banks include non-interest banks, microfinance banks, development banks, mortgage banks and such other banks as may be designated by the CBN from time to time.

Guidelines for some of the specialized financial institutions, e.g., microfinance banks primary mortgage institutions and finance companies have been issued under a separate cover. Guidelines for other categories of non-interest banking will be issued upon request which shall be consistent with international best practice.

The emphasis of this guideline is on Non-Interest Financial Institutions operating under the principles of Islamic Commercial Jurisprudence, one of the categories of Non-Interest Financial Institutions (NIFI). In addition, other guidelines in the conduct of banking under the principles of Islamic commercial jurisprudence, e.g., operational, corporate governance, product compliance, risk management and capital adequacy, etc. will be issued in due course.

NIFI means a bank or Other Financial Institution (OFI) under the purview of the Central Bank of Nigeria (CBN), which transacts banking business, engages in trading, investment and commercial activities as well as the provision of financial products and services in accordance with any established non-interest banking principles.

Non-interest banking and finance models are broadly categorized into two:
1. Non-interest banking and finance based on Islamic commercial jurisprudence.

2. Non-interest banking and finance based on any other established non-interest principle.

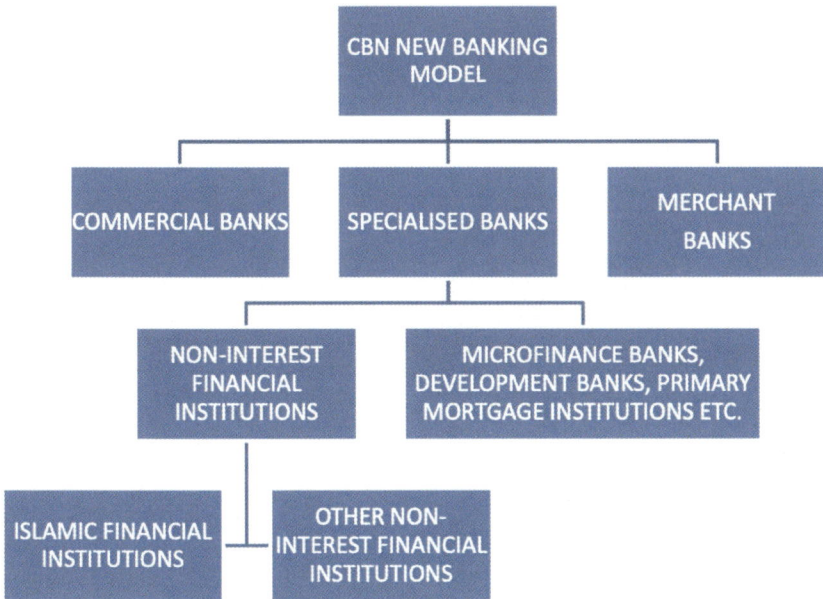

Islamic banking as one of the models of non-interest banking, serves the same purpose of providing financial services as do conventional financial institutions save that it operates in accordance with principles and rules of Islamic commercial jurisprudence that generally recognizes profit and loss sharing and the prohibition of interest, as a model.

Other non- permissible transactions include those involving any of the following:

- uncertainty or ambiguity relating to the subject matter, terms or conditions;
- gambling;
- speculation;
- unjust enrichment;
- exploitation/unfair trade practices;
- dealings in pork, alcohol, arms & ammunition, pornography and;
- other transactions, products, goods or services which are not compliant with the rules and principles of Islamic commercial jurisprudence.

Given the increasing number of requests from persons, banks and other financial institutions desiring to offer non-interest banking products and services based on Islamic commercial jurisprudence in Nigeria, the CBN has developed these guidelines for the regulation and supervision of institutions offering Islamic financial services (IIFS) referred to in this guideline.

All non-interest financial institutions under this model are required to comply with these and any other guidelines that may be issued by the CBN from time to time.

The reference to IIFS for the purpose of these guidelines means:

   i.   Full-fledged Islamic bank or full-fledged Islamic banking subsidiary of a conventional bank;
   ii.   Full-fledged Islamic merchant or full-fledged Islamic banking subsidiary of a conventional merchant bank;
   iii. Full-fledged Islamic microfinance bank;
   iv.   Islamic branch or window of a conventional bank;
   v.   Islamic subsidiary, branch or window of a non-bank financial institution;
   vi.   A development bank regulated by the CBN offering Islamic financial services;
   vii. vii. A primary mortgage institution licensed by the CBN to offer Islamic financial services either full-fledged or as a subsidiary; and
   viii. A finance company licensed by the CBN to provide financial services, either full- fledged or as a subsidiary.

2.0 OBJECTIVE

2.1 The objective of these guidelines is to provide minimum standards for the operation of IIFS in Nigeria.

1.2 Accordingly, these guidelines are applicable to IIFS only and do not seek to regulate other non-interest financial institutions which may be established from time to time.

3.0 LEGAL FRAMEWORK

3.1 Legal Basis

These guidelines are issued pursuant to the Non-Interest banking regime under Section 33 (1) (b) of the CBN Act 2007; Sections 23(1) 52; 55(2); 59(1)(a); 61 of Banks and Other Financial Institutions Act (BOFIA) 1991 (as amended) and Section 4(1)(c) of the Regulation on the Scope of Banking Activities and Ancillary Matters, No. 3, 2010. It shall be read together with the provisions of other relevant sections of BOFIA 1991 (as amended), the CBN Act 2007, Companies and Allied Matters Act (CAMA) 1990 (as amended) and circulars/guidelines issued by the CBN from time to time.

3.2 Corporate Powers

A non-interest financial institution under this model shall ensure that its Memorandum and Articles of Association (MEMART) state that its business operations will be conducted in accordance with the principles and practices of Islamic commercial jurisprudence.

4.0 LICENSING REQUIREMENTS

A non-interest financial institution under this model shall be licensed in accordance with the requirements issued by the CBN from time to time.

4.1 Applications for the grant of license shall be accompanied by evidence of a technical agreement executed by the promoters of the proposed institution with an established and reputable Islamic bank or financial institution. The agreement shall explicitly specify the role of the two parties and shall subsist for a period of not less than 3 years from the date of commencement of operations of the licensed IIFS.

4.2 A license to undertake Islamic banking business operations may be issued by the CBN upon such terms and conditions which authorize the operation of a non-interest financial institution on a regional or national basis for banks, or any other basis for other financial institutions.

4.3 An IIFS with regional banking authorization shall be entitled to carry on its banking business operations within a minimum of six (6) and a maximum of twelve (12) contiguous States of the Federation, lying within not more than two (2) Geo-Political Zones, as well as within the Federal Capital Territory (FCT).

4.4 An IIFS with national banking authorization shall be entitled to carry on banking business operations within every State of the Federation including the Federal Capital Territory (FCT), Abuja.

4.5 The detailed licensing requirements can be obtained directly from the Financial Policy and Regulation Department (FPRD), Central Bank of Nigeria, Abuja or downloaded at www.cbn.gov.ng.

5.0 FINANCING MODES AND INSTRUMENTS

IIFS shall transact business using only financing modes or instruments that are compliant with the principles under this model and approved by the CBN.

6.0 COMMISSIONS AND FEES

6.1 An IIFS may charge such commissions or fees as may be necessary in accordance with the principles under this model and the Guide to Bank Charges.

6.2 The funds received as commissions and fees shall constitute the bank's income and shall not be shared with depositors.

7.0 ESTABLISHMENT AND OPERATION OF AN ISLAMIC SUBSIDIARY, WINDOW OR BRANCH OF A CONVENTIONAL BANK

7.1 Conventional banks and other financial institutions operating in Nigeria may offer or sell products and services in line with the principles under this model through subsidiaries, windows or branches only.

7.2 An Islamic subsidiary of a conventional bank or financial institution shall be established in line with the licensing requirements for the establishment of a full fledged non-interest financial institution.

7.3 Similarly, an Islamic window or branch of a conventional bank or financial institution shall be established and operated in line with the guidelines on windows/branches issued by the CBN.

7.4 Cross-Selling of Products/Services and Shared Facilities
The Islamic subsidiaries, windows or branches may operate using the existing facilities or branch network of the conventional bank. The subsidiary, window or branch shall however, not sell products/services that do not comply with the principles under this model.

7.5 Execution of Service Level Agreements in Respect of Shared Services
Conventional banks or other financial institutions with Islamic subsidiaries, branches or windows shall execute Service Level Agreements (SLA) in respect of shared services with their subsidiaries, branches or windows.

7.6 Intra-Group Transactions and Exposures
All transactions and exposures between an Islamic subsidiary, window or branch of a financial institution and the parent shall be in accordance with the principles and practices under this model.

8.0 CORPORATE GOVERNANCE

8.1 All licensed IIFS shall be subject to:

Guidelines on corporate governance for non-interest financial institutions issued by the CBN;

The provisions of the Code of Corporate Governance for Banks in Nigeria issued by the CBN and any subsequent amendments thereto; and

All relevant provisions of BOFIA 1991 (as amended) and CAMA 1990 (as amended).

8.2 All licensed IIFS shall have an internal review mechanism that ensures compliance with the principles under this model. They shall also have an Advisory Committee of Experts (ACE) as part of their governance structure. The detailed guidelines for the appointment, operation, qualification, duties and responsibilities of member of the ACE are contained in separate guidelines to be issued by the CBN.

9.0 CBN ADVISORY COUNCIL OF EXPERTS

9.1 There shall be an advisory body to be called CBN Advisory Council of Experts to advise the CBN on matters relating to the effective regulation and supervision of IIFS in Nigeria. The qualification, duties, responsibilities etc of members of the Council are contained in guidelines to be issued by the CBN.

10.0 CONDUCT OF BUSINESS STANDARDS

10.1 Branding

In line with the provisions of Section 39 (1) of BOFIA 1991 (as amended), the registered or licensed name of an IIFS shall not include the word "Islamic", except with the consent of the Governor of the CBN. IIFS shall, however, be recognized by a uniform symbol designed by the CBN. All the signages and promotional materials of IIFS shall bear this symbol to facilitate recognition by customers and the general public.

10.2 Approval of Contracts, Products and Services

All contracts, products and services offered or proposed to be offered by IIFS shall be reviewed and approved by each institution's ACE. The introduction of new products/services shall require the prior written approval of the CBN.

10.3 Product Literature

An IIFS shall state in its product literature/marketing materials the ACE (indicating names of all the members) that certified the product or services being offered.

11.0 PROFIT SHARING INVESTMENT ACCOUNTS

11.1 An IIFS shall ensure that relevant disclosures are made to Profit Sharing Investment Accounts (PSIA) holders in a timely and effective manner and also ensure the proper implementation of investment contracts.

11.2 An IIFS shall inform its prospective PSIA client(s) operating under profit- sharing, loss-bearing contracts, in writing that the risk of loss rests with the client(s) and that the institution will not share in the loss unless there is proven negligence or misconduct for which the institution is responsible.

11.3 IIFS with PSIAs may maintain a Profit Equalization Reserve (PER) which would serve as an income smoothing mechanism and risk mitigation tool to hedge against volatility of returns to investment account holders. They may also maintain an Investment Risk Reserve (IRR) to cushion against future losses for PSIA holders.

11.4 The basis for computing the amounts to be appropriated to the PER and IRR should be pre-defined and disclosed.

12.0 AUDIT, ACCOUNTING AND DISCLOSURE REQUIREMENTS

All IIFS shall comply with relevant provisions of the circular issued by the CBN on disclosure requirement by financial institutions and other disclosure requirements contained in CAMA 1990 (amended) and BOFIA 1991 (as amended). In addition, they shall comply with the relevant standards on disclosure issued by standards- setting organisations including the following:

- Accounting and Auditing Organisation for Islamic Financial Institutions (AAOIFI);
- Islamic Financial Services Board (IFSB); and

- Nigerian Accounting Standards Board (NASB).

12.1 All IIFS shall comply with the requirements of section 29 of BOFIA 1991 (as amended) and applicable guidelines/directives issued by the CBN as well as the relevant provisions of CAMA 1990 (as amended) regarding the appointment, re-appointment, resignation, rotation, change and removal of auditors.

12.2 All IIFS shall comply with the Generally Accepted Accounting Principles (GAAP) codified in local standards issued by the NASB and the International Financial Reporting Standards (IFRS)/International Accounting Standards (IAS). For transactions, products and activities not covered by these standards, the relevant provisions of the financial accounting and auditing standards issued by the AAOIFI shall apply.

12.3 Where there is a conflict between the local and international standards, the provisions of the local standard(s) issued by NASB shall apply to the extent of the inconsistency. All IIFS shall have an internal review and audit mechanism to examine and evaluate on periodic basis the extent of compliance with the rules and principles pertinent to this model.

13.0 PRUDENTIAL REQUIREMENTS

13.1 Minimum Capital Adequacy Ratio

All IIFS shall maintain a minimum Capital Adequacy Ratio (CAR) as may be prescribed by the CBN from time to time. The minimum Capital Adequacy Ratio (CAR) for IIFS shall be consistent with the prevailing CAR as may be prescribed for conventional banks and financial institutions by the CBN from time to time.

13.2 Liquidity Management

13.2.1 All IIFS are required to put in place appropriate policies, strategies and procedures which ensure that they maintain adequate liquidity at all times to fund their operations.

13.2.2 IIFS shall not invest their funds in interest-bearing securities or activities. They are required to invest their funds in eligible instruments for the purpose of meeting the CBN prescribed minimum liquidity ratio. Liquid assets shall be held in line with the provision of section 15 of BOFIA 1991 (as amended), provided they comply with the principles under this model.

13.3 Other Prudential Requirements

All IIFS are expected to comply with other prudential requirements on exposure and concentration limits as may be prescribed by the CBN from time to time and standards of best practices.

14.0 RISK MANAGEMENT

All IIFS are required to put in place appropriate policies, systems and procedures to identify, measure, monitor and control their risk exposures. In addition, they are required to put in place a risk management system that recognizes the unique risks faced by IIFS such as displaced commercial, fiduciary, transparency, reputational, equity investment and rate of return risks. Further details and guidance are provided in documents issued by the CBN and international standard setting organizations including:

i.   CBN Prudential Guidelines;

ii. Risk Management Guidelines issued by the Basel Committee on Banking

Supervision; and

iii. IFSB Guiding Principles of Risk Management for Institutions Offering Only

Islamic Financial Services.

15.0 ANTI-MONEY LAUNDERING AND COMBATING OF THE FINANCING OF TERRORISM (AML/CFT)

15.1 All IIFS and their promoters are required to screen shareholders, customers, counterparties, transactions, products and activities against the proceeds of crime, corruption, terrorist financing and other illicit activities using legal and moral filters.

15.2 All IIFS are required to have effective AML/CFT policies and procedures and comply with relevant statutes and guidelines for combating money laundering and the financing of terrorism issued by the CBN and other relevant agencies.

16.0 GENERAL

16.1 Consistent with the CBN objective of promoting financial inclusion in Nigeria, no IIFS shall engage in act(s) or practice(s) that appear inimical to the achievement of this overall objective as well as the integrity, credibility and long term interest and sustainability of the Islamic financial services sub sector.

16.2 Discrimination on grounds of faith or ethnicity or any other grounds in the participation by individuals or institutions as promoters, shareholders, depositors, employees, customers or other relevant parties in any transaction regarding a non-interest financial institution, whether based on Islamic or other model, is strictly prohibited.

16.3 In line with extant banking laws, the CBN shall provide level playing field for all categories of financial institutions under its regulatory purview without discrimination or special favors.

GLOSSARY OF TERMS

In these guidelines, unless the context requires, the terms below shall have the following meanings:

S/N	Term	Meaning
1	Profit Equalization Reserve	An amount appropriated by a NIFI out of the gross income of the profit sharing investment before allocating the entrepreneur's share in order to maintain a certain level of return on investment for the investment account holders and to increase
2	Investment Risk Reserve	An amount appropriated by a NIFI in a profit sharing investment activity out of investment account holder's income, after allocating the entrepreneur's share, in order to cushion against future investment losses for the investment account holders.
3	Displaced Commercial Risk	This is the risk that arises when a non-interest bank is under commercial pressure to pay its investors- depositors a rate of return higher than what should be payable under the "actual" terms of the investment contract. This can occur when a non-interest bank under-performs during a period and is unable to generate adequate profits for distribution to the account holders.
4	Fiduciary Risk	This is the risk that arises from an institution's failure to perform in accordance with explicit and implicit standards applicable to its fiduciary responsibilities, which could lead to legal risks.
5	Transparency Risk	This is the risk of incurring loss due to bad decisions based on incomplete or inaccurate information or lack of transparency.
6	Reputational Risk	This is the risk that the irresponsible actions or behaviour of the management of a non-interest financial institution will damage the trust of the institution's clients.

S/N	Term	Meaning
7	Equity Investment Risk	The risk arising from entering into a partnership for the purpose of undertaking or participating in a particular financing or general business activity as described in the contract and in which the provider of finance shares in the business risk.
8	Rate of Return Risk	This is the risk associated with the potential impact of market factors affecting rates of return on assets in comparison with the expected rates of return for investment account holders (IAHs).
9	Non-interest Window	A non-interest window is defined as a dedicated unit of a Conventional bank or other financial institution that provides fund management (investment accounts), financing, and investment and other banking services that are compliant with the principles under this model.

Appendix 5: Books of Interest

This is a partial list of books I have found informative or drawn on, in alphabetical order.

10 Steps to Restoration	Brett Johnson
A Biblical Economics Manifesto	James P Gill, MD and Ronald H Nash, Ph.D
Anointed for Business	Ed Silvoso
Biblically Responsible Investing	Robert Netzly
Business Unlimited	Gunnar Olson
Coins left over	Eugene Strite
Completing Capitalism	Bruno Roche & Jay Jakub
Daring the Live on the Edge	Loren Cunningham
Doing Business God's Way	Dennis Peacocke
Debtor's Prism (Article)	Margaret Atwood, Wall Street Journal, 20 Sep. 2008
Finances– Who is in control?	Gottfried Hetzer
Generous Living: Finding Contentment through Giving	Ron Blue with Jodie Berndt
God is at Work	Ken Eldred
Keys to Heaven's Economy	Shawn Bolz
Keys to Kingdom Resources	Shawn Bolz
Kingdom Economics	Brett Johnson
Money & Wealth in the New Millennium	Norm Franz
Money, Greed and God	Jay Richards
Money won't make you rich	Sunday Adelaja
Not another rich idea	Eugene Strite
Passing the Plate	Smith, Emerson, and Snell

For the execs who only read the last page if it has a picture. You made it to the end.

God revealed himself through his work

Motivation for Work	Method of Work	Outcomes of Work	Collaboration with Mankind

Real work created wealth through Societal Value Chains

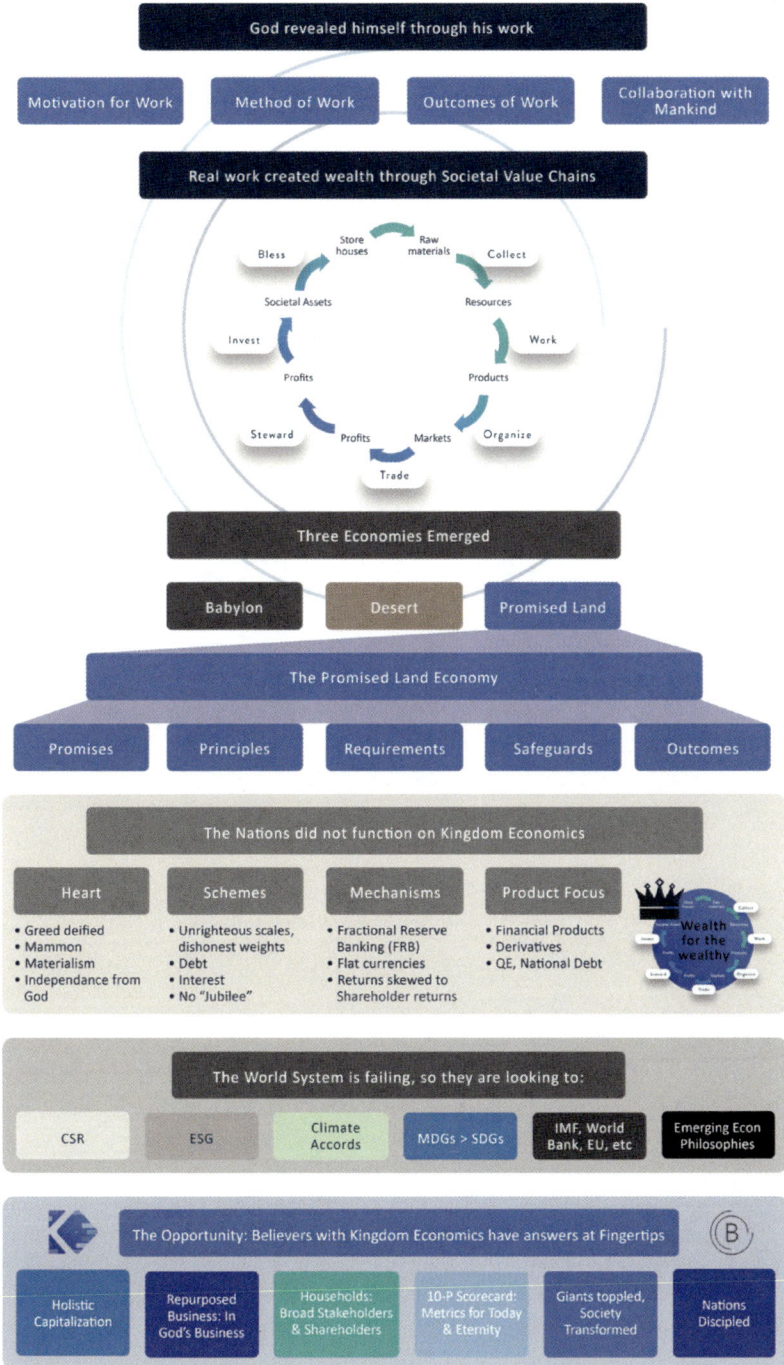

Three Economies Emerged

Babylon	Desert	Promised Land

The Promised Land Economy

Promises	Principles	Requirements	Safeguards	Outcomes

The Nations did not function on Kingdom Economics

Heart	Schemes	Mechanisms	Product Focus
• Greed deified • Mammon • Materialism • Independance from God	• Unrighteous scales, dishonest weights • Debt • Interest • No "Jubilee"	• Fractional Reserve Banking (FRB) • Fiat currencies • Returns skewed to Shareholder returns	• Financial Products • Derivatives • QE, National Debt

Wealth for the wealthy

The World System is failing, so they are looking to:

CSR	ESG	Climate Accords	MDGs > SDGs	IMF, World Bank, EU, etc	Emerging Econ Philosophies

The Opportunity: Believers with Kingdom Economics have answers at Fingertips

Holistic Capitalization	Repurposed Business: In God's Business	Households: Broad Stakeholders & Shareholders	10-P Scorecard: Metrics for Today & Eternity	Giants toppled, Society Transformed	Nations Discipled

Made in the USA
Monee, IL
21 January 2022

ed9dee15-c023-4ebd-aafc-bcfebf8f8afcR01